Sermons On The Second Readings

Series I

Cycle A

**James L. Killen, Jr.
Richard W. Ferris
William G. Carter
Jeff Wedge
Rick Brand**

CSS Publishing Company, Inc., Lima, Ohio

SERMONS ON THE SECOND READINGS, SERIES I, CYCLE A

Copyright © 2004 by
CSS Publishing Company, Inc.
Lima, Ohio

All rights reserved. No part of this publication may be reproduced in any manner whatsoever without the prior permission of the publisher, except in the case of brief quotations embodied in critical articles and reviews. Inquiries should be addressed to: Permissions, CSS Publishing Company, Inc., P.O. Box 4503, Lima, Ohio 45802-4503.

Scripture quotations unless marked otherwise are from the *New Revised Standard Version of the Bible*, copyright 1989 by the Division of Christian Education of the National Council of the Churches of Christ in the USA. Used by permission.

Library of Congress Cataloging-in-Publication Data

Sermons on the second readings. Series I, Cycle A / James L. Killen, Jr. ... [et al.].
    p. cm.
Includes bibliographical references.
ISBN 0-7880-2324-1 (perfect bound : alk. paper)
    1. Bible. N.T. Epistles—Sermons. 2. Sermons, American—21st century. 3. Church year sermons. I. Killen, James L. II. Title.

BS2635.54.S47 2004
252'.6—dc22

2004014771

For more information about CSS Publishing Company resources, visit our website at www.csspub.com or e-mail us at custserv@csspub.com or call (800) 241-4056.

ISBN 0-7880-2324-1   PRINTED IN U.S.A.

Table Of Contents

**Sermons For Sundays
In Advent, Christmas, And Epiphany**
From Expectancy To Remembrance
by James L. Killen, Jr.

Introduction	15
Advent 1	17
Expectancy	
Romans 13:11-14	
Advent 2	23
A Hope For Peace	
Romans 15:4-13	
Advent 3	31
Look Who Is Standing At The Door	
James 5:7-10	
Advent 4	37
A Gift For You	
Romans 1:1-7	
Christmas Eve/Christmas Day	43
Grace Has Appeared	
Titus 2:11-14	
Christmas 1	49
The Incarnation: What And Why?	
Hebrews 2:10-18	
Christmas 2	57
With A Song In Your Heart	
Ephesians 1:3-14	

Epiphany 1   65
(Baptism Of The Lord)
    Someone Is Trying To Get Through
    Acts 10:34-43

Epiphany 2   73
Ordinary Time 2
    Thank God For The Church
    1 Corinthians 1:1-9

Epiphany 3   79
Ordinary Time 3
    Removing Obstacles
    1 Corinthians 1:10-18

Epiphany 4   87
Ordinary Time 4
    Different
    1 Corinthians 1:18-31

Epiphany 5   95
Ordinary Time 5
    How Does It Work?
    1 Corinthians 2:1-12 (13-16)

Epiphany 6   101
Ordinary Time 6
    Still Under Construction
    1 Corinthians 3:1-9

Epiphany 7   107
Ordinary Time 7
    The Reward
    1 Corinthians 3:10-11, 16-23

Epiphany 8   113
Ordinary Time 8
    Dealing With Criticism
    1 Corinthians 4:1-5

Transfiguration Of The Lord   121
(Last Sunday After Epiphany)
    Remembering Jesus
    2 Peter 1:16-21

**Sermons For Sundays
In Lent And Easter**
Temptation Of The Palms
by Richard W. Ferris

Preface   129

Foreword   131
    by Dr. Gene R. Thursby

Ash Wednesday   133
    A Christian's Resumé
    2 Corinthians 5:20b—6:10

Lent 1   139
    Adam's Legacy
    Romans 5:12-19

Lent 2   145
    Abraham Believed God
    Romans 4:1-5, 13-17

Lent 3   151
    Access Denied
    Romans 5:1-11

Lent 4   157
    Light Is As Light Does
    Ephesians 5:8-14

Lent 5   163
    Enjoy The Scenery
    Romans 8:6-11

Passion/Palm Sunday   **169**
    Temptation Of The Palms
    Philippians 2:5-11

Good Friday   **175**
    After Good Friday
    Hebrews 10:16-25

Easter   **181**
    Taking You Up With Him
    Colossians 3:1-4

Easter 2   **187**
    Living Hope
    1 Peter 1:3-9

Easter 3   **193**
    Because
    1 Peter 1:17-23

Easter 4   **199**
    Sheep That Count
    1 Peter 2:19-25

Easter 5   **205**
    The Church That Jesus Built
    1 Peter 2:2-10

Easter 6   **211**
    King Of The Mountain
    1 Peter 3:13-22

Ascension Of The Lord   **217**
    The Eyes Of Your Heart
    Ephesians 1:15-23

Easter 7   **223**
    A Holy-wood Ending
    1 Peter 4:12-14; 5:6-11

Sermons For Sundays After Pentecost (First Third)
The Gifted
by William G. Carter

Pentecost   231
    The Gifted
    1 Corinthians 12:3b-13

Holy Trinity   237
    A Name Not Taken In Vain
    2 Corinthians 13:11-13

Proper 4   243
Pentecost 2
Ordinary Time 9
    No Shame
    Romans 1:16-17; 3:22b-28 (29-31)

Proper 5   251
Pentecost 3
Ordinary Time 10
    Uncle Abraham
    Romans 4:13-25

Proper 6   259
Pentecost 4
Ordinary Time 11
    Still Sinners, Still Forgiven
    Romans 5:1-8

Proper 7   265
Pentecost 5
Ordinary Time 12
    Thank God, We're Already Dead
    Romans 6:1b-11

Proper 8   271
Pentecost 6
Ordinary Time 13
    Slaves Of A Different Master
    Romans 6:12-23

Proper 9   277
Pentecost 7
Ordinary Time 14
    At War With Myself
    Romans 7:15-25a

Proper 10   283
Pentecost 8
Ordinary Time 15
    No Longer Damned
    Romans 8:1-11

Proper 11   289
Pentecost 9
Ordinary Time 16
    Speaking Of The Spirit
    Romans 8:12-25

Sermons For Sundays
After Pentecost (Middle Third)
Complete Joy
by Jeff Wedge

Introduction   297

Proper 12   301
Pentecost 10
Ordinary Time 17
    Effective Suffering
    Romans 8:26-39

Proper 13   309
Pentecost 11
Ordinary Time 18
    Families In Christ
    Romans 9:1-5

Proper 14   315
Pentecost 12
Ordinary Time 19
    Beautiful Feet
    Romans 10:5-15

Proper 15   321
Pentecost 13
Ordinary Time 20
    Irrevocable Gifts
    Romans 11:1-2a, 29-32

Proper 16   327
Pentecost 14
Ordinary Time 21
    Body Parts And Pride
    Romans 12:1-8

Proper 17   335
Pentecost 15
Ordinary Time 22
    Heaping Coals And Virtues
    Romans 12:9-21

Proper 18   343
Pentecost 16
Ordinary Time 23
    Doing Well And Doing Good
    Romans 13:8-14

Proper 19   **349**
Pentecost 17
Ordinary Time 24
    Life, Death, And Judgment
    Romans 14:1-12

Proper 20   **355**
Pentecost 18
Ordinary Time 25
    Struggles, Death, And Christ
    Philippians 1:21-30

Proper 21   **361**
Pentecost 19
Ordinary Time 26
    Complete Joy
    Philippians 2:1-13

Proper 22   **369**
Pentecost 20
Ordinary Time 27
    Bragging Rights
    Philippians 3:4b-14

**Sermons For Sundays
After Pentecost (Last Third)
Worthy Of God
by Rick Brand**

Preface   **377**

Proper 23   **379**
Pentecost 21
Ordinary Time 28
    No Idea
    Philippians 4:1-9

Proper 24　　　　　　　　　　　　　　　　**385**
Pentecost 22
Ordinary Time 29
    Always?
    1 Thessalonians 1:1-10

Proper 25　　　　　　　　　　　　　　　　**391**
Pentecost 23
Ordinary Time 30
    The Cloak
    1 Thessalonians 2:1-8

Proper 26　　　　　　　　　　　　　　　　**397**
Pentecost 24
Ordinary Time 31
    Worthy Of God
    1 Thessalonians 2:9-13

Proper 27　　　　　　　　　　　　　　　　**403**
Pentecost 25
Ordinary Time 32
    Further On Up The Road
    1 Thessalonians 4:13-18

Proper 28　　　　　　　　　　　　　　　　**409**
Pentecost 26
Ordinary Time 33
    The Day Of The Lord
    1 Thessalonians 5:1-11

Reformation Sunday　　　　　　　　　　　**415**
    When Is Being Right Wrong?
    Romans 3:19-28

All Saints' Sunday　　　　　　　　　　　　**421**
    Say What?
    1 John 3:1-3

Christ The King   **427**
    The Power Of God
    Ephesians 1:15-23

Thanksgiving Day   **433**
    Thanks Be To God
    2 Corinthians 9:6-15

Lectionary Preaching After Pentecost   **439**

U.S. / Canadian Lectionary Comparison   **441**

About The Authors   **443**

Sermons On The Second Readings

For Sundays In Advent, Christmas, And Epiphany

From Expectancy To Remembrance

James L. Killen, Jr.

Introduction

When a visitor stands in the public square of the ruins of ancient Corinth, he or she may be overwhelmed by two apparently contradictory feelings coming all at once. On the one hand, there may be a great sense of awe. This is the place where Paul founded one of the most vital congregations of the ancient church, the place where the people lived to whom Paul wrote letters that are now part of our Bible. The place may be one that has always seemed far away, unreal, almost mythological to us. On the other hand, there may be a dawning consciousness that this place where those history-making things happened is part of the same world that you live in, it is a place on the other side of the same little planet that you live on, and the things that happened there were parts of the same continuum of human history in which you are a participant.

The more we learn about ancient Corinth — and Joppa and Caesarea and Bethlehem and Jerusalem and Rome and the other places where the biblical events happened — the more we will realize that those places really were parts of our world and the things that were going on in them during those long ago times mentioned in the Bible are not as different as we might have thought from the things that are happening around us today. The things that were going on in their culture were much more similar than we might guess to the things that are going on in our culture. The things that were going on in their churches are things that go on in our churches. And the things that were going on in their lives are the things that are going on in our lives.

The other impression also tells us something that we need to know. The things that happened there were charged with eternal significance because the living God was at work in them — and so are the things that are happening in our world and in our lives today. Our lives and our world's history are parts of the same drama that was going on then. And, the same God who was active in those happenings is still God today and still active in the same ways. The God who was made known to us through Jesus Christ is still God. The One who reached out to people through the Holy Spirit is still reaching out to us today, making us aware of the reality of God, assuring us of God's love for us, doing saving works in our lives, calling us out of whatever hurtful or wasteful uses we are making of our lives into new life in Christ, and challenging us to become participants in the work that God is doing to bring in God's new age. The events of our own lives either are, or can be, charged with the same eternal significance that made the biblical events important.

For this reason, the things that Paul and the other Bible writers said are very relevant to our lives. It can be exciting to try to see what they are trying to show us and to realize that they are not just talking about something long ago and far away. They help us to discover what the living God is doing in our world today in all kinds of situations, from humanity's great struggle with suffering and oppression to the petty squabbles and nit-picky criticism that are parts of everyday church life. They help us to see the real experiences of our daily lives in the light of God's eternity. They lead us through the discoveries that are parts of living in a growing relationship with God.

The lessons selected for reading in the seasons of Advent, Christmastide, and the Sundays after Epiphany lead us from expectancy through discovery to remembrance. And the remembrance of Jesus always leads us back again to expectancy, and the drama goes on. We are parts of the same drama that was going on in places like ancient Corinth. Let us try to find ourselves in it and to discover the new meaning it can give to our lives.

Advent 1
Romans 13:11-14

Expectancy

Christmas decorations are beginning to appear everywhere and the children are getting excited. Children love this time before Christmas because it gives them something for which to look forward. We all like to have something exciting and good for which to look forward, don't we? We enjoy expectancy. That is the great thing about the season of Advent. It is a season of expectancy. It is a season of looking forward expectantly to the celebration of the birth of the Savior. But it is even more than that. It is a time for entering into the expectancy that should be a part of the lives that Christians live every day of the year.

Our scripture lesson is full of expectancy. Paul is telling the Romans, and us, to look forward to something that God is going to do. "... you know what time it is, how it is now the moment for you to wake from sleep. For salvation is nearer to us now than when we first became believers" (Romans 13:11). What did Paul mean by that? Some of us are accustomed to looking back to the day on which we first believed, the day when we accepted the Christian faith, and calling that the day on which we were saved. But here is Paul, writing to believers and telling them that their salvation is still in the future. What did he mean by that?

One thing that Paul must have had in mind is the belief that there will be a coming "day of the Lord" when Jesus will return and all of God's loving purpose for the world will be accomplished. Paul believed that day would come during the lifetime of many of the people to whom he wrote. Obviously, that didn't happen.

And yet, Paul's writings reflect the fact that there is a definite orientation toward some future fulfillment that is a part of our Christian faith. Paul believed that God is bringing in a new age of righteousness, a new day when all of God's loving purpose for us and for our world will be fulfilled and that we are living in the dawning of that new day.

That belief is reflected in what Paul wrote in Romans 8. In that pivotal chapter, he does indeed speak of salvation as something that has been given to believers. "There is therefore now no condemnation for those who are in Christ Jesus" (Romans 8:1). "When we cry, 'Abba! Father!' it is that very Spirit bearing witness with our spirits that we are children of God, and if children, then heirs, heirs of God and joint heirs with Christ ..." (Romans 8:15-17). And finally, nothing in the whole creation "will be able to separate us from the love of God in Christ Jesus our Lord" (Romans 8:39).

But in that same chapter, he speaks of a yearning for and a movement toward a future salvation, "If the Spirit of him who raised Jesus from the dead dwells in you, he who raised Christ from the dead will give life to your mortal bodies also ..." (Romans 8:11). And, "... we ourselves, who have the first fruits of the Spirit, groan inwardly while we wait for adoption, the redemption of our bodies" (Romans 8:23). Clearly, our salvation is something that is still going on, something we can hope for and anticipate and reach out toward.

But our scripture lesson for today comes from a part of the letter in which Paul is not talking primarily about personal salvation but about the participation of the Christian community in the life of the larger community in which they lived. Also in Romans 8, Paul makes it clear that the movement toward the fulfillment of God's purpose has social dimensions. "For the creation waits with eager longing for the revealing of the children of God; for the creation was subjected to futility, not of its own will but by the will of the one who subjected it, in hope that the creation itself will be set free from its bondage to decay and will obtain the freedom of the glory of children of God. We know that the whole creation has been groaning together in labor pains until now ..." (Romans 8:19-22). So God is at work in the whole creation to move it toward some future salvation.

I hope that you can catch enough of a vision of what Paul was trying to show us to get excited about it. That vision can help us understand what we are doing when we celebrate the season of Advent. Here we are, almost 2,000 years after the birth of Jesus, participating in an observance that has to do with looking forward to the coming of salvation. Yes, the Savior has come and the gift of salvation has been given. But the difference that gift is meant to make, both in our lives and in our world, is something that has yet to be brought to fulfillment. That fulfillment is something that we should hope for and look forward to expectantly. And we are called to participate in the work that God is doing to bring salvation to completion.

In our reading for today, Paul says, "Wake up. It's almost morning. Let's get ready to live a life that is appropriate for the new day. Let's lay aside the works of darkness. Let's put away things like reveling and drunkenness. Instead, put on the Lord Jesus Christ, put on new life in Christ like you would put on a new garment, and make no provision for the contrary way of life in the flesh."

What would it mean for us to live in that kind of active expectancy? Let's talk about that for a while. It may help us to get the picture of what Paul is trying to tell us.

What would it mean for us to live as if we believe that God is at work in our world to bring the whole world to some kind of new and better life? For one thing, it would mean taking a much more positive attitude toward the unfolding of human history than lots of us have. Do you remember the Y2K commotion? You have probably all but forgotten it now, but it caused quite a furor when it was going on. You will remember that, as our world approached the year 2000, someone realized that, through the short-sightedness of what is supposed to be one of our most future-oriented industries, all of the world's computers were expected to go haywire as the new millennium arrived. In a computer-dependent society, we thought that was going to throw the whole world into chaos. That anxiety, together with a re-emergence of some very primitive old superstitions about the coming of a new millennium, caused lots of people to go into a tizzy. Some were preparing for the year 2000 in a way that was reminiscent of the ways in which some people prepared for nuclear war, complete with hoarded food and water and weapons to shoot your neighbors if they tried to take any of your stuff. Looking back on it, it all seems very foolish. But it caused a lot of real consternation when it was happening. You know, lots of people always look forward to the coming of the future with a similar kind of dread. It is unknown and so they think of it as threatening.

But Christian people should look forward to the future with a confidence that comes from knowing that the future is in God's hands and that God will be at work for our salvation in the future as in the past.

That is not to say that the future can always be counted to bring only good things to us. As we look at the things that have happened since Y2K, we will see that some of them have been good and some have been bad. We have endured September 11. That was about as bad as it gets short of a nuclear war. And we have seen the Holy Land enveloped in a heartbreaking conflict that has given new meaning to the psalmist's admonition to "Pray for the peace of Jerusalem" (Psalm 122). We have experienced the anguish of our country's involvement in Iraq. But in all of these things, we can be confident that God is still at work to bring good out of evil and new life out of chaos and death — and we can also be confident that God has some things for us to do so that we can participate in God's saving work.

We can take a similar attitude toward our own lives. When we are very young, it is easy to stay excited about the future because every new day seems to bring some new experience and some bright new possibility. At least that is true for the most fortunate young people. It was true for lots of us. But sometimes, as life goes on, things slow down. Life may seem to stagnate into the "same old same old." The burdens and the threats of it may make us stop looking forward to the future with much happy anticipation. We may have a hard time finding any reason to get excited about the future.

But so long as we know that God is at work in our lives leading us toward the fulfillment of our best possibilities, we can know to approach each new day ready to discover what surprise we will find there. Many people have found that it works that way. When the adventure that is our youth is over, when we realize that we have climbed about as far up our career ladder as we are going, when some limitation forces us to realize that some door we had always hoped would open never will, then many have learned to stop and look around and explore other dimensions of life, to take adventures into beauty or meaning or relationship of service. Many who have done that have found God at work there; opening unexpected new vistas and possibilities to them.

Many have discovered that when they had gone as far as they could in the pursuit of what Paul would have called "the life of the flesh" and reached a point of success — or limitation — or disillusionment — then God is there to lead us into a new adventure that Paul would have called "the life of the spirit." God always has more to offer to us as soon as we are ready to receive it — and as soon as we are ready to work with God to reach out for it. There is a kind of spiritual retreat that is called a Crusseo or a Walk to Emmaus that has been a very meaningful experience to many people. At the end of those retreats, the participants are invited to share any reflections they may want to share with the group. Quite often, people in that situation tell of experiences of renewal in which the religious faith they had professed all of their lives has taken on new meaning for them and given the whole adventure of life a new freshness.

The promise that God will be there in our future to carry on the work of our salvation extends even into those conditions of life that most people think are completely empty of possibility. An alcoholic who bottoms out may think he or she has reached the end of his or her rope. But then, with the help of a spiritual program, he or she may discover not only the way to sobriety and sanity, but also the way to a new spiritual aliveness that he or she never knew was possible. More than a few people who have dealt with cancer, sometimes even with terminal cancer, have caught a new vision of the real meaning of life that has enabled them to make the last of life much better than the first.

In fact, the promise extends even beyond this life. God is not limited by our deaths. We can dare even to approach the ends of our lives in faithful expectancy. A Texas pastor was talking with an older member of his church when the conversation shifted to a certain family whose young daughter had been injured in an accident and was apparently brain-dead. They had felt compelled to terminate her life support. The situation had been a burden on the hearts of all who knew them. When the subject came up, the older man looked off into the distance and said, "You know, preacher, I used to work in the oil fields." At first the pastor thought the man had found the subject too hard to talk about and had changed the subject. He soon found out that was not so. The man went on. "I was always a boomer. I liked to be where things were coming on. Once I was working in an oil field that had 23 rigs pumping. But they began to shut rigs down. I transferred to another oil field that only had eight rigs working, but they were drilling new wells and making new explorations. I like to be where things are booming. That is the way I feel about life. As long as things are booming here, I am ready to stay and make the most of it. But when things start to running down in this life, I will be ready to go on to the next place because I believe God will have something exciting going on there." He had learned the secret of expectancy.

When we are able to believe that God is alive and at work to save in this life and beyond it, we will soon discover that we have received the gift of expectancy — and that can make a great big difference in our lives.

**Advent 2
Romans 15:4-13**

A Hope For Peace

We will soon be singing Christmas songs full of joy and goodwill and love and peace. Someone asked some little children what love is and one said, "Love is what you hear in the house at Christmas time if you stop opening presents and listen for a while" (from PreachingToday.com, May 15, 2002). That is important to us, isn't it? That is really the way we want it to be.

But that is not always the way it is. There are estrangement and againstness and hostility in our world and it is especially painful to us at Christmastime. Maybe there is some tension between some people you love, some friends getting a divorce, some members of your family who are in conflict with one another — or maybe one who has separated from the family for some reason. That is always painful but it is especially painful at Christmastime when we want everyone we know to be part of one happy circle of love. It is really painful when you are one of those who are in conflict with someone who is important to you. Are there people or groups in your circle who are set against each other at your office, in your club, or in your church? Don't you wish that everyone could get along?

And what about your community? Are there tensions between racial groups or economic groups in your community? Some conflicts can be really dangerous as well as painful. There always seems to be a war going on somewhere in the world, and recently it seems that our country is always involved in it in one way or another. The whole world is grieving because war is raging in the part of the world that we are accustomed to calling the "Holy Land." Not long ago, the Church of The Nativity, the place where tradition tells us Jesus was born, was occupied by one group of combatants and besieged by another group. Do things like that break your heart, as they do mine? Especially at Christmastime, we wish that everyone could learn to get along and to live in peace with one another. We wish there really could be peace on earth and good will among all people.

But that is more than just a Christmas wish. It is a part of the Christmas promise. It is a part of what we are invited actually to hope for, especially in this season of expectancy.

It was a part of Paul's vision of the saving work of God that God is working to overcome all of the divisions between the peoples of the earth and to gather them into one harmonious whole. The letter to the Ephesians speaks of God's "plan for the fullness of time, to gather up all things in him, things in heaven and things on earth" (Ephesians 1:10). Paul was especially concerned about the hostility that existed between Jews and Greeks in his society. It was a bitter division that could turn violent. It was probably that hostility that eventually caused Paul's death. But Paul found that conflict very painful because he loved both his own people, the Jews, and the people to whom he was a missionary, the Gentiles. He yearned for their reconciliation and he believed that it had been accomplished, or at least made a real possibility and as a part of God's promise, through Jesus. Again in Ephesians, we read, "He is our peace; in his flesh he has made both groups into one and has broken down the dividing wall, that is, the hostility between us" (Ephesians 2:14). And in the letter to the Galatians, Paul shares his vision for something that God was causing to be true, first in the church and then in the world. "There is no longer Jew or Greek, there is no longer slave or free, there is no longer male or female; for all of you are one in Christ Jesus" (Galatians 3:28).

In our scripture lesson for today, we are coming near the end of Paul's greatest letter. He has witnessed to the good news of God's saving work with great power and clarity. Then he moved into several chapters having to do with the practical matters of living out that faith in the real world. As he approaches the end of that section, he quotes three lessons from the Hebrew Scriptures that point forward to a reconciliation between Jews and Gentiles. He makes this a part of the hope he is leaving with his readers. "May the God of hope fill you with all joy and peace in believing, so that you may abound in hope by the power of the Holy Spirit" (Romans 15:13). He also makes it a part of the faith they are called to live out in their lives in the real world. "May the God of steadfastness and encouragement grant you to live in harmony with one another, in accordance with Christ Jesus, so that together you may with one voice glorify the God and Father of our Lord Jesus Christ" (Romans 15:5). Paul sees the reconciliation of humankind as a part of the vision of the good future toward which God is moving us and also a part of the hope that should already be shaping our lives.

But what does that offer us in our real world today? What can it have to do with those real conflicts that are making our hearts hurt right now? And what can we do about it?

First, believe the promise and claim the hope that there can be peace. When we talk about the conflict in the Holy Land, we often hear people say, "Those people have been fighting over there for thousands of years and they always will." We can't let ourselves give up to that. Peace is still a real possibility for those people and for all people because of something that happened in that very land. You have heard that the Bible says, "There will be wars and rumors of wars." Look that up in Matthew 13:7 and you will find that Jesus did not say that wars are parts of the plan of God but rather that, when we hear of wars, that does not mean the world is coming to an end. God is at work in the world to bring peace. Believe that peace can happen in this real world. Believe that it can happen in your community and your church and your family and in your life, too. If we don't believe that peace is possible, it won't be. It is part of the promise of God. Trust the promise and live expectantly.

Paul believed that, in the church, all kinds of people could and should be reconciled and live together in mutual love. He spent a lot of time talking about that because he thought it was important. Paul believed that the church should live in the world in a way that would be both an example and an agent of the new possibility God offers to the whole world. Yes, there will be problems. But they can be worked out. Paul gives lots of practical guidance about how to do that in this last half of the letter to the Romans. Sometime, read Romans 12 and see how much practical help it offers. Yes, there will be differences within the church; differences of "gifts," differences of disposition, differences of opinion. Paul believed that there is room for difference within the church. When different people live together in love, the differences become sources of enrichment and creativity. Loving harmony in the church is important. It is worth working for because the church is called to live in the world as a "beach head" of God's new age.

It is important for us to take seriously the possibility of reconciliation and love in our own personal lives and relationships. The place to start is with being reconciled to God. The problem behind the problem in many of our conflicts is some incompleteness in ourselves, some bitterness, some anxiety, some lack of self-esteem that makes us defensive. As we move into a trusting relationship with the living God, we will find God healing our hurts and taking away our bitterness, replacing our anxiety with the ability to trust, affirming our personhood with God's love, and, in more ways than we can list, moving us toward wholeness. With wholeness will come the freedom to take the risk of venturing out into relationship. A healthy self-love will tell us that we should not allow ourselves to be abused or exploited, but the possibility of a better relationship is worth the vulnerability that comes with reaching out to others. The others to whom you reach out may not be ready for peace, but, as Paul said, "If it is possible, so far as it depends on you, live peaceably with all" (Romans 12:18).

The next step is actually to become a peacemaker. Jesus said, "Blessed are the peacemakers for they will be called children of God" (Matthew 5:9). Reach out to work for reconciliation every chance you get. Most of us think, "How could I be a peacemaker?" Let's think about that.

We could start by trying to be reconciled to those people with whom we are in conflict in our personal lives and relationships. You know who those people are, don't you? They are the people who once did something hurtful to you and whom you have not forgiven. They are the friends or relatives from whom you have grown away. They are the people with whom you are in conflict over some significant issue whom you have allowed yourself to think of as enemies. That is the place where peacemaking can be most difficult because you will have to overcome bad feelings, not only in yourself, but in the other. And reaching out to try to be reconciled may result in your being hurt again. We really feel the things that go wrong in this area of our relatedness. We are tempted just to leave those relationships broken so that we won't risk being hurt again. But it is reconciliation at this level that brings the most immediate reward. And if we can't make peace in our own relationships, how can we hope to make peace in our world? How would it be if we each made a list of the people with whom we need to be reconciled and made some effort to offer a hand of friendship to each of them during this happy season? How would it be if we each sent a Christmas card to each of the people on our lists with some message of genuine warm wishes written in it? Maybe nothing would come of it. Maybe it would get an unpleasant response. But maybe it would be the beginning of a reconciliation that could make both your life and theirs better.

Then we should look for ways to move out into the community in which we live and do the work of a peacemaker. What would happen if every time you hear someone "bad mouthing" someone with whom they are in conflict, you would say something like, "You know, you folks need to get over this and work things out"? What would happen if every time you hear someone depersonalizing and berating members of another race or group, you would say something like, "They are people just like we are"? Or "Have you tried to see things from their point of view?" You might take some flack for doing that, but then, you might do some good, too. Look for every opportunity to help people work out their conflicts.

Christian people and Christian churches ought to be actively involved in working for peace in communities and in the world.

There are lots of things a church can do to help bring reconciliation between groups in a community, from helping to establish a climate of opinion that wants peace and justice, to facilitating conversations between conflicting groups and sometimes actually acting as mediator. If there is anything the church can do, we ought to do it. It is part of our mission.

Is there anything we can do to help to bring about peace between nations in conflict in our world? We can teach the way of love that Jesus taught us. It actually can become a strategy for moving toward peace. There was a time when we might have thought that the solution to the world's problems would be to convert everyone to the Christian faith. Every Christian will want to share the faith that has brought him or her to fullness of life with every person he or she can. But in today's world, massive attempts to convert people of other religions to ours could be a source of greater conflict, not less. And, sadly, the situation in Northern Ireland and in some other places leads us to know that having everyone professing the Christian faith may not be the same as having everyone living the life of love. We should, however, do all that we can to teach all nations, beginning with our own, the way of respect for others, commitment to justice for all, and willingness to dare to trust and to work toward reconciliation. A certain Hindu by the name of Gandhi once took the principles taught by Jesus and used them to change the course of the history of his nation. We could also use them to change the history of the world. It may be necessary for us to become involved in the politics of peace. Sadly, it is necessary for nations to be ready to go to war. But war never accomplishes peace. We can do all we can to influence our nation not to believe that military might and economic intimidation can solve the problems of the world and then go on to discover and then do the things that actually can.

Peace is a real possibility in our lives and in our world. God is working to accomplish it. And there are things that we can do to participate in what God is doing. There is a church building, actually, it is a German army base chapel in Landsberg, Germany, that preaches an architectural sermon on reconciliation. As people enter the courtyard through the steeple, they pass a display of massive wooden plaques hung on the wall, each saying in one of the many languages of the world, "Be reconciled to God." The building preaches other symbolic sermons as worshipers are led finally to the altar behind which is a banner with an abstract representation of Christ on the cross with the hands of people of all colors reaching out to him and the words that say, in German, "And I, when I am lifted up from the earth will draw all people to myself" (John 12:32). The chapel itself is a witness to the possibility of reconciliation.

In a few weeks, when we again hear the scriptures read in which the angel spoke of peace on earth and good will among people, we may still experience sadness because we know that the peace we wish for has not yet come to our world or to our families or to our lives. But sadness will not have to lead to despair. God is at work in our lives and in our world, and that gives us reason for hope. "May the God of hope fill you with all joy and peace in believing, so that you may abound in hope by the power of the Holy Spirit" (Romans 15:13).

Advent 3
James 5:7-10

Look Who Is Standing At The Door

Imagine a happening with me. The scene is a fine restaurant all decorated for the holidays. It is noontime and the restaurant is crowded. Five well-dressed businessmen are seated around a round table enjoying drinks after an expensive lunch. They are entrepreneurs. Each has been successful in building up a business and operating it in a way that has made him wealthy. Since it is the holiday season, they have gathered for a celebration. But they are not celebrating Christmas or Hanukkah. They are celebrating their own success. They take turns politely inviting each other to tell their stories. Each in turn tells of how he has come from some kind of situation of disadvantage, either real or imagined, and, by his own shrewdness and willingness to take risks and by hard work has become a successful man. They all listen attentively and wait for their turn to tell their stories. They all speak just a little louder than they need to, as if in the hope of being overheard. It is a celebrative ritual they enjoy indulging in on special occasions.

In fact, the people at the nearby tables do overhear. For the most part, they share in the admiration. These men are telling stories that the culture has taught everyone present to call success stories. There are, however, some who overhear but do not share in the admiration.

Two businesswomen at the next table overhear and are honestly jealous. They, too, are trying to achieve a similar kind of success. They share hushed comments about how they intend to crash that "good old boys' club" and make them take notice.

The waiter overhears too and, in spite of his impeccable courtesy, he does not admire. He recognizes one of the men, but is not recognized by him. He once worked for his company. He had received a commendation for his work two weeks before he was laid off as a part of the company's program of downsizing. He was told that the company had to get lean and mean to meet competition. He doesn't think his former boss looks too lean. He has lots of bad feelings. He is hoping to find a new job that will get him back on some company's ladder. But, right now, he is just hoping for a generous tip.

The woman who is collecting dishes from the tables has bad feelings, too. She is a single mother, holding two jobs to support her family. She is very anxious because she can't give her children the quality time she knows they need. She thinks it is really unfair that some people have so much and some others have so little. No, not everyone who hears is celebrating.

As a matter of fact, some of the people at the table are not really able to put themselves completely into the celebration. One is a younger man who has scored some spectacular early successes in business. He is proud of himself, but he does not yet feel entirely comfortable in this winner's circle. He knows he still has to prove himself in the long haul.

Another of the men has just made a risky investment to expand his business using lots of borrowed money. If the enterprise is successful, he will reap huge profits. But if it is not, he will be very vulnerable. He knows that all of the men at the table know about this situation. He knows that, if his venture fails, it may well be one of these men who will move in to take advantage of his misfortune. He really does not feel that he is among friends. But none of that is mentioned. He speaks of his new enterprise as a sure thing and the others congratulate him for it.

A third man feels thoroughly uncomfortable. He really doesn't feel a part of this scene. He has indeed been successful in business. He would be frank to tell a friend that his success has been three-fourths good luck and only one-fourth his ability to stumble into the right decisions at the right time. He is deeply grateful for his good fortune and he feels a real responsibility to manage it for the good of all whose lives are touched by his enterprise. These are two attitudes that the others at the table would not understand, so he does not mention them. He just participated half-heartedly in the celebration. This man's problem is that he is a Christian. He is grateful for his good fortune and intends to keep on working to be a successful businessman, but he finds the values and the attitudes and the competitive arrogance of his companions foreign to his way of life. He goes along because it is expected, but he will be glad when this lunch is over.

That was not a true story. It is not something that happened just like that at some particular time. But it could have. It wasn't hard to imagine, was it? The elements of that story are all around us every day and we see them. In that sense, it was truer than a story about one particular event.

But the big question is: What does it have to do with our scripture lesson or with the season of Advent or with anything that we are supposed to be talking about in church? Much more than you may think.

Paul contrasted two ways of life: the way of the flesh and the way of the Spirit. Other biblical witnesses refer to the way of the flesh as the way of the world. One of every Christian's greatest challenges is to keep living according to the Spirit, that is to say, living a life that is being shaped daily by a relationship with the living God, while everyone else around us is living a very different kind of life. That is hard to do. The temptations and the influences and the intentional pressures of our culture are always pulling us or pushing us to live like everyone else and making it costly not to do that.

What is this "way of the world" that we have to cope with? Paul's use of the expression, "living according to the flesh," has given lots of us the idea that it must have something to do with sex. But the letter of James goes to some trouble to describe it in another way. What James describes has a remarkable resemblance to the things that we imagined going on in the restaurant. It is life committed to material gain and dominated by envy and competitiveness. Listen to some things that the letter said in the passage just before the one we read.

"Those conflicts and disputes among you, where do they come from? Do they not come from your cravings that are at war within you? You want something and do not have it; so you commit murder. And you covet something and cannot obtain it; so you engage in disputes and conflicts. You do not have, because you do not ask. You ask and do not receive, because you ask wrongly, in order to spend what you get on your pleasures. Adulterers! Do you not know that friendship with the world is enmity with God? Therefore whoever wishes to be a friend of the world becomes an enemy of God" (James 4:1-4). A little later, he hoots at those who say, "Today or tomorrow we will go to such and such a town and spend a year there, doing business and making money" (James 4:13), as if they could really be in control of their future. And in the beginning of the chapter from which we read our lesson, he said, "Come now, you rich people, weep and wail for the miseries that are coming to you" (James 5:1).

All of a sudden our own culture and perhaps some aspects of our own lifestyles are on the stage on which the biblical drama is being played out.

What does James want to tell Christians who are living in the midst of cultural circumstances like these? Don't give in. Keep living the life of faith and of love that you have learned from Christ, even in the midst of the competitiveness and greed and envy of our culture. And don't let envious and competitive attitudes invade the fellowship of the church. Keep supporting each other in the way that you learned from Jesus. And be patient in enduring any stress or abuse that comes from being "different."

James reminds the Christians that Judgment Day is coming. That is one of the themes that is always a part of the observance of the season of Advent. The time of the coming of the Lord is always a time of judgment in which the things that are wrong with our lives are shown for what they are and we are called to get our lives right. James reminded the early Christians that the way of the world that is so tempting and troublesome will fall under judgment and be shown wanting, and the way into which Christ called them will prove to be real life at its best. James warned his readers not to let themselves be drawn into the ways of the world that will fall under condemnation because "the Judge is standing at the doors" (James 5:9).

We suppose James must have been wrong about that. Judgment day has not come yet — or has it? Judgment doesn't come just on one terrible day at the end of time. Judgment is one aspect of every meeting with the Lord. It is going on all of the time, and it is going on for our own good. All of the awesome biblical images of the final judgment can be taken as descriptions of something that happens right in the midst of our everyday lives. Judgment can happen in lots of different ways. There was really a lot of judgment in the story we imagined, wasn't there? A business failure, the loss of a job, a situation of disadvantage, or any other experience in which the system you depend upon lets you down can be a judgment day. Any day on which you wake up and realize that the life you have invested yourself in has not delivered what it promised, and that you don't like the life you have, and that you really don't like yourself as you have become is judgment day. We are wise to recognize those experiences as times when the Lord comes to show us what is wrong with our lives and to call us to better lives.

What is the message for today? Take a good look at the lifestyle of our culture and recognize all of the things in it that are contrary to a life shaped by a relationship with the living God whom we know through Jesus of Nazareth. Don't let yourself be drawn into the world's way of thinking about things and of acting and of living. It really won't lead to happiness — in spite of what it keeps telling you. Follow the way of Jesus, the way of faith and love, no matter what it costs you. That will lead to the life that really is life at its best.

Where should we start? We might start by taking a good look at the way in which we are planning to celebrate Christmas. Some of you have already thought of that, haven't you? It would be easy to get drawn into an experience of envy and competitiveness that could spoil your season. Open the door and welcome the judge who will help you to get things into a right perspective.

But some may be wanting to cry out, "Wait! Why must we be talking about such a somber subject as judgment during this season when we want to be happy and celebrate Christmas?" The answer is that it is part of our preparation for a real celebration of Christmas. The first verses of our scripture lesson for today spoke of waiting patiently for the coming of the Lord. It is part of God's way of dealing with us that judgment comes before the Savior comes so that we can know our need for the salvation. That is the function of judgment. It is not to condemn us. It is to prepare us. The one who comes brings forgiving of our sins, healing of our sickness and brokenness, and the possibility of a better life. It is important for us to realize that those things don't just have to do with a salvation in some realm of abstract spirituality or with salvation after we die. The forgiving of sins, the healing of brokenness, the offer of a better life has to do with the real things that are going on in our real lives. It has something to offer to people like the ones in the little story of the businessmen's lunch with which we began. It has something to offer to you that has to do with the things that are hurting in your life.

We will be wise to open the door of our lives because the Judge is standing at the door — and so is the Savior.

Advent 4
Romans 1:1-7

A Gift For You

Christmas is almost here. There is probably a Christmas tree in your house somewhere and there are probably presents appearing under it, all brightly wrapped and labeled. No doubt you have snooped around enough to see which packages have your name on the tag, and you may have begun to try to guess what is in them. If you have guessed what is in the package, you probably can't wait for the day to come for you to open it. If you haven't been able to guess what is in it, you are probably even more eager to open it.

During Advent, this season of expectancy, we have been looking forward to Christmas and trying to anticipate what it really can mean to us. A part of that meaning is that there is a gift waiting for you. It is a very special gift. It is something chosen especially for you by someone very special. It is the most valuable thing that anyone could ever have. It will open a really new and exciting possibility for you that will change the rest of your life. But, once you have guessed what is in it, you may decide not to open it. I hope you will choose to open it — but you may not. Let's talk about that.

Our scripture lesson puts things into perspective. We have read the very first verses of one of the most important books in the whole Bible. Paul wrote his letter to the Romans late in his ministry when his faith and his understanding of the good news were mature. He was making a very careful effort to sum up everything of importance that he had been sharing with people all over the ancient world. He was sending this letter to the people in Rome where he hoped to go. He really didn't know the people there and he felt a need to tell them ahead of time who he was and what he was about. But what emerged may really have been a letter addressed to all of the people of the Roman Empire. It is a very important summary of the meaning of everything that followed from the birth of Jesus which we will be celebrating soon.

Paul addressed his letter to the Romans, but those who incorporated it into our Bible identified it as scripture through which the living God can still speak to us. It is addressed to us as well.

Paul is so eager to share his message that he can hardly contain himself. The address of a letter would ordinarily say something very simple like, "Paul, an apostle of Jesus Christ, to the people at Rome. Greetings." But Paul expands the address into an awesome run-on sentence that introduces all of the themes of the letter like the prelude to a symphony might.

He introduces himself and explains that he has been called to be an apostle, that is, a missionary, to the non-Jewish people of the world.

Then he introduces the gospel he preaches, good news about the saving work of God, begun long ago and coming into focus in the life of Jesus Christ, through whom, he said, he had received grace and responsibility to share that grace with the Gentiles, and to bring them to faith.

Then he tells who the message is for. It is for those in Rome and for us who are called to belong to Jesus Christ, called to be saints. That is the gift God has chosen for each of us. That is what God wants for you because God loves you.

Now you see what I meant when I said you might not want to open that package. When Paul mentions being saints, some of us instinctively begin to back away and start singing that old Bob Dylan song, "No, no, no, it ain't me, babe. It ain't me you're lookin' for, babe." Sure, we want to be Christians. We want to do whatever we must to know we won't go to hell when we die. We will even come to church and bring our children to Sunday school so they will grow up to be decent people and not do drugs. But we would like to keep our religion separated from the rest of our lives so it won't get in the way. This business of being saints goes way beyond what we have in mind. Is that what you are thinking?

Let's talk about that. Let's talk about what it means to be a saint and what it doesn't mean. The idea we have in mind about what it means to be a saint is different from what Paul meant. But the idea some of us have in mind about what it means to be a Christian is different from what Paul had in mind, too. Let's talk about what it means to be called to be a saint and then let's talk about why we ought to choose to answer that call.

The word "saint" means "one who is set apart for the service of God." In the early church, it came to be another name for a Christian.

When most of us think of saints, we think of people who are represented in statues in some churches. It also conjures up some images that are totally unattractive and also totally inaccurate.

A saint is not someone who is perfect. Read the stories of the biblical saints. They were very human. Even Paul himself was headstrong, impulsive, and inclined to be a little arrogant — and he had a temper. But God accepted them as they were and worked with them and used them in the service of God's high purpose.

A saint is not some super-human being who lives up to a standard that no real person could achieve. The Christian faith will make some differences in your life. But after those differences are made, you will still be you. And being "real" is a part of what it means to be a Christian.

A saint is not someone who can't have any fun. You will see that some of the things that are characteristic of the lives of the saints make it easier, not harder, to have fun. The saints are more likely to experience real joy in living than anyone else. One pastor always made it a point to tell his confirmation classes to remember two things. One is that fun is not sin. And, the other is that sin is not fun.

A saint does not have to go into a monastery or become a missionary. In fact, God has an urgent need for saints who are business people, engineers, teachers, politicians, doctors, managers, farmers, and workers in every kind of field you can imagine. It is through just such people that God works to change the world.

But being a saint does require commitment. There is the rub. That little religion that never gets in the way of the rest of our lives never has been any kind of real Christianity. It is just an easy little substitute for a religion that we have dreamed up for our own convenience. The biblical faith has always required commitment. The Christian faith requires us to venture out into life daring to trust the reality and the love of God instead of hanging on to the tangible little things we try to use as life preservers. The Christian faith requires us to march to the beat of a different drummer; it requires us to let our lives be shaped by an ongoing, daily interaction with the living God rather than by all of the little cultural things that are shaping most other people's lives. And the Christian faith requires us to be committed to a purpose bigger than our own little purposes. It requires us to intentionally invest our lives in accomplishing the purpose of God for us and for the whole creation. That is a big requirement.

Some of us are not willing to make that kind of commitment. We are so caught up in the little commitments of our little lives that we can't see any other calling as anything but an imposition. A pastor was talking with a man about becoming a Christian. The man said, "Preacher, I don't know about that. You know, I like my beer." Well the jury is still out on whether or not it is an okay thing for Christians to drink beer. Some say, "Yes." Some say, "No." But if the fellow couldn't think of anything bigger than whether or not he would have to give up beer, he hadn't really gotten the picture of what it means to be a Christian. To answer the call to be a saint — that is, to be a Christian — does require commitment. It requires a commitment that lots of people really may not be ready to make yet. That is why some people may not be ready to open that gift from God that is represented by the coming of Jesus.

But there are some good reasons for choosing to open that package no matter what the cost. There are some things in there that you may really want — or that you may come to want as your life goes on. Let's talk about those things.

There is freedom in that package. When we think of "being saved" we ought not just to think of being saved from some abstract thing called "sin." God actually works to save us from the things that are really messing up our lives, like the guilt that keeps us from being able to like ourselves, or the anxieties that make us afraid to venture out into life and relationships, or the selfish ambitions that make slaves of us and drive us mercilessly, or the bitterness that makes all of life taste bad, or the hatreds that could make us do destructive things. To get free from those things can make a big difference in our lives. But the freedom that we gain through the Christian faith is not primarily freedom from something. It is primarily freedom for something. It is freedom *for* new life in Christ.

There is happiness in that package. Ask any random group of people what they want most out of life and the majority of them are likely to say, "Happiness." There is a special kind of happiness in the package for you. No, there is no promise that everything is always going to come out like you want it to. There may actually be more troubles and not less. But there will also be an assurance that life as a whole is a good gift from God that we should receive gratefully and enjoy fully. You know, in this pleasure-oriented culture of ours, there are lots of people who cannot really enjoy anything. The Christian faith can teach us how to enjoy life even when circumstances are not what we could wish for them to be.

In that package there is also the ability to love. That is something all of our hearts hunger for. Stephen Covey, whose book, *Seven Habits of Highly Effective People,* was a best seller for a long time, told about an experiment he sometimes performed with his students when he was teaching in a college. He required them to think through what they would do if they had only the rest of the semester to live. He said that the exercise often produced some profound responses and the dominant central theme, the underlying principle, was love.[1] Love is something that we all want in our lives. But many of us don't have a very clear idea about what love is, much less the ability to do it. Part of our inability to love has to do with our unwillingness to make commitments. God has sent Jesus to show us what it means to love, and God surrounds us with love, God's love and other loves, that can love us into the ability to share love. That is the pearl of great value that we all yearn for. It is in the package.

And purpose is in the package, too. Robert A. Raines began his book, *New Life in the Church,* by lamenting the lack of purpose in the nation, in the church, and in most of us as people. He compared us to plankton, the little plants that live in the sea and drift thousands of miles wherever the current takes them with no power or will of their own to direct their destiny.[2] In order to be truly human, we need a purpose to live for that is big enough to be worth the investment of our lives. When we read the newspaper and learn of wars and corruption and suffering and all sorts of things going wrong in our own hometowns and around the world, we want to cry out, "Why doesn't somebody do something about all of this?" God is at work in the world to do something about it — and God calls those who are set apart for his service to participate with God in building a better world. Yes, it can be costly to get involved in that, but it can give you a purpose for your life that is worth living for.

Freedom, happiness, love, purpose, those are some very valuable gifts. Who knows what else you will find in your own personal gift from God? It is something that God wants for you because God loves you. God picked it out for you and put it under the Christmas tree with your name on it. It is all part of the calling to be saints, people set apart for the service of God. But it will require commitment. Commitment is an essential part of answering the call. Things just won't work without it. I can understand that when you have guessed what is in that package some may not want to open it. But I hope you will.

---

1. Stephen R. Covey, *The Seven Habits of Highly Effective People* (New York: Simon and Schuster, 1990), p. 132.

2. Robert A. Raines, *New Life in the Church* (New York: Harper and Row, 1961).

**Christmas Eve/Christmas Day
Titus 2:11-14**

Grace Has Appeared

A little baby was born nearly 2,000 years ago under very unimpressive circumstances. He was born to poor working people living in an oppressed country. He was born while the parents were on a journey that was required by a tyrant, and they had to stay in a stable instead of in a home. The baby was laid to sleep in a trough from which cattle usually ate. And yet, Christians down through all of those years have believed that there was something very special about that birth. We have believed that, in that event, something from God dropped into our world and the circles of significance of that event spread throughout the world like ripples spread across the surface of a pool when a pebble is dropped into it. Those circles of significance are still spreading today.

What is the significance of that birth and of the life that followed from it? What have its results been? And what may they yet be? Our text tells us a lot about the significance of that event. But we will have to work our way through it slowly and analyze it a few words at a time.

It starts by saying, "Grace has appeared...." Grace is the freely given love of God. That one who has created galaxies beyond our ability to imagine has done something to make God's love known.

That is really important. It answers that most basic question that every person asks. From the moment we are born, we begin to look out at the world that surrounds us and ask, "What is all of that out there? What is it all about? How does it relate to me? And, how should I relate to it?" The answer we come up with to that basic question will do more than anything else to determine the shape of our lives. And the answer is not always easy to guess. The world around us gives mixed signals. People come up with lots of different answers. As a result, people live lots of different kinds of lives.

But Christians believe that, in the coming of Jesus, that greater reality which is present in all of the little realities that bump up against us, did something special to make us able to know that God loves us, and that God loves everybody, and that life is a good gift given to us by God. Think about the love of the ones who love you most. Then, think about a love even bigger than that coming from the one who gives you life and comes to meet you in every new day of life. That is grace. Learn to believe that and to live as if it is true and that belief will make a big difference in your life.

That is why the text goes on to say, "Grace has appeared, bringing salvation." Salvation means a lot more than many people think it means. It means more than having your guilt atoned for so that you can go to heaven after you die, wonderful as that is. It also means being set free from the power of fear and greed and hate and indifference and all of the other things that can mess up our lives and generate all of that guilt. It means being liberated for a life of freedom and purpose and love. If you learn to live trusting God's love, God will enable you to live in love. That interaction will become a lifelong process of having your life shaped and fulfilled by God. It is a very complex process because it works itself out differently in the life of every person. But it is also a very simple process because it is always a working out of the impact of God's love on your life.

Think of a message that brought you the news of a new possibility that changed your life, a college scholarship, a new job, acceptance of a marriage proposal. Then think of another new possibility many times better than any of these. That is salvation.

God's love works to save in the life of each individual person. But God's love also works to save the whole world and to build a new and better world. It is important for you to know that God loves you, you as an individual person, and that God wants to do a saving work in your life. It is important for you to know that the birth of that little baby, and the life, work, death, and resurrection of Jesus that followed from it, and all of the many, many things that can mean, are for *you* in the most personal possible way. It is important for you to take that into your life and let it do all of the saving work that it can for you. But it is also important for you to know that it was meant for everyone else in just the same way that it was meant for you.

The text goes on, "The grace of God has appeared, bringing salvation to all." — "For all!" God loves everybody just like God loves you and God wants fullness of life for everybody just as God wants fullness of life for you. As you grow in love and learn to love as God loves, you will learn to love others as you love yourself and to want fullness of life for all others just as you want it for yourself. That love will be a part of what shapes your life. It will generate in you a commitment to justice and well-being for all people and it will also generate in you a compulsion to share with others the good news that is shaping your life, the good news that the grace of God has appeared bringing salvation to all. Think of the thing that stirs up the greatest commitment within you, love for your country, love for your family, love for life. Christ hopes to stir up in you just that kind of commitment to the salvation of the world.

That will indeed reshape our lives. "The grace of God has appeared, bringing salvation to all, training us to renounce impiety and worldly passions and to live lives that are self-controlled, upright, and godly...." Yes. God works in our lives to make us into the very best people we can be. That is part of the process of the salvation that Jesus came to bring into our lives.

Our culture has taught us to be skeptical of morality. It has taught us to resist being told what to do and to insist on the freedom to do just whatever we choose to do. It has also taught us to use that freedom to indulge ourselves. But our culture has not always produced people who are either very noble or very happy. All of us have working in our lives some of the influences of that culture — all of us. That is part of what we need to be saved from.

God's love works within us to make us want a better life, to set us free for a better life, and to enable us to live a better life. Yes, the moral teachings about what is right and what is wrong may come from beyond ourselves. But love, working in us, makes us see the reason for them so that we take them into ourselves. Instead of being dominated by rules made by others, we are reshaped from the inside out by convictions and commitments that we have made our own. We learn to live better, more truly human, more genuinely happy lives that are really our own. Faith and morality grow together. It is not that we have to be good so that God will love us. It is that, once we have discovered God's love and taken it into ourselves, God's love works within us to make us good. Think of athletes training for the Olympics. They subject themselves to rigorous disciplines and do it gladly because they want to accomplish something that is important to them. Training in righteousness is like that.

But wait. The last time we repeated our text, we left something out. "The grace of God has appeared bringing salvation to all, training us to renounce impiety and worldly passions, and in the present age to live lives that are self-controlled, upright, and godly ..." — "in the present age." Today is the only day you have to live and today is the day for your salvation and for the living out of life in its fullness. Yes, God acted almost 2,000 years ago to show us God's grace. But, the same God who was made known to us then is still God right now. What God did then, God is still doing now. Think about waking up tomorrow morning, before you ever go to the breakfast table, or, if that doesn't work for you, think about walking out your door to go to school or to work or wherever you are going tomorrow. Now think of that as the beginning of the day when God wants to do a work of salvation in your life and, through your life, in the world.

God is still at work in our world and in your life to bring salvation to you and to all. Right now is the time for you to respond to God's saving work so that it can make a difference in your life, and right now is the time for you to commit yourself to God's saving work so that God's saving work can make a difference in the world. It is true that right now may not seem like a good time for salvation. It never does. There are always lots of things in our world and in our culture and in our lives that are working against it. But that will always be true. If you are ever going to live life in its fullness, today is the day to do it. God is working with you to make that a real possibility for you. And there has never been a time when the suffering and the need of God's people all over the world cried out more urgently for the building of a better, more just world. God is at work now as always to accomplish that. And today is the day on which God calls you into participation in that work.

But today is not the end of the story. "God's grace has appeared bringing salvation to all, training us to renounce impiety and worldly passions, and in the present age to live lives that are self-controlled, upright, and godly, while we wait for the blessed hope and the manifestation of the glory of our great God and Savior, Jesus Christ." Today is the day for salvation but salvation teaches us a hope that keeps us looking forward to something more. Having sampled fullness of life in Christ, we look forward to fulfillment. Having caught a vision of the world as God wants it to be, we look forward to its actually becoming what God is making it. That may mean that we are looking forward to something that will happen beyond our lifetime. That gives a new dimension to our lives. When we are investing ourselves in something that reaches beyond our lifetimes, we will find that we are living bigger lives with bigger meanings. And the promise of our faith is that God has something good in store for us beyond this life. Even in the fulfillment of Christmas there is still the expectancy of Advent. Expectancy is a part of our faith. Because we know that the future is in the hands of God, we look forward to it with hope and we commit ourselves to the accomplishment of all that God is working to bring about in our lives and in our world.

Think of a time when you will know that the end of your life is coming near. Will you be able to believe that the investments you have made of your life and your love will yet bear dividends for you and for others even beyond the end of this life? Or, will you have to believe that it has all been lost? God wants to bless us with the knowledge that our time is lived out in the context of God's eternity.

The author adds another sentence which adds a significant dimension for all of us who are called Christians and members of the church. "He [Jesus] it is who gave himself for us that he might redeem us from all iniquity and purify for himself a people of his own who are zealous for good deeds." God has given us a role to play in the drama of salvation. We are called to be a special people set apart for the service of God. We are to live out an example of the possibility that God has opened to all people. We are to live lives through which others can see the grace of God that has appeared bringing salvation for all. And we are to be zealous of good works so that God can work through us to carry forward the work he began in this world through Christ. Think of a time when you were given responsibility for doing something really important, something you thought was worth whatever it cost to do it, something in which you found great satisfaction. That is what it means to be part of the church. That is another dimension of the adventure in faith into which God has called us.

Is your brain hurting from overload? The writer of the book of Titus has put a lot of meaning into a few verses. But all of that is part of what follows from the precious simple event that we celebrate on Christmas Day. With shepherds and Wise Men, we gather around the manger and gaze at a newborn baby. And we know that there is something special about this baby and about this birth. In it, "The grace of God has appeared, bringing salvation to all, training us to renounce impiety and worldly passions, and in the present age to live lives that are self-controlled, upright, and godly, while we wait for the blessed hope and the manifestation of the glory of our great God and Savior, Jesus Christ. It is he who gave himself for us that he might redeem us from all iniquity and purify for himself a people of his own who are zealous for good deeds." The next time you find yourself standing by a manger scene, look at the figure that represents the baby and whisper to yourself, "Grace has appeared."

(Consider asking an associate or a lay reader, perhaps one of a different gender from the preacher, to read the scripture passages that are scattered throughout this sermon. It will give an interesting dialogical quality to the presentation.)

**Christmas 1
Hebrews 2:10-18**

The Incarnation: What And Why?

We have just remembered again the beautiful story of the birth of Jesus. We have been reminded of the miracle of the virgin birth. Most of us have been satisfied just to remember and wonder and enjoy. But there is a meaning behind that event that we need to know. Christian scripture and tradition tell us that, in the birth of Jesus, an aspect of God's own being took flesh to dwell among us as one of us. One of our favorite Christmas carols has us singing, "Veiled in flesh the God-head see; hail incarnate deity, pleased as man with men to dwell, Jesus our Emmanuel." What does all of that mean? And what should it mean to us? It is important for us to know. The book of Hebrews tells a story that will help us understand. But first, let me tell you another story.

I will tell you a parable. There was a certain college track team that could not win a track meet. In their particular league, there was a special event that was unique to their area. It was an obstacle course similar to the obstacle courses that are part of military training. Every athlete was expected to run it. That was the team's worst event. They almost had a tradition of finishing last in that event — or of not finishing at all. The college was well endowed and they continued to have a track team because they could offer attractive scholarships. But, they were so famous for losing that only those athletes who couldn't get a scholarship anywhere else would come. They also had a record for changing coaches several times a year. Coaches came and went through the motions halfheartedly until they could find another job where they could coach a winning team. If they didn't quit before the year was over, the college administrators fired them at the end of their losing season because the alumni who contributed to the support of the athletic program believed that they should be able to buy a coach who could produce a winning team. The news media sports reporters finally began to make their own sport of composing derogatory jokes about the losingest team in the league.

Then one year a certain young man with an outstanding athletic record came and applied for the position of coach of the track team. The administration was so surprised at getting an applicant that they did not have to seek out and bribe to come that they gave him the job. At the first practice, a cynical team member asked, in the hearing of the whole team, "How long are you going to be here, one week or two?" The coach answered in the hearing of the whole team, "I am here for my whole career if the alumni will let me stay. I believe you can win and I am here to help you do it. Don't wonder about me. I am with you. I am going to be here. Are you?" At first, the team didn't believe him. But he acted like he meant it. He came to each workout and practice session with real enthusiasm. He told the team members, "There are two things I want you to do. Believe you can win and live like winners." The team members joked about the coach's platitudes in private. But he acted as if he meant for them to take it seriously.

The coach worked hard. He tried to make a friend of each team member. He worked with them individually, analyzing their needs and showing them what to do. Finally, the day came for the team to work on the obstacle course. The coach told the team members to watch as he ran the course to show them how it should be done. The coach had one of the team members hold the stop watch and keep his time. He ran the course perfectly and, to everyone's surprise, his time broke the league record. The coach said, "If I can do that, you can do it, too. I am a guy just like you." The team members were impressed — but they didn't believe it.

At the end of the season, they finished last again. They could not even finish the obstacle course. The alumni yelled for the dismissal of "that preachy coach," but there was no one else who would consider coming. The sports pages began to announce that the losingest team had another losing coach. To everyone's surprise, the coach was offered another job in spite of his losing season — but he didn't take it. He said to the team members, "I told you I am with you and I meant it. Now believe you can win and live like winners." Some of the team members began to take him seriously and to work harder. Bit by bit, the team's attitude changed. Finally the time came for the team to run the obstacle course in practice. The coach followed his tradition and ran it before them. Then he stood at the finish line and shouted, "Come on now; if I can do it, you can do it." And one by one, they did it. They began to believe that they could win and to live like winners. They won several preliminary competitions.

But the change had escaped the attention of the alumni and the administration. By then, they had made a joke of the preachy coach and his platitudes. One prominent big contributor to the athletic fund found another person whom he persuaded to apply for the position of coach. The coach was terminated just before the final track meet. The team members were shocked. They didn't quite know what to do. But when they came to the track meet, they saw their old coach in the stands. Every time a team member was about to compete, he heard the old coach shouting, "Come on. I believe in you. You can do it." Each team member did his best. And when the time came for the team to run the obstacle course, the old coach found a way to position himself just beyond the finish line so he could be heard yelling, "Come on now. You can do it." And they did. They won the meet. The team members made it their tradition to shout, "Believe you can win and live like a winner." They became a winning team.

The New Testament book of Hebrews tells a story that is similar to that in many ways but much more cosmic in its scope and much more important in its implications for us. The book of Hebrews is a hard book to read. It is full of mixed metaphors and references to ancient traditions that most of us don't remember or understand. Actually, you have to dig around in all of that to find the story line in the book. But when it finally emerges and you see it, it is exciting.

The story begins by assuming our human need. We want to live good and productive lives. We want to live in a good and right relationship with God and with life and with ourselves and with others. But it is hard to do that. Many things in life and within ourselves work against us. We find ourselves living lives of which we are not proud and with which we cannot be happy. We feel like we are parts of that losing team. We can't win. We feel the condemnation that always seems to rest on the losers. But God acted to reach out to us, to make known to us the things that God is always doing for our salvation.

It is important to remember that God is the primary actor in this story. God sent one who was an aspect of God's own being to lead us to life. The opening verses of Hebrews say, "... in these last days, [God] has spoken to us by a Son whom he appointed heir of all things, through whom he also created the worlds. He is the reflection of God's glory and the exact imprint of God's very being, and he sustains all things by his powerful word" (Hebrews 1:2-3a). This one, who will be called "the pioneer" because he came to lead us into faith and life, is God with us. It is important to remember that.

But it is also important to remember that same one became one of us and one with us. He came to identify with us. Like the track coach in the parable, he came saying, "I am with you. I am committed to you. I am one of you." The text says that Jesus was not ashamed to call us brothers and sisters. "Since, therefore, the children share flesh and blood, he himself likewise shared the same things ..." (Hebrews 2:14).

Living as one of us, he experienced life as we experience it. The text says, "It was fitting that God, for whom and through whom all things exist, in bringing many children to glory, should make the pioneer of their salvation perfect through sufferings." He even experienced temptation. Later, the book says he was in every respect tested as we are (Hebrews 4:15). He experienced uncertainty, anxiety, pain, loneliness, and all of the other things we experience. "Because he himself was tested by what he suffered, he is able to help those who are being tested" (Hebrews 2:18). Having identified with us and shared our life situation, Jesus was able to accomplish several important things for our salvation.

The text says he made "a sacrifice of atonement for the sins of the people" (Hebrews 2:17). Whenever we read about atonement in the Bible, we are reading about God forgiving our sins and not holding our guilt against us. This is a very important part of the saving work of God. It is one of the things that is represented by the suffering of Jesus. It tells us that we are accepted by God as we are. No, it does not say that our sins were okay. But it does say that God has set our past failures aside so that he can start with us where we are and lead us into a better life.

Hebrews also tells us that the pioneer lived the life that we are called to live and did it under our circumstances to show us that it can be done. Like the track coach in the parable, he ran the obstacle course that is set before us to show us how to do it and to show us that we can do it. He was "in every respect tested as we are, yet without sin." What kind of life is this that he lived to set an example for us? It was a life of faithfulness to the purpose of God. "Jesus, the apostle and high priest of our confession, was faithful to the one who appointed him, just as Moses was 'faithful in all God's house'" (Hebrews 3:1-2). He lived a life of commitment to God's purpose for himself and for the whole creation. That is the kind of life we are called to live. That kind of life will take different shapes for different people, but it will always be a life of faith and of love. Jesus has shown us that we can live that kind of life under our circumstances no matter how difficult they are.

He has also shown us that we need not allow ourselves to be intimidated by the threat of death, either by the ultimate death that ends our lives or by the little deaths with which we are so often threatened by those who want to control us. He died rather than allow the threat of death to turn him aside from his commitment to God's purpose. He did that "... so that through death he might destroy the one who has the power of death, that is, the devil, and free those who all their lives were held in slavery by the fear of death" (Hebrews 2:14-15).

Can you see why it was necessary for the Son of God to become one of us and to live under our circumstances? It made it possible for him to suffer for our sins and to set us free from guilt. It made it possible for him to show us the life for which we were created and to demonstrate that we can actually live it under our human limitations and circumstances. And it made it possible for him to set us free from the fear that so often keeps us from living in obedience to God's higher purpose.

But then the story enters another phase. After the death and resurrection of Jesus, he returned to being with God and being an aspect of God's own being. He went where God is. The book of Hebrews uses traditional ancient imagery and talks about Jesus sitting at the right hand of God in heaven, making sacrifices for us in the heavenly temple, and representing us before God. That can translate into an image of the one who once was one of us now being an aspect of God who comes to meet us and to interact with us in all of our interactions with life.

Now we find ourselves reckoning with the great question that all of us ask and answer without knowing it every day when we walk out the door to meet life and to live it. We have to ask: How will life deal with me? Will it afflict me, or condemn me, or be indifferent toward me?

The book of Hebrews tells us that, even though many hurtful and cruel things may happen to us in life, the one who stands behind all of those experiences, the one who counts, is one who loves us enough to be committed to our salvation, one who understands what we are going through because he has been through it too, one who forgives our sins and accepts us as we are, one who expects much of us, and one who believes in us and is pulling for us — like the track coach sitting in the stands and shouting, "Come on, you can do it." That enables us to go to meet life with confidence and expectancy. The book says, "Since, then, we have a great high priest who has passed through the heavens, Jesus, the Son of God, let us hold fast to our confession. For we do not have a high priest who is unable to sympathize with our weaknesses, but we have one who in every respect has been tested as we are, yet without sin. Let us therefore approach the throne of grace [let us approach every experience of our lives] with boldness, so that we may receive mercy and find grace to help in time of need" (Hebrews 4:14-16).

Later the book actually comes close to the image of the parable of the track coach saying, "... let us also lay aside every weight and the sin that clings so closely, and let us run with perseverance the race that is set before us, looking to Jesus the pioneer and perfecter of our faith, who for the sake of the joy that was set before him endured the cross, disregarding its shame, and has taken his seat at the right hand of the throne of God" (Hebrews 12:1a-2).

Now do you understand why Christmas was necessary? Do you understand some of what it means that God is God with us? Can you begin to catch a vision of what it can mean for you to live a life in which God is with us? Can you hear someone shouting from the stands, "Come on, you can make it!"?

Christmas 2
Ephesians 1:3-14

With A Song In Your Heart

What kind of a song does your heart sing as you go through your days? Almost everyone sings some song. Of course, we may sing different songs from time to time, depending upon what is happening in our lives, but most of us have one song that is our song, a song that expresses our feeling about life. Some people dance to meet life, singing something like, "Zip-a-dee-doo-dah, zip-a-dee-ay; My, oh my, what a wonderful day." Others drag themselves into life singing something like, "Nobody knows the trouble I've seen." Do you see what I mean? It makes a difference. Many of us have been walking around for several weeks now humming or whistling or singing Christmas carols. That helps, doesn't it?

In many churches, it is customary to begin every worship service with a hymn of adoration. There may be lots of different moods and acts of worship during the service, representing different human experiences and different aspects of our interactions with God. But, everything comes into perspective more effectively if the congregation starts by remembering that the worship all takes place in the presence of the living God who is great and good and loving. Adoration puts us in the presence of God and reminds us of what we know about God and sets the stage for everything else.

The writer of the letter to the Ephesians evidently believed that everything should start with adoration. Our scripture lesson, the passage just after the address, the passage that is intended to set the stage and to establish the tone for the whole book, is a hymn of adoration. No, it is not actually a hymn that is intended to be sung.

But it is an act of adoration that is intended to perform the same purpose.

The passage starts with a traditional blessing of God, a variation of the blessing with which Jewish people were accustomed to starting their Passover prayers. "Blessed be the God and Father of our Lord Jesus Christ." The hymn then incorporates several of the most joyful themes of the Christian faith. God has made known to us the mystery of his will. God has a good and loving plan for the whole creation and he is working to bring it to fulfillment. God is working to draw all things together into a harmonious unity. There is a place for us in that plan. God chose us before the foundation of the world to be adopted as God's children. He has provided for our redemption, the forgiving of our sins, and he is at work to make us holy and blameless before him in love. We who have believed, who have set our hopes on Christ, have claimed our inheritance and are privileged to live in praise of God. A person who can sing that hymn with confidence has plenty to be happy about, no matter what is going on in his or her life.

Can you sing that kind of a song?

It makes a difference what song your heart sings. A certain man who served in the Air Corps during the Second World War told his son later of his experience after being shot down behind enemy lines. He was captured and confined in a prison camp where the prisoners were subjected to exceptional cruelty. He told his son that the only thing that made him able to endure the ordeal was the songs he had learned in Sunday school when he was growing up. He really had not been much of a churchman but he remembered the hymns and gospel songs that assured him that God is God and that God loved him and cared what was happening to him. He kept remembering those songs and either humming them or singing them when he could, and they helped him to keep everything in perspective and to find the strength to carry on.

A Choctaw Christian woman was dying of cancer in a hospital far from her home and from her people. But her daughter was there, and her daughter stood by her bed during the last hours singing Christian hymns in the Choctaw language, and the woman was able to die with God's promise of eternity in her heart.

And blessed is the person who is able to experience good fortune with a hymn of adoration in his or her heart. In the context of adoration, good fortune evokes gratitude rather than pride or insatiable appetites for more and more. Gratitude is a really happy way of relating to good fortune. It allows us to enjoy fully without slipping into any of the greedy excesses of our culture.

Look at the themes that are parts of the act of adoration in Ephesians. If they are really parts of our song, they can make a great difference in our lives.

The wisdom that God has shared with us teaches us that we do not live our lives in the midst of a chaos of dangerous accidents or under the brazen skies of an indifferent reality. Instead, we live out our lives in the presence of a greater reality who knows and cares and loves. And that one is engaged in significant ways in the dramas of our lives and of human history.

We are also assured that behind and within all of the different things that are going on around us, there is a movement toward the accomplishment of some good purpose that we may not be able to see clearly but that is always there before us. Yes, terrible things happen in our world, stupid, cruel, irrational things that cause awful suffering. And bad things happen in our individual lives, too. They happen because of the freedom God has allowed to exist in the creation. But God has not abandoned the creation. God is still working in it all to pull things together and to move things toward some good future. One observer of the tragic conflicts between Palestinians and Israelis in the Holy Land asserted that, even in this destructive againstness, God is working to draw things together eventually into loving unity. Believing that in the center of our hearts can give life new meaning — and hope. When you have given yourself to the accomplishment of some good purpose and been disappointed by your inability to accomplish it, you can find encouragement in the knowledge that you were not alone in working for that good. The one who called you into that commitment will keep on working through others until everything really good is accomplished.

And when you, yourself, feel defeated, rejected, and hurt, you can know that there is a special place in God's love and in God's plan for you. The adoration from Ephesians tells us that God knew you before the beginning of all things and that God wants something good for you and God is working in your life to achieve it. It may not be the particular good that you have chosen for your goal in life, but, if it is not, it is something better. And God is at work in your life to make it possible. That should invite you to go to meet life in openness and expectancy. Sing a song of adoration and it will make a difference in your life.

But how can we sing a song of adoration? Our experiences of life do not always seem to call for it. The truth is that we all choose what song we will sing. Our circumstances do not always determine it. Look around and you will see that it is true. Look around and you will see people who have everything but the right song who live as if they have nothing. You will also see people who seem to have nothing but a song who are living as if they have everything. Look around and see if it is not true.

But there has to be some reason for choosing to sing a song of adoration. There are too many people who seem to be making up their own songs without regard to reality, just to psyche themselves up or to escape from reality. That can't be right. But we have to make a decision about what we believe about reality. There has to be some truth in it. The song that we sing has to be true. It doesn't always have to be true in the way that theorems in physics and mathematics are true. It can be true in the way that poetry is true. But we have to be able to believe that it is true.

What reason do we have to believe that the affirmations in the Ephesians adoration are true? God has shown us that it is true through Jesus Christ. The text says, "With all wisdom and insight, he has made known to us the mystery of his will, according to his good pleasure that he set forth in Christ ..." (Hebrews 1:8-9). God has made known the real meaning of life in Jesus Christ. Yes, it takes an act of courageous faith to believe that what was shown to us in Jesus is true. But we can look for further evidence at the lives of those people whose lives sing his song. Can we dare to believe that they are the ones who have really discovered the truth about everything? Can we dare to let that song set the tone for our lives?

It is true that life will sometimes call us to sing other kinds of songs. There will be times for singing fun songs or the blues, lament, songs of protest, love songs, and patriotic songs, and lots of other kinds of songs. Life is rich and varied and so is the music of our participation in it when we dare to experience it deeply. But, if the song of adoration is the main theme of our lives, all of the other themes become parts of the symphony. If we allow one of those other songs to be the main theme, our lives will play a different symphony.

The Apostle Paul was a man whose life sang a hymn of adoration. Scholars are still squabbling over whether the letter to the Ephesians was written by Paul himself or by one of his followers who hoped to represent him. But, almost everyone agrees that the letter represents Paul's teachings well. It is also safe to assume that the hymn of adoration with which the letter begins also represents the song that Paul's heart sang throughout his life and work.

Do you remember the story of Paul? As a young man, he was called Saul. He had all of the advantages — a prominent family, a good education, status in the Jewish community, and Roman citizenship — and that was really something special. But Saul was an angry young man. Who knows where that kind of anger comes from? He focused his anger on the early Christians whom he regarded as a threat to his people's way of life. He stood and watched and approved as Stephen was stoned to death for witnessing to his Christian faith. He became a leader in the persecution. But he must have had some misgivings because he seemed to have been accumulating some subconscious guilt feelings that were at war with his anger. Finally, this tormented soul got a warrant for the arrest of any Christians he could find in Damascus. But on his way to that city, he had an encounter with the risen Christ who asked, "Why are you persecuting me?" He was struck blind and taken by members of his party to Damascus. There, a brave Christian named Ananias, one of those whom Saul had come to arrest, came to him and shared the Christian faith with him. Paul accepted the Christian faith as his own faith. He experienced God's freely given love. He knew himself forgiven for all of the bad things he had done. He was given a new way of life and a new purpose to live for and he found great joy in it.

Paul's life was no longer an easy one. He traveled all around the ancient world enduring all sorts of hazards, to share the Christian faith. The young man, who had once had all of the advantages, suffered beatings, imprisonment, shipwrecks, persecution from his own people, and abuse from the Roman authorities. But he did his work with a joyful song in his heart. Even when he knew his death was coming near, he said, "I have fought the good fight, I have finished the race, I have kept the faith. From now on there is reserved for me the crown of righteousness" (2 Timothy 4:7-8). I am sure that the people to whom he ministered heard the song that his life sang as well as the message that his lips spoke. This must have been part of the reason that the people listened.

The eighteenth century in England was not a happy time for many people. It was the time of the beginning of the Industrial Revolution, a time when many people were uprooted and moved to urban centers where they worked long hours at hard labor for very little pay. Lots of people lived in poverty during those days. But the eighteenth century was also the time of the Wesleyan revival in England. The Wesleyan evangelists told the poor people, who felt like outsiders, that God loved them and gave his Son to die for them and that salvation, both now and hereafter, was possible for them. It gave them a new outlook on life. And the Wesleyan revival produced thousands of hymns intended to let the poor people sing the new faith that they had found. Imagine miners, who hardly ever saw the sun, walking together to the mines singing songs like, "Jesus! the name high over all, in hell or earth or sky: Angels and men before it fall, and devils fear and fly. Jesus! The name to sinners dear, the name to sinners given; it scatters all their guilty fear; it turns their hell to heaven." The songs made a difference in the lives of the people and, eventually, in the quality of life in the nation.

Have you known some who always had a positive attitude toward life no matter what was happening to them? Have you known some who always seemed to be grateful to be alive? Have you wished that you could be like them?

Each of us chooses what song his or her life is going to sing. And we always make that choice in the absence of any conclusive evidence about which is the "right" song. A big part of choosing a song is choosing what kind of life we want to live. That gives us good reason to dare to believe what God has shown to us about the meaning of life and to choose for the theme of our lives a hymn of adoration. Let's learn to hear each new sunrise calling to us, in the words of the liturgy, "Lift up your hearts." And let us learn to respond joyfully, "We lift them up unto the Lord." Then let us move into each new day singing, "Joy to the world...."

**Epiphany 1
(Baptism Of The Lord)
Acts 10:34-43**

Someone Is Trying To Get Through

Someone is trying to get through to you. Someone with an important message for you is trying to get in touch with you. It would be greatly to your advantage to make contact with the one who is trying to get through to you.

That is what Epiphany is all about. This is the season of Epiphany in the church year. "Epiphany" is a Greek word that means the showing forth of God, or God's self-revelation. Epiphany means that God is trying to get through to us to make God's self known to us, to help us experience the reality of God and to help us discover what life can be like if we allow our lives to be shaped by our relationship with God.

We really need to let God get through to us. By trying to help us experience a relationship with God, God is trying to help us to meet one of the biggest needs of our lives. God is trying to help us to answer a big question that every one of us asks — and eventually answers — in the very center of our being. The question is too big to put into words. If we had to put it into words, it would sound something like, "What is life really all about?" or "How is everything out there related to me and how should I relate to it?" or "Who am I and how do I fit into everything?" Many of us may never in our lives have asked those questions in words. But every one of us lives her or his way through a quest for an answer and every one of us comes up with some kind of an answer and, for good or for ill, the answers we come up with shape our lives.

If you want to do something interesting — and very significant — look at the ways in which the people you know are living their lives and try to guess what kinds of answers they must have come up with to the question about the meaning of life. Then, when you have gotten good at it, ask those same questions about yourself.

God wants to give us the answer to our big question. But the answer we need is not something that can be just stated in words and explained and believed, though that may be a part of the process. The answer that we need is something that has to be shown to us so that we can experience it.

Just as the big question cannot adequately be put into words, the answer can't be adequately put into words, either. But, again, if we had to put it into words, it might sound something like this: "There is a great someone out there who is in and behind all of the little things that surround us in life and that someone is God. God is great and powerful beyond our ability to imagine and God loves us like a parent loves a child. If we learn to trust that great someone and to love that great someone and to try to know and to do what that great someone wants us to and to let our whole lives be shaped by our relationship with that great someone, then our lives will be good in a way that we just can't imagine until we have experienced it."

Now you can see why the message that we need to hear can't just be delivered in words. We have all heard those words, or others like them, a thousand times, haven't we? But lots of us seem not to have really gotten the message yet, at least not completely, because our lives have not really been reshaped by the message behind them. That is why God keeps trying to get through to us to make God's self known to us. That is what we really need to know. We don't just need to know about God, we need to know God. We need to experience the reality of God and to experience our relationship with God in a way that will reshape our lives from the inside out.

God has been trying to get through to us and to be known by us since the beginning of time.

God created everything that is. Just looking at the vastness and the intricacy and the beauty of all that God has created should make us able to know that God is. In fact, many people have been able to come to their first experience of the reality of God while marveling at the creation that we see around us and within us. It can also make us able to know a lot about God. The Apostle Paul believed that people should be able to tell a lot about what is right and what is wrong just by looking at the order of the creation. He wrote, "What can be known about God is plain to them, because God has shown it to them. Ever since the creation of the world, his eternal power and divine nature, invisible though they are, have been understood and seen through the things he has made" (Romans 1:19-20).

God has also been trying to get through to us through the experiences of our lives and the history of the human race. The people of Israel learned to experience God in that way, and they have left us a fascinating record of the things they have learned through those experiences.

But at one particular time in human history, God did something really special to help us know God in a way that would help us to come to a new understanding of God and a new relationship with God. God came to live among us as one of us. God was born among us in the form of a helpless little baby. His parents named him Jesus, which means "The Lord's Salvation." The event itself was not very impressive. But God made it known to a few people — the child's parents, some shepherds, some astrologers from a distant country, and a few others — that something really special was happening in the birth of this baby. God was being shown forth among us in a surprising new way.

About thirty years later, that baby had grown up into a young man. One day, he came to a place by the Jordan River where his kinsman, John, was preaching repentance and a baptism for the cleansing of sins. Jesus came and asked to be baptized. John recognized him as the one who was to make God known to all people, and he did not want to baptize him. But Jesus insisted. He knew that his baptism would be a very special happening. It would enable him to stand with a needy human race in their need so that he could begin to minister to them. After Jesus was baptized, the Spirit of God came upon him and the voice of God was heard saying, "This is my Son ..." (Matthew 3:17).

Soon after that, Jesus began his ministry. He went around his country telling people about God's love and doing loving things, like healing the sick, so that people could experience the reality of God's love. Jesus taught that we should live trusting God and obeying God and loving God as if God is our king and that, if we do, we will experience a new kind of life and participate in building a new kind of world.

Many people were drawn to God by his message. But, for one reason or another, some could not receive it. They hated the one who came to show us God's love. They hated him so much that they killed him. And he loved them — and us — so much that, to show us how much God loves us, he died. God would not let the story end there. To show us that Jesus had indeed shown us God, God raised him up out of death.

But that was not the end of God's trying to get through to us and to make us able to know God. The same God who once came among us in the visible form of the man, Jesus, continues to live among us in the invisible form of the Holy Spirit and to do the same works that Jesus did among us. As the Holy Spirit, God continues to work among us through people, especially the people who have come to know God and to live lives that are shaped by their relationship with God. God continues to work especially — but not only — through the church, which is the fellowship of those who are committed to living lives shaped by their relationship with God. God continues to work through such people to make God known.

Our scripture lesson for today tells about part of a very important event that took place in the story of God's trying to get through to us. For some time after the death and resurrection of Jesus, the faith that Jesus taught was shared only among the people with whom Jesus had lived, his own people, the Jews. But God had really sent Jesus to make God and God's new possibility known to all people. God spoke to Peter, one of the leaders of the followers of Jesus, and told him to go and talk with a group of people who were not Jews. They were people who wanted to hear about Jesus. They were gathered in the home of a Roman army officer named Cornelius. Even though it broke all of the traditions of his people,

Peter went, in obedience to God, and shared the Christian faith with them. Our scripture lesson is a summary of what he said. There must have been much more. Eventually, the people gathered there in the house of Cornelius came to experience the reality and the presence of God. They received the Holy Spirit just as the Jewish Christians had. When Peter saw that they had indeed come to know God, he baptized them into the Christian faith. That was the beginning of the church's mission to make God known to all of the people of the world.

God is still trying to get through to everyone. God is still trying to get through to us. Why is it so hard for God to get through to us? Maybe we have just not been tuned in. Maybe we have been so preoccupied with other things that we have just not been paying attention when God has tapped us on the shoulder or spoken into our ears. Or maybe God's message has gotten drowned out in all of the static that confuses our ability to receive. After all, there are an awful lot of voices whispering — talking — shouting in our ears and trying to tell us what life is all about. It can be confusing. And an awful lot of us are living confused lives, lives that fall far short of that good life that God wants for us.

But God is still trying to get through to us — and we need to let God get through to us — and we need to let our discovery of God bring us into a new set of relationships with God and with life so that our lives can be all that they can be.

How can we do that? How can we tune God in so that God can get through to us and be known to us? When and how can that happen?

It could happen to us as we are sitting in church. After all, that is really what church services are for. It could actually happen. When you come into a church, remember that God is really there. The preacher is not just talking about something or someone who is somewhere else — if anywhere. The preacher is trying to introduce you to someone who is really there and who wants to get in touch with you. Remember to look beyond the words that are spoken to see the realities that they represent. Remember, when you go through the motions of rituals, like the service of the Lord's Supper, to see yourself actually living through the relationships and interactions that the ritual is trying to dramatize. If you give it a chance to happen, God may actually get through to you while you are sitting in church.

But don't stop "tuning in" when you leave the church building. Remember, God is in the church, but God is everywhere else, too. Remember the things that you heard in church and keep watching to see if any of them will give you a new way of understanding the things that happen to you in your daily life. God really is there in and behind all of the other things that surround you in life. God is trying to get through to you through the experiences of your daily life. God may finally get through to you as you drive to work or as you sit in class or as you wash the dishes or as you do whatever you do day by day. Just stay open to the presence of God.

When, at last, you find yourself experiencing the reality of God, even if you just experience it a little bit, stop and pay attention to what you are experiencing. Don't just push it aside and go on to more pressing things. It is interesting that one part of the call to prayer to which Muslim people respond several times a day says, "Nothing is more important." We all need to remember that nothing is more important than getting in touch and staying in touch with the living God. Pay attention to your experience of God and move it to the center of your life and let your life be very intentionally reorganized around it. That will be a growing experience for you. You will learn more and more about God and about yourself and about life as you live daily in relationship with the living God.

When you find yourself living a new kind of life that is shaped by a relationship with God, live it openly and unashamedly and joyfully. When people ask you what shapes your life, talk about your faith freely. It really is not impolite to talk about your religion unless you cut down someone else's religion. Share what you have discovered. You just may be the agent through which God may get through to some others, just as Peter was the agent by which God got through to Cornelius and his friends.

When God finally gets through to you, it can make a difference in your life. Then you may make a difference in the world you live in. To see how that might work, let's go back to the story of Peter and Cornelius.

Cornelius was an interesting person. He was a high officer in the Roman army of occupation sent to govern the troublesome people of Palestine. But Cornelius had actually adopted the religion of the people he was sent to govern and he practiced it quite devoutly. He had probably been raised in the Roman version of the Greek religion that had many gods, all of whom had some very human failings, and all of whom could be managed by people who knew how to do it. He was a participant in a power structure that he knew was oppressive to everyone — even those, like himself, whom it favored. He must have found something attractive about a religion committed to the worship of one God who made the heavens and the earth and who was committed to justice for all people.

But we can imagine that there were still some deep needs in his life. He must have heard of Jesus and he must have felt a deeper sadness than most because he had probably been required to participate in the execution of other innocent people, following the orders of some powerful person who thought it would be expedient. There must have been lots of painful guilt feelings. There must have been a deep yearning for some way to peace, both peace in the world and peace in his heart.

When he heard the message of peace through Jesus Christ and of forgiveness of sins, and when he then experienced those things through the Holy Spirit, we can know that it must have made a big difference in his life. If he then began to exercise his power in love, that may have made a difference in life for many people.

But the same encounter made a difference in Peter's life. Peter probably knew more than anyone else in the world at that time about Jesus Christ and about the Christian faith. But he had continued to be contained within the Jewish traditions about not associating with people of other races. When God sent him to preach to Cornelius and his friends, God pushed back the horizons of Peter's faith. Soon after that, the Christian church began to reach out to the non-Jewish people of the world — and that made a big difference for lots of people in the world — including us.

Someone really is trying to get through to you — and to all of us. Someone with an important message about an exciting new possibility really is trying to get in touch with you. God is trying to get through. It really would be good for you to tune in.

**Epiphany 2
Ordinary Time 2
1 Corinthians 1:1-9**

Thank God For The Church

Try to visualize yourself on the way to church. Not too difficult? Let's make it a little harder. Imagine that the year is 55 A.D. and that the place is the city of Corinth in Roman Greece. You are a member of the thriving church that has grown up there and you are on your way to a meeting at the house of Gaius. Lots of people will be gathering both from the church that usually meets at the house of Gaius and also from the churches that meet in the houses of several other Christians. News has been passed around that a letter has come from Paul and everyone is eager to hear what Paul will have to say about the things that are going on in the church.

It is late afternoon and you are walking from your house on the edge of the city nearest to the harbor to the house of a prominent citizen near the center of the city. A gentle breeze blows in from the gulf. You reach a high point on the road and pause to look around. You are surrounded by very fine buildings. Some remnants can be seen of the buildings of the old Greek city that the Romans destroyed before refounding it again a hundred years later. You look back toward the gulf to see the sun setting over the water. The harbor is crowded with ships. Corinth is located on a narrow isthmus between two major bodies of water. Many shippers choose to drag their ships overland the few miles between the two or to offload and then reload cargo to make their trip shorter and safer. The port is busy. Corinth has become the business and commercial center of Greece. It will never become the intellectual and cultural center that Athens is, but it is probably the second most important city in the country. This is a busy and prosperous new city. There is little old aristocracy. There is opportunity to move up in business. There is an openness to new ideas and new people. There are many people from many parts of the world here. It is an interesting place to live.

As you turn back to continue your walk, you look up and see the high mountain, Acrocorinth, hovering beyond the city. On it are the ancient fortifications and ornate temples. One of the most prominent is the famous temple of Aphrodite that has made Corinth famous for giving a religious sanction to the sexual permissiveness that is a part of the Greek culture of the day. That is a problem for the church. It is only one of the many problems that come from living in a pluralistic culture.

Finally, you arrive at the house where the church will be meeting. It is a beautiful villa with a large courtyard. The church at Corinth is unique among the early churches in that it has among its members a few of the wealthy and prominent citizens of the city. Of course most of the members, like most of the early Christians in other places, are poor, hard working servants. Some are well educated and hold responsible positions, but they are still clearly of the lower social and economic classes. Some of the newer members of the church still feel awkward about coming into this fine home. Most are not accustomed to being welcomed into the homes of the prominent, except possibly as servants. But all are welcomed. Paul, who was the founding apostle of this church, made it clear that there should be no distinctions among the followers of the way. Everyone remembers that he said, "There is no longer Jew or Greek, there is no longer slave or free, there is no longer male and female; for all of you are one in Christ Jesus" (Galatians 3:28).

Paul was a very important person to most of the members of the church in Corinth. You remember Paul. He was an intense and energetic person, very deeply committed to what he was doing and saying. He had once been a devout Jew who actually persecuted the church. But after his conversion, he became the chief missionary to the non-Jewish world. He had learned how to articulate the teachings of the Christian faith and to interpret them to people from all sorts of national and religious origins. You remember when Paul came to Corinth. It was a number of years ago. He was on one of his missionary journeys and he recognized the openness to the gospel and also the strategic importance of this place for the spread of the Christian faith. He was clearly excited about the possibilities he saw in the church in Corinth. He spent a year-and-a-half here preaching the good news of Jesus Christ, instructing the converts in the Christian faith and life, and training the people in churchmanship. Paul made a large investment of his energies in this church before moving on. Clearly, he thought it had an important mission to accomplish in the spread of the Christian faith throughout the world.

But Paul left several years ago. Things have changed at Corinth. Some of you who remember Paul are fiercely committed to his teachings. But other teachers have come. Divisions have grown up in the church. Some people are being influenced by the culture and trying to incorporate Gnostic philosophy into the faith and others are trying to interpret Christian freedom in ways that would sanction irresponsibility and even immorality. Some are getting carried away with the ecstatic aspects of the faith and behaving as if it is all about speaking in tongues. Some have real questions that need to be answered about how to live as Christians in their pluralistic world. And some are confused about what to believe about the resurrection. Tensions have developed between the church and Paul. Paul is living in Ephesus now, doing there the same kind of work he did in Corinth. Everyone knows that the letter will address these issues. Although you are all anxious to hear what he will say, there is a certain amount of dread in your anticipation. Paul is known for speaking plainly and you all know that there are some things going on in the church that Paul does not like.

You enter the courtyard and greet the other members of the fellowship. Most are a little more reserved than they usually are, especially those who you know disagree with you about some of the issues Paul is sure to address. Ordinarily, there might have been a love feast or a time for the sharing of witnesses. But this time the letter from Paul will be the primary order of business. Everyone joins in singing some psalms and someone leads a prayer. Then one of the church leaders announces the letter, unrolls the scroll, and begins to read. The anticipation is electric.

The letter starts in a traditional way. Yes, Paul is careful to state the address in a way that makes it clear that he thinks of himself as an apostle by the will of God. He mentions his Christian brother, Sosthenes, whom you know and who is with him in Ephesus. He goes on to address the church as if he thinks you are all something special, people sanctified in Christ, called to be saints, that is, called to be set apart for the service of God, and parts of a larger fellowship that is developing throughout the ancient world. He wishes you all the very best he knows to wish you: grace, the freely given love of God, and peace, wholeness, and salvation from God the Father and the Lord Jesus Christ. The address sets the stage with an affirmation. Then Paul goes on to give thanks for the church. He gives thanks for all of the good things that are happening among you and for the gifts and the promises that God has given to you. He also gives thanks for the faithfulness of God who called you into fellowship with him which, he is sure, will lead you through to the fulfillment of his promise.

You feel yourself relaxing a little. You look around and see that others are relaxing a little, too. One fellow, with whom you recently had a heated argument about one of the big issues facing the church, looks at you and smiles. You all know that the letter has just begun. Paul is still going to have a lot to say about all that is going on among you and it will not all be complimentary. But the context has been set in a positive way. You are the church. God is at work among you. Paul knows that and appreciates it. Paul loves you and God loves you. Now you can deal with the issues that need to be dealt with.

Now stop imagining that you are in ancient Corinth. Remember all of the things we have said about that church, because we will be studying lessons from 1 Corinthians for several weeks and all that we have said will be useful background. But now you can see yourself as a part of your own church in the here and now. How much of what has been said still applies?

Is your church not, like the church at Corinth, a church called into existence by God for the purpose of doing God's work in the world? Have you not learned of the saving grace of God through this church? Have you not been taught the Christian way of life here? And have you not seen to it that your own children and others who came into the church were enabled to learn those things, too? What are the special gifts that have been given to your church that give it unique abilities to serve God? What makes your church special?

What is unique about the community in which your church lives and works? What are the unique stresses it puts upon the lives of those who try to be faithful? What are the greatest needs of the community to which your church ought to respond? What unique possibilities do you see in your community to serve God? How can your church best participate in the worldwide mission of the Christian church?

Can you see that, if Paul had indeed been the founding pastor of your church, he might have some of the same excitement about your church's possibilities that he had about those of the church in Corinth?

But now we have to ask the other question, too. Are there any things going on in your church that are interfering with its ability to carry out its mission? Are any of the same things going on in your church that went on in Corinth? Are there any party divisions within your church? Are there people caught up in the worship of personalities, some who liked the last pastor better than the present one and others who are anxious for the coming of the next pastor because they don't really like any of the pastors they have had. Are there theological differences within your church, some who believe that others just do not hold right beliefs? Are there jealousies between people and groups because each of them thinks that their part of the church's work is more important than the others? Are there arguments about the right way to worship? Are there selfish people who insist upon their own rights without regard to the effect of their exercise of freedom on the lives of others? Are there some who act as if they are either spiritually or intellectually a little better than others? Are there some who are embarrassing the church by not living up to the teachings of the faith? Are there some who are taking liberties with the teachings of the faith? All of these things were going on in Corinth. Are there other things that are going on in your church that hinder the effectiveness of the church in doing its work?

Things like that are going on in your church, aren't they? They go on in all churches. And some of us are very disillusioned because of them. Some of us are tempted just to give up on the church and to withdraw into the "solitary spirituality" that so many in our culture advocate and maybe even to feel superior about doing it. But that is no answer.

Paul will go on in his letter to tell us that we ought not to become complacent about these things. The work that the church has to do in the world is too important for us to tolerate petty little things that detract from its effectiveness in its mission. We ought to be very intentional about working these things out. And we can work them out if we approach them in faithfulness to the Christian gospel and in love for each other.

But the most important thing for us to remember is that the church is the *church*, the fellowship of those set apart for the service of God and commissioned to do the work of God in our communities and throughout the world. We, like Paul, must be able to take a full and honest look at the church as it is and still give thanks for the church and hold on to the confidence that God, who is faithful, will finally be able to help the church become what God wants it to be and to do what God wants it to do. Commit yourself to helping the church become what God wants it to be. But start by giving thanks for the church. End by giving thanks for the church. And, while you are doing everything in between, give thanks for the church.

Epiphany 3
Ordinary Time 3
1 Corinthians 1:10-18

Removing Obstacles

Our church has an important mission. Our church was called into existence to witness to the good news of God's love that was shown to us in Jesus Christ. Our church exists to share God's love, to bring people into a fellowship in which God's love is shared, and to help people grow into followers of Jesus. There are people, perhaps many people, within the reach of our church who are hungry for the love of God that we were given to share. Our church has been commissioned to teach the way of love that is the hope of the world. Most of the people of the world probably don't yet realize how urgently they need to learn the way of love, but the need is great and urgent. Our church has a very important mission. Our church's mission is just about the most important thing going on in our community and in our world today.

That being the case, doesn't it make sense that we should organize the whole life of our church around the accomplishment of that mission? And, doesn't it make sense that we should be careful not to let anything go on in our church that would hinder the accomplishment of that mission?

Can you think of any things that could go on in our church that would appear to contradict the good news of God's love that we have been called to share? Can you think of any things that could go on in our church that would turn people away rather than drawing them into the love and the new life that we are supposed to offer them? Can you think of any things that *are* going on that may be turning people away?

Paul wrote his letters to the Corinthians, in part, because he had heard that some things were going on in that church that contradicted the gospel and that were a hindrance to the mission of that church. In his letters, he tried to bring those things to the surface and to set them in the context of the Christian faith so that the Corinthian Christians would know what to do about them. The things that Paul said to the Corinthians can help us to get things into proper perspective, too.

Paul stated the problem. He had heard that there are divisions in the church and that the people are quarreling with one another rather than being united in the same mind and purpose.

At first glance, it appeared that something like denominations were emerging as the churches meeting in different houses in the city chose to give their allegiance to one or another of the leaders of the church with whom they were familiar. Some were still dedicated to Paul, the one who had organized their church and brought many into the Christian faith. Others were attracted to another leader who had come after Paul, an attractive young man named Apollos who had received an excellent education in Alexandria, one of the greatest centers of learning in the ancient world. He would have been expert in relating the Christian faith to popular Greek philosophies. Still others had been in contact with Cephas, Peter, the one who had been the leader of the followers of Jesus and who would represent a more conservative kind of Jewish Christianity. And there seemed to have been some who took a superior attitude and said, "We belong to Christ," just to get above the other divisions.

These could indeed have been divisions along the lines of significant theological differences — or they could have been divisions based on the personal attractiveness of the several leaders. But, in fact, it eventually became apparent that neither of these was really what was dividing the church. Differences don't have to cause divisions. Differences of opinion can be lived with in a community of loving people who are committed to one common purpose. Paul suspected that something else was going on in Corinth.

There were lots of other differences in the church in Corinth. There were people of different races and national origins, people of different religious origins, people of different socio-economic classes, and people of different dispositions. All of these caused differences with regard to certain aspects of the Christian faith. Some seem to have been incorporating some kind of Greek "wisdom" philosophy into their faith and claiming to be superior to others. Some were interpreting Paul's teachings about grace as an excuse for moral laxity. Some were using their Christian freedom in ways that were causing problems for other Christians. Some who had received the gift of speaking in tongues were claiming to be superior to other Christians. All of these were significant issues — but none of them was the real problem that was dividing the church. They were just the excuses for acting out the real conflicts.

What was actually going on in Corinth? Surprisingly, it was something very similar to something that goes on in our society.

You see, Corinth was a major center of commerce, a business-oriented city. And it was a new city whose life was not built around any old aristocratic structures. Some people had become very rich and some people were very poor and there were some people on each step of the ladder in between. And, it was a place where upward mobility was possible. People could climb the social and economic ladder. Many people were preoccupied with doing just that — and many others were trying to think of reasons for claiming to be superior to others in some other ways. There was competition for status and honor. There was lots of "networking" to form advantageous relationships. That was what was really going on in many of the conflicts that were dividing the church in Corinth.

Does any of that sound familiar to you? There is a lot of that going on in our culture, too, isn't there? If a person's real religion is what is shaping his or her life, then there are many whose real religion has to do with their commitment to getting ahead, even though they profess the Christian faith. It is hard to keep the things that are really important to us from influencing the shape of our religion.

This competitive jockeying for positions of honor and stature had evidently invaded the church in Corinth. Petty jealousies, snobbishness, and quarreling were being played out in the conflicts over real issues. Divisions were appearing within the church. People outside of the church could probably see what was happening better than those who were inside the church. The quarreling made the church unattractive to some who needed to be attracted to the Christian faith. And the snobbishness of some probably made others feel unwelcome.

Does any of that ever happen in our church?

It would be easy for us to start pointing fingers at one another. That would be exactly the opposite of the results this sermon and Paul's letter to the Corinthians hope to accomplish. Instead, let us each look within and see if there are any attitudes or ways of action in our lives that might contribute to conditions that could hinder the mission of our church.

Are there any personal conflicts between us and any other members of the church that we have not yet resolved? Are there any hurt feelings that we insist upon remembering and allowing to create againstness, any personality conflicts that we have not been able to overcome with simple acceptance, any old arguments that should have long since been laid to rest? Are we allowing any things like that to get in the way of the friendship that should be the quality of life in the church? Are we allowing things like this to influence our dealing with the real issues that must be decided in the church rather than thinking them through in terms of the really relevant factors?

If we are old members of the church, or major contributors, or prominent citizens, or people with some other kind of status in the church, do we expect to be honored? Do we expect a little more attention to be paid to our opinion than to others when decisions are being made? Do we think the church ought to organize its life to meet our needs more than to meet the needs of new people who should be attracted into the church? Do we insist on sitting in our favorite pew and make anyone else who sits there feel like a trespasser?

On the other hand, if you are not a part of what you perceive to be the "in" group in the church, do you resent those who are? Do you let that resentment get in the way of your participation in the life and fellowship of the church?

Are there some members of the church you wish would go away? Are there some kinds of people you hope will not come to your church?

These attitudes can be very subtle. They can work in our lives without our ever recognizing them for what they are. But they can play havoc with the ability of the church to witness to the love of God and to bring people into a loving relationship with God and God's people.

Paul said some things to the Corinthians that can help us to get all of those attitudes into perspective.

First, he reminded the Corinthians — and us — that we all have our status in the presence of God as a gift of grace. None of us can claim any standing in the presence of God because of who we are in the community or because of what we have done or because of our goodness or our wealth or our education or even because of our faithfulness. We are saved by grace. Paul said, "God chose what is foolish in the world to shame the wise ... so that no one might boast in the presence of God" (1 Corinthians 1:27, 29). Paul did not say that to cut us down. After all, we have been freely given the role and status of beloved children of God. That is far better than anything we could achieve or claim for ourselves. We should find great joy and self-confidence in that. But, since the best thing that we have is something that has been freely given to us and to others, none of us ought to feel superior to others. We are all parts of one family.

Second, Paul reminds us that the real sign of Christian maturity is not some kind of intellectual or spiritual or cultural sophistication, but the ability to love. The most beautiful chapter in this letter is chapter 13, the chapter that starts with the words, "If I speak in the tongues of mortals and of angels, but do not have love, I am a noisy gong or a clanging cymbal" (1 Corinthians 13:1). Later in the chapter, Paul gives one of the best descriptions of love that can be found anywhere. "Love is patient; love is kind; love is not envious or boastful or arrogant or rude. It does not insist on its own way; it is not irritable or resentful; it does not rejoice in wrongdoing, but rejoices in the truth. It bears all things, believes all things, hopes all things, endures all things" (1 Corinthians 13:4-7). Doesn't

Paul have a beautiful way of stepping on our toes? Paul draws his picture of love and then says, "That is what is supposed to be going on in the church."

In another place, when an issue came up about the Christian's freedom to do certain things, Paul said, "Yes, we ought to claim our freedom. But we ought to use our freedom in loving concern for others and be careful not to do anything that will be a hindrance to others" (1 Corinthians 9 and 10).

Again and again, Paul reminds the people that they should put their mission first and be of one mind and purpose.

Paul provides us with three beautiful images of what it means to work together in the service of the Lord. He insisted that he and Apollos, far from being competitors, were actually partners. He uses one image drawn from farming. He said, "I planted, Apollos watered, but God gave the growth" (1 Corinthians 3:6). A little later, he draws an illustration from building, saying, "... like a skilled master builder I laid a foundation, and someone else is building on it" (1 Corinthians 3:10). But perhaps the most beautiful image of all comes when he compares the members of the church with different spiritual gifts to different members of one human body. He says, "Now you are the body of Christ and individually members of it" (1 Corinthians 12:27).

Paul makes it very clear that he believes that diversity will strengthen the church if people will love each other and live in a shared commitment to one purpose.

Some time ago, St. Pius X Catholic Church in Tulsa, Oklahoma, placed an advertisement in the *Tulsa World* inviting the lapsed to return to church. The ad especially welcomes "singles, twice divorced, under thirty, gay, filthy rich, black and proud, poor as dirt, can't sing, no habla Ingles, married with pets, older than God, more Catholic than the pope, workaholics, bad spellers, screaming babies, three times divorced, passive-aggressive, obsessive-compulsive, tourists, seekers, doubters, bleeding hearts ... oh, and you" (*Christian Century*, July 2-10, 2002, p. 8). Someone asked, "If they all came, could they all get along?" Paul would answer, "If they have the love of God in their hearts, they can."

What will people find when they come to visit our church? Will they find us sharing love with one another and working together in the service of one purpose? Will they find us eager to welcome them into the fellowship and to make a place for them? Let us pray that they will.

Epiphany 4
Ordinary Time 4
1 Corinthians 1:18-31

Different

The Christian faith is supposed to make a difference in our lives. If it doesn't, why should we bother with it? If the Christian faith is supposed to make a difference in our lives, then we should expect that Christians will be different. And, Christians are supposed to make a difference in the world. We know these things — and yet, we tend to want to minimize the difference. We want to be like everyone else — not to offend anyone — to make our faith more attractive to others. But it is the difference that gives the Christian faith its power to save. We would do well to remember just how radically different the Christian faith is from the way in which most of the other people we know live and to let that difference turn our lives into adventures in becoming and in changing things.

Paul said he came to preach the message of the cross and to preach it so that its power can come through.

Do you remember what the cross is all about? It is easy for us to forget, to turn it into a symbol of our religion — or a piece of jewelry. Remember where we got that symbol. The cross was an instrument of cruel torture and execution. A certain young rabbi, who came to show us a new way to live, was executed on the cross for being different and for trying to make a difference — and in that event, the eternal God, who made the heavens and the earth demonstrated God's self-giving love for us. The cross is not just a piece of jewelry or a symbol of a religion. It is the memory of an event whose meaning just keeps on unfolding for those who pay attention to it.

Paul said that message of the cross sounded like foolishness to most of the people to whom he was talking. The Greeks had one way of thinking about everything and the Jews had another, but the cross didn't fit into any of their ways of thinking. He said the cross was a stumbling block to the Jews and foolishness to the Greeks, something that got in the way of their accepting the Christian faith. The Corinthian Christians must have been tempted not to talk too much about the cross. They must have been tempted to turn Christianity into an attractive philosophy that sophisticated people would like.

That same thing is true for us today, isn't it? If we really take seriously the most essential aspects of our faith, won't most of the people in our own culture find it foolishness, something contrary to the way they usually think and act, something they would want to reject? (And isn't there something within even those of us who profess faith that argues with our faith and feels the same way about it?) Let's look at what this message of the cross really has to say to us.

First, it talks to us about God. The truth is, that is a problem for lots of people. No, there are not many people who claim to be atheists. Most of us say we believe there is a God — but most of us live as if there is not one. Most of us live lives shaped only by our relationships with those things that we can see and touch — and put in the bank. The idea of actually living lives that are shaped by a relationship with some great invisible reality that is beyond our understanding and our control is foreign to most of us. And the wisdom of our day argues against it, too. Science tells us that only things that can be proven "empirically" can count. Law tells us that our community affairs must be conducted in ways that are entirely secular. And, popular culture — the stuff that comes over the television — is eager to push God out of the way because most people associate God with some moral expectations that they find troublesome. Taking God seriously puts us at odds with our culture right off the bat.

Then when we talk about a God who loves us and demonstrates that love is an act of costly commitment, we are really talking a foreign language for lots of people. As we look out at life, many of us see something that is entirely indifferent to us. Others see something that just lays there and waits to be exploited. And many of the rest of us see life as something hostile that attacks us and against which we have to defend ourselves. To see life as the gift and embodiment of someone who loves us and wants what is good for us is a real stretch. But when we think of the giver of life as one who loves us enough to suffer for us, that is really hard to take in.

And if our culture has a hard time understanding what the message of the cross says about God and about all reality, we have an even harder time taking in what it tells us about how we ought to live. It calls us to live in ways that are exactly opposite to the ways in which we are most inclined to live.

The message of the cross calls us to live trustingly. To live in faith means to live trusting the love of God that was demonstrated in the suffering and death of Christ. The wisdom of our day tells us we had better not trust. We had better not trust many people, if any. And, we had better not trust the institutional structures of business or of government or even the church. With more and more of those institutions that we need to trust letting us down and giving us reasons not to trust them, we find it awfully hard to move out into life trusting something we can't see.

The message of the cross tells us to live lovingly. There are still some of us who know that the verb "to love" does not just mean "to have sex with," but when we talk about living in love, we don't have a very clear idea of just what that could mean. We suspect that it has to do with some kind of unrealistic sentimentalism.

And the message of the cross tells us to live in commitment to something bigger than ourselves. It tells us to take up our own cross, that is, to be ready to suffer if we have to and to live in commitment to the purpose of God. That is pure nonsense in our culture. Our culture tells us that life is about getting all you can for yourself no matter what you have to do to get it and that all suffering is to be avoided at any cost.

In his day, Paul said the message of the cross is foolishness — to those who are perishing. We can see that in our day, too, the message of the cross is foolishness to most people. But that is because most people are perishing. The reasons for which the cross seems like foolishness are the reasons why people are perishing — the reasons why we are perishing.

But wait! Who is perishing? What are we talking about? Those who live according to the wisdom of our world look to us like they are thriving and prospering. Those who are best at it live in big houses and drive big cars and don't seem to have a worry in the world. And the businesses and institutions and countries that live in that way seem to get respect and to have the power to control others. So it would appear.

But look again. A certain young man went into the highly competitive field of commercial real estate because he admired the wealth of those who were successful in that field. But as he got to know some of those successful people, he realized that most of them were living over-stressed lives, empty of any real satisfaction, and that no one he knew had a happy family life. He took warning and changed vocations.

What is really going on in the lives of those who live as if God has abandoned the world and who live defensive or exploitative lives, empty of love and committed only to selfish little goals? Are they really living — or are they perishing?

And what is going on in your life as the result of your own participation in that way of life? It is hard not to get drawn into participating in it to some extent. What is it getting you? Is what is getting you what is really good about your life — or is what is really good coming from another source?

And what is it getting for our world? Are the structures of community life and public morality and business life and national life really healthy — or are things beginning to fall apart? Think hard about that.

The message of the cross is foolishness to those who are perishing. That is why we are perishing. But to those who are being saved, it is the power of God. It is time for us to talk about that, isn't it?

What does it mean that the message of the cross is the power of God for those who are being saved? It means that it can lead us into a relationship with God that can make life work. It can make life really good in this world and give us the promise of eternal life in the world to come. It means that the message of the cross can lead communities and nations into a way of living together that could actually bring peace with justice in this world. The Bible writers had experienced this new life and they wrote to bear witness to it and to tell us how to enter into it. Paul ends one passage of scripture saying, "[God] is the source of your life in Christ Jesus, who became for us wisdom from God, and righteousness and sanctification and redemption" (1 Corinthians 1:30). All of those are religious words that mean, with God's help, they had finally gotten it right.

But that is still a bold claim: The message of the cross is the power of God for salvation. Why should we believe it? Why should we bet our lives upon it — because we know that is where this whole conversation is going. We really need to know.

Well, let's ask again: What has been your experience? Earlier we asked what you had found to be the results of living according to the skepticism and cynicism and selfishness of the world. We have all participated in some of that. We know what it got us. But most of us have at least sampled the ways of relating to life that the message of the cross has taught. Have you sampled, even just in brief moments, the awe of realizing that there is some greater reality out there beyond the little things we can see and touch, some invisible reality that holds things together and makes them work? Have you even experienced the freedom that comes with being able to trust? Have you ever experienced being loved? Have you ever experienced sharing love with others? Have you ever gotten involved in the service of something bigger than yourself and experienced the new meaning that gives to your life? What were those experiences like? Didn't you find those experiences making you really alive in a new way?

Try to imagine what life would be like if those were the dominant attitudes and motives and qualities of your life. Wouldn't that be life at its best? Wouldn't that be salvation? Do you know anyone who seems to be living that kind of life more fully than you are? Does that person's life have about it qualities that you would like in your own life?

And what about the salvation of the world? We have all seen things falling apart because people keep exploiting and threatening and abusing each other for their own advantage and profit. Many of the important structures of life in our society, things like the medical care system, the legal system, and the welfare system, are in danger of falling apart because people have been exploiting them. Where have you seen the opposite thing happening? Have you seen communities and families where people were able to live together trusting each other and loving each other and where people worked together for the good of everyone? What was life like in those situations? It was really good, wasn't it? Can you imagine what life would be like if every community, every church, every family, yes, if the whole world learned to live that way? Wouldn't that be a kind of salvation for the world?

When Paul said that the message of the cross is the power of God for salvation, he was saying that God acted in Jesus Christ to show us a better way of life and to put us in touch with one who can help us actually to be able to live it. It is interesting that he spoke of those "who are being saved," not of people who have been saved. He and the other early Christians knew themselves as people who were in the process of moving from one way of life to another, and he experienced that as the process of being saved.

But, now, what are we going to do about that? It requires a decision of us — and it is not an easy decision to make. It requires a commitment of us — and it can be a costly commitment. Can you actually believe that this message that will seem like utter foolishness to most of the people around you — and probably also to certain parts of what is within you — is the way to fullness of life? Are you willing to leave the familiar old ways of living and to be really different? You will not need to act superior or to be offensively different, but you need to be willing to be made deeply different from the way you may have been and from the way most other people are, different in your basic ways of understanding life and of relating to life and everything in it, different in your ways of putting life together and making it work. Are you willing to venture out believing that the way you are following will lead to fullness of life and salvation?

Then are you willing to invite others to come and be different with you? Are you willing to work to make the world different as God wants it to be different? If you will, you can become a part of the hope of the world.

A certain man, we will call him Bill, told how he happened to become a Christian missionary. His story started when he was an aggressive young businessman, riding the wave of a booming economy in a city that was enjoying spectacular economic growth. He was intent on getting rich. He presented himself to others — and to himself — as a successful man who had everything going for him. But, in fact, everything was falling apart for him, his marriage, his business, his life.

At just that time, Bill went to one of those gatherings where businessmen go to make profitable contacts, and there he met an old friend who had been very successful in business and was then living in another state. They talked for a long time. The old friend invited Bill to come to visit him. They made an appointment. When the day for the appointment came, Bill flew his private plane to his friend's city, expecting to have some opportunity to make some money. The friend met him at the airport and drove him to a bank. He ushered him into a conference room where they met two other businessmen. So far, everything was going as Bill had expected.

But when the conversation started, Bill got a surprise. His friend told him that, during their previous visit, he had realized that Bill was going through some things that he had gone through. He told how he had been caught up in scrambling after material wealth as if that were the most important thing in his life, and how he finally realized that he was just about to make a mess of his life. Then he told how he had found peace and a truly fulfilling life through the Christian faith. The other two men at the meeting shared similar stories. Then they engaged Bill in a conversation about what was going on in his own life. The "meeting" lasted several hours. Before it was over, Bill was able to deal honestly with the fact that his life was disintegrating and to enter into the new possibility that his friends were trying to share with him. Bill had been a church member for a long time, but he had never moved his faith to the center of his life. He did that as he knelt with the three other men in the conference room of a bank and prayed.

In the months that followed the meeting, everything changed for Bill. The three men who had shared their faith with Bill had been able to allow their lives to be reorganized from the inside out while they continued in their same family and business situations. Their transformations had transformed their world. But it was too late for Bill. His old life collapsed. But he had found what he needed to build a new one. Bill eventually found himself living in a foreign country doing the work of a Christian missionary, living a life that was radically different from his old life, a life shaped by radically different values and commitments. But, Bill said he had never been happier. He was a different person, a person whose life was shaped by the message of the cross that he once would have called foolishness. He was different — and he was glad.

We are called to be different, too.

Epiphany 5
Ordinary Time 5
1 Corinthians 2:1-12 (13-16)

How Does It Work?

There is a very nice book for children that is titled, *The Way Things Work*. It uses cartoons and diagrams and simple explanations to help young children understand the operation of such things as a magnet, a light bulb, a water faucet, and even a car engine and a computer. These are things that children see working every day. They even have to work with some of them. It is important for them to understand how these things work so that they will understand how to work with them.[1]

We need to know how the Christian faith works, too. We know that the Christian faith can make a difference in our lives, but how does it do that? How does it work? At first the answer to that question seems obvious. If you just follow the rules and live according to the wisdom of the Christian faith, it will change your life. That seems obvious. But that is not the right answer. There is wisdom and there are rules in the Christian religion and they have important roles to play, but they are not what changes our lives, at least not alone. The thing that really makes the difference in a Christian's life is a relationship, an ongoing relationship with the living God.

In the Corinthian church in Paul's day, there were Jewish Christians who wanted to keep following the Jewish traditions and obeying the Jewish religious laws. And there were Greek Christians who valued the Greek philosophies that are still influential today. There were also some who believed that there was a kind of secret wisdom that some people had that made them superior to everyone else.

I suppose that in every age and in every culture there have been traditional wisdoms that people have valued. Until well into the twentieth century, the teachings of Confucius were cherished as the traditional wisdom of China. An educated man was one who had passed advanced examinations on the teachings of Confucius. Anyone who hoped to advance in any profession or in civil service had to pass those examinations, even if he was applying for a job as an engineer. They valued that traditional wisdom.

And new eras can produce their own wisdoms. During the '60s, people like Alan Watt and Carlos Castinada and Baba Ram Dos undertook to produce a wisdom for the counter-culture. It scared the bejeebers out of parents whose children were young people during that era. People seem to like to have some kind of "wisdom" to follow.

But Paul said that wasn't what was important. Now understand, Paul was not an advocate of "dumbing down." Some have said that there is a tendency in our culture today to muddle everything down to the very lowest possible level of intellectual and cultural activity so that no one will expect too much of us. That is not what Paul was suggesting. He was simply saying that learning the wisdom of a culture or of a religion is not what makes the difference in our lives — and a "wisdom" that makes some people feel superior to others is counter-productive.

Now, as a matter of fact, there is a kind of wisdom that is spoken of in the Bible. It is a major theme in some parts of the Old Testament like Psalms and Proverbs and Ecclesiastes and Job. And it has a role to play in the New Testament faith, as Paul said. But it is different from the wisdom that is written in old books or taught by teachers of philosophy. It is the living wisdom that is at work in the mind of God, the wisdom according to which God created the heavens and the earth, the wisdom that God made known to us in Jesus Christ in whom "the Word became flesh and lived among us" (John 1:14). We get in touch with that wisdom by learning to live in a relationship with God. Oh, yes, we have a book. And the book has laws and proverbs and lots of other things in it. The book is the collection of the witnesses of the faithful to what they had learned by experience in relationship with God. It is the purpose of the book to lead us into our own relationship with God.

Paul speaks of living according to the Spirit. He speaks of proclamation with demonstrations of the Spirit and of power and of being taught by the Spirit interpreting spiritual things to people who are spiritual. Paul means something very specific by that. He is not talking about just being religious in a general sort of way. He is talking about reaching out, through that spiritual capacity that is present in each of us to enable us to relate to that which is beyond us. That is what really makes the difference. That is how the Christian faith works. It works by enabling us to live life day by day in an active relationship with the living God. That relationship can reshape our lives.

How does that work? It does not work by giving us some special straight phone line to God so that we can get the right answers to all of our questions and then tell everyone we are infallible because we have been talking with God. It comes, rather, from living in humble openness to that reality who is great beyond our understanding and in willingness to obey when we think we understand the will of God for us.

That can be done through prayer and worship and the study of the Bible. These spiritual disciplines really come to life when you realize that you are having a conversation with someone who really is there.

It can also work itself out in our daily interactions with life. Once we have learned from the Bible what sorts of things God does, we can watch to see when any such things are happening in our lives. When we see those things being done again, we can know that it is God who is doing them and respond in a way that will allow God's saving work to be done in us and through us. The Old Testament writers believed that God worked through happenings in the history of the people of Israel, like the escape from Egypt and the invasion of the Babylonian armies. If God can work in events like that, he can work through things that happen in our everyday lives, too. If we learn to live through our daily interactions with life as interactions with the living God, then our lives will become spiritual adventures and our interactions with God can make a big difference in our lives. Let's talk a little bit now about just how that can work.

Living a spiritual life adds a new dimension to every experience of life. It is like being married. It is a realization that you are not alone. There is someone else who is there with you in life, caring about what you do and about what happens to you, wanting what is good for you. There is someone there whom you don't want to hurt or disappoint, someone whose expectations you want to live up to. There is someone there with whom you can talk, someone who will help. That realization alone can make a big difference in your life. If you are married, you know what a difference it can make for there to be someone there with you and for you. Knowing that God is there can make a similar difference.

Perhaps the biggest difference living in relationship with God can make is that you will know someone loves you. That makes a big difference.

A group of Christian men went into a prison to conduct a retreat for the inmates. It was part of a program called KAIROS. At the end of the retreat, one of the men told what it had meant to him. He said, in all of his life, he had never felt that anyone had loved him. His father left the family when he was only five years old and he felt that somehow he must have been to blame. He kept wanting and needing his mother's love — but he never got it. He said he thought there must be something he had to do to win love and he kept trying to do everything he knew to do to win love from someone, but he never felt love, not at any time in his life. Eventually he dropped into cynicism. He didn't believe in God and he didn't believe that anyone loved him. He didn't talk about what he had done that got him put him in prison, but it must have been related to that. After the men had spent three days with him, sharing their friendship and their faith, he said he finally knew that there is a God and that God loves him. He said that would make a big difference in his life.

Knowing we are loved makes a big difference in all of our lives. Life at its best, the fullness of life that God wants for us, is the life of love, and loving has to start with knowing that we are loved. Paul said that the experience of knowing that we are loved is a pivotal part of the life of the Spirit. In Romans (8:14-17) and in Galatians (4:6-7) he speaks of the Spirit of God witnessing with our spirits and enabling us to call God "Abba," Father, and knowing that we have been adopted as children of God. Once we know that God loves us, we can experience God's love coming through to us in all sorts of real-life experiences, from the love that is shared in our families to the gift of a new sunrise. And knowing that we are loved can make all of the difference in the world.

Eventually the Holy Spirit will lead us out, in the strength of our new enablement, into loving involvement with others and with the world as a whole. The Bible will help us see that God cares deeply about things like injustice and human suffering. When the nightly news — or an encounter with someone who is in need — brings us face to face with injustice and suffering, we will find ourselves caring about those things, too. We will find ourselves wanting to do something about them. We will find our little self-centered lives being turned inside out in commitment to the greater purpose of God for the whole creation. And that commitment will lead us into the experience of needing to grow in many ways we had never expected and being driven back to God to seek help for our becoming. That can make lots of differences in our lives.

Can you see now the shape of the unique wisdom that leads us into relationship with the living God? Lots of devout people want to take the Bible or some other written source book as the embodiment of wisdom and to let obedience to the Bible shape their lives. It is better to take the Bible as our guide on a journey in relationship with God. I cannot emphasize enough that this doesn't mean we can forget about the Bible or disregard anything it says. Paul had a problem with people thinking they could forget about the teachings of the Bible since they were living under grace. He kept saying, "No, no, no, we are talking about the fulfillment of the law and the prophets, not about forgetting them." The Bible introduces us to God and tells us about God so that we can recognize God at work in our lives. And the Bible teaches us how we ought to respond to God when we encounter God in our lives. And the Bible helps us to know when we have wandered off of the track following some whim of our own or some influence that comes from the wrong source. But the thing that reshapes our lives is not a set of written rules. It is a relationship with someone who is alive and at work in fresh, creative ways in our lives and in our world. That makes a great difference in the quality of our lives. Instead of just obeying rules received from the past, we move into the future, eager to discover where our relationship with God will lead us — and that may be a unique experience for each of us.

Duke Ellington was one of the greatest composers and conductors of jazz music in recent history. It is said of him that he would often seek out creative musicians who he thought had something fresh to offer and recruit them into his band — even though some of them would be a little hard to work with. Then he would compose music that would give them opportunities to make their unique contributions. Most composers wrote their music, then sought skilled musicians who could follow orders to play it. But Duke Ellington brought his creative musicians into the process of composition and together with them brought exciting new music into being.

The wisdom of God is like that. God, whom we know because of things that have happened in the past, is still at work creating a new future. And God is eager to involve us in that creative process if we will learn how to reach out spiritually and to be engaged by the Spirit of the living God. Getting involved in that process will make a big difference in our lives — and it will enable us to help God make a big difference in the world. That is how it works. That is how the Christian faith makes a difference.

There is an Alcoholics Anonymous group that has a very significant way of ending a meeting. They spend their meetings talking about the twelve-step program, which is really an application of the life-changing dynamics of the Christian faith to their particular problem. Speakers take turns telling how the program has worked for them to encourage others to give it a chance to work in their lives. Then they close their meeting by joining hands, praying the Lord's Prayer in unison, and then shouting all together, "Keep a-coming back. It works if you work it." We need to know that is true of the Christian faith as a whole. It works if you work it.

---

1. David Macaulay, *The Way Things Work* (Boston: Houghton-Mifflin, 1988).

**Epiphany 6
Ordinary Time 6
1 Corinthians 3:1-9**

Still Under Construction

People print all sorts of things on T-shirts, from advertisements to obscenities to affirmations of faith. One fellow was seen wearing a T-shirt with the words, "Christian Under Construction," printed on it. We can all appreciate what he meant by that. We can talk about the difference faith in Christ is supposed to make in our lives and about how it is supposed to work and even about the samples of the new life in Christ that we have already experienced. But, most of us know that we are not yet what God wants us to be. At our best, we are Christians under construction. And, that is all right. That is a good way to be. The changes that God will make in our lives don't happen all at once. It is a good thing to know that we are in the process of becoming what God wants to make us and to participate in that process very intentionally and joyfully.

In our scripture lesson for today, Paul reckons with the fact that the Christians at Corinth, to whom he is writing, are still Christians under construction. He has been talking about new life in the Spirit and about the Spirit interpreting spiritual things to those who are spiritual. Then he comes down to earth and says, "But, you folks obviously aren't there yet. If you were, you wouldn't be arguing about petty little things like which pastor you like best." He says, "I could not talk to you as spiritual people. I must speak to you as people who are still in the flesh, as infants in Christ." Paul seems impatient at this and disappointed in the Corinthians. But eventually Paul came to understand that this is just part of the process, something that has to be worked with. By the time he wrote the letter to the Romans, which embodies the most mature statement of his teachings, Paul was able to speak eloquently of the process of growing into Christian maturity, a process through which God leads us. He spoke of the hope that "the creation itself will be set free from its bondage to decay and will obtain the freedom of the glory of children of God" (Romans 8:21).

If you really get to know a congregation of the church today, you may have an experience very much like Paul's. When you first visit the church, you may look around at the friendly, attractive people, all dressed up in their Sunday clothes and think, "This is a fine-looking group of Christians." But, as you get to know the people and learn what is really going on in their lives, you will discover that things are not always as they appear to be. You may hear some people expressing some attitudes that do not seem to you to be compatible with the Christian faith, some social snobbishness, some racial prejudice, some impatience and lack of sympathy with the poor of the community and the oppressed of the earth, some hate pretending to be patriotism. You may begin to suspect that some people's lives are being shaped by an anxious pursuit of affluence rather than by trusting obedience to the love of God. You may discover some person struggling to overcome a drinking problem and the whole family having to cope with the effects of that. Some family that seemed at first to be everybody's ideal may turn out to be a blended family made up of the leftovers from two painful divorces and the parents may be working very hard to put something good together under difficult circumstances. Still another family may have an adolescent child who is using drugs. Others may be trying to rebuild their lives after being devastated by some catastrophe like a business failure or the death of a spouse.

When you first discover that the church members are not all what they first appeared to be, your initial reaction may be to think that they are all hypocrites — and some of them may be. But look again. You will discover that many of these same people actually are taking the Christian faith seriously and that they do hope that it will make a difference in their lives. They really have no other reason for being in church. Each of their lives is a story that is still being written, and God is one of the participants in the action that is going on. They are Christians that are still under construction.

Jesus himself understood that the change doesn't take place all at once. In the first part of his Sermon on the Mount (Matthew 5), he keeps trying to move us up to the next level of spirituality. He said, "You have heard that you must not murder, but I tell you that you must not be angry with another person or insult anyone or call anyone depersonalizing and degrading names. You have heard that you must not commit adultery but I say to you that you must not even lust." Finally he said, "You have heard that you must love your neighbors and hate your enemies. I tell you that if that is the best you can do, you are not doing very much. You need to learn to love everyone whom God loves and to love them like God loves them. Be perfect, be mature in love, even as your heavenly Father is perfect." How is that for a goal? It is obviously something into which we will need to grow — and it will take a lot of growing. John Wesley, the founder of the Methodist movement, took that teaching seriously and made "going on to perfection" one of the important aspects of his explanation of the Christian faith.

So, it's okay to be a Christian under construction. As a matter of fact, a little later on in the chapter, Paul is going to use that very image to describe what is going on in the Corinthian church and among the Corinthian Christians. In this construction project, God is the builder, but there are certain things that we need to do to participate in the process. Let's talk about what we need to be doing to be "Christians under construction."

First, you need to remember where you already are in the process. You are not an outsider trying to work your way in. You do not have to qualify for anything. That is not what this is about. You are already a child of God. You are already a member of the club. That is already yours. God has given it to you because God loves you. If you will remember that, it will completely change the way you will feel about what is happening as you try to grow in faith.

Second, accept yourself as someone who still has some growing to do. God knows all about you and God still accepts you as you are and loves you just as you are. You must learn to accept yourself and to love yourself in spite of all you know about yourself. Now there is a big difference between accepting yourself as you are and deciding that you are as good as you need to be. You need to be very aware that you still have a lot to learn and a lot to become. But, knowing that God already accepts you and loves you and being able to accept yourself and love yourself as you are will actually make it a lot easier for you to be honest about who you are and to reckon with the things that are wrong and to be willing to let go of the things that you need to let go. Acceptance takes the threat and the shame out of the process and sets you free to get on with the construction project.

It is good to look forward to all that God still has to give to you. But it is best not to be tied to any particular notion of what that is. Our perception of the goal may change as we move along. Early in the process, we may be looking forward to liberation and blessedness, happiness, and maybe goodness. Later, we may find ourselves hoping to love more completely. Then later on, we may be more concerned about being more able to serve the purposes of God. All of these hopes are appropriate in their times. Just keep looking forward to the new visions that God will show you and to the new fulfillments into which God will lead you.

Be careful to do your part. Growing spiritually is something that God helps you do, but you have to do your part. Keep on practicing spiritual disciplines like prayer and Bible study and participation in the worship life of your church. Participating in prayer groups and growth groups with other growing Christians can help a lot. These things give God an opportunity to get through to you. They help you to keep on interpreting the meaning of your daily life experiences in the light of your Christian faith. Keep on asking what God is trying to show you. Keep on asking what God is doing in your life and in the world around you. Keep on asking how you can become a participant in what God is doing. That will keep a growing edge on your relationship with God.

And keep on making the big moral and ethical decisions of your life in the light of what you know about the Christian faith. It would be nice if we could count on ourselves just spontaneously to do the right thing in all of the different situations of our lives, to do what is right because we want to, because it comes naturally to us. But most of us are not there yet. It will often be difficult for us to know what is the right thing to do in the important situations of our lives and it will often be stressful and costly for us to do it. We will have to keep on doing the hard work of making moral choices. We will have to consider all of the factors involved and ask what Christian love requires us to do. It will get easier as we go along. But most of us will have to keep on making ourselves live like we know Christians ought to live until we come to a place where doing what is right comes naturally.

We can never separate the moral and ethical decisions that we have to make from our spiritual life. If we try to do that, it will separate us from God and cause us to drop into shallowness, artificiality, and hypocrisy. Christians under construction have to keep on working at doing what is right.

Now, if you want to increase your theological vocabulary, you may want to know that the name theologians give to the process of growing in faith is "sanctification." It is part of the process of salvation. The first step in our salvation is called "justification." That is the joyful discovery that Christ has died for you and that God loves you and has forgiven you and accepts you just as you are. It is the experience of having been freely given the status of a child of God. The process of sanctification moves us on from there as God works in our lives to help us learn actually to live like children of God. Both of these are very important.

An older pastor once gave a talk on the subject of sanctification to a group of growing Christians. Then he invited them to ask any questions they had on the subject. One person asked the pastor to give his personal witness and to tell what the doctrine of sanctification has meant to him. He asked if they wanted him to tell how he had gone on to perfection. While they were laughing, he had a chance to think about it. Finally, he said, "Even though I have been a pastor for many years and have earned a doctor's degree and have written books, I still consider myself spiritually a work in progress."

He went on to say that this had meant the most to him during some really bad times in his spiritual life when some major disappointments had caused him to drop into anger and depression and to live in a secret gloom for a long time. He said those experiences had forced him to reckon with the shallowness and limitedness of his own spiritual life. He had known people who had lost their faith in times like that. But he said he was able to hold on to his faith because he believed that God would eventually lead him through to a better time. He knew that he could not just indulge himself in feeling bad. He recognized the fact that he was off the track and he would have to accept responsibility for getting back on it. He said God frequently gave him a boot and said, "Come on now, get over it." But he knew that he would not have to do it alone. God was working in his life and God would help him to get over his bad experience and to move on to wholeness.

Then the pastor thought for another minute and added that he had long since stopped thinking of himself as climbing some kind of a spiritual ladder. That was no longer important to him. But, even in his old age, he was still looking forward to the future expectantly, believing that God still had more to show him, believing that God would keep on making his life an experience of discovery and becoming. And he said he expected that to continue even after his death.

The experiences that show us that we are not yet what God wants us to be sometimes feel like unhappy experiences to us. But they should not. They are just the experiences that remind us that we are still Christians under construction. They teach us to keep looking forward with joyful anticipation to the new experiences and to the fuller life that God still has yet to give us.

Epiphany 7
Ordinary Time 7
1 Corinthians 3:10-11, 16-23

The Reward

The Rock opera, *Jesus Christ, Superstar*, pictures Jesus in the Garden of Gethsemane, asking God if it is really necessary for him to die on the cross. In deep anguish he prays, among other things, "I'd have to know, I'd have to know, my Lord, if I die, what will be my reward?" We don't think or talk much about the reward of the Christian life. I suppose we feel reluctant to ask because we think that, if we are being Christian just for what we get out of it, we are probably doing it for the wrong reason. But the question sometimes occurs to most of us, doesn't it? And in our scripture lessons for today, Paul mentions a reward. So let's let ourselves ask the question just this once. What is the reward that comes to those who live the Christian life?

There is a reward. When we think about the Christian's reward, we usually think of something that waits for us beyond this life, something we don't quite know how to describe because it is hidden behind a veil and probably cannot be adequately described in the words and concepts we have developed to describe things in this life. That expectation has been important to Christians down through the ages. It was important to Paul. Later in his first letter to the Corinthians, he wrote, "If for this life only we have hoped in Christ, we are of all people most to be pitied" (1 Corinthians 15:19). The hope for the hereafter has been very important to people in our day, too. Jonathan Kozol wrote a book about the lives of desperately poor people living in a slum of a great city. The book was titled *Amazing Grace* because the author said the lives of these people were so empty of hope or of promise that they could only find meaning for their lives in the promise of heaven they heard in their little church.[1] That promise of a reward in heaven can also mean a lot to people living under oppression or going through debilitating illness and also for most of the rest of us as we approach the end of life. The promise of a reward beyond this life is important.

But there can also be a reward, a wage for work well done and for a life well lived, in this world, too. The Corinthian Christians were interested in that, maybe more interested than they should have been. Corinth was a busy, cosmopolitan city, a center of commerce, a place where people could move up the ladders of affluence and of status. Lots of people were thinking about that sort of thing — and some of them let that kind of thinking get mixed up with their religion. Those who were so interested in "wisdom" were, for the most part, really just looking for an excuse for feeling superior to others. Yes, they were interested in knowing what would be the reward of their righteousness. Finally, Paul said, "Okay, okay. If you want to talk about rewards, we will talk about rewards."

Paul said that a foundation has been laid and each of us is invited to build upon it. We will be rewarded on the basis of how well we build.

Paul said that he had laid the foundation by preaching to them the gospel of Jesus Christ. If a person or a community builds on any other foundation, they are building something that cannot last. No other foundation can support the structure. So what are we to build on? We are to build on a knowledge that God is, and that God loves us all, and that God is at work in our lives and in our world to save.

As individuals and as churches — and as a universal church — we are called to build something on that foundation. Each of us is to build a life. Together, we are to build a church, and as a whole human race, we are to build a world. We do build those things. We each do build lives. We do build churches — and the church. Yes, and we are the ones who build the world we live in. We might as well accept responsibility for doing the jobs and do them as well as we can.

People and communities build in lots of different ways with lots of different materials. Of course, some don't think much about building anything. They just kick back and let things happen as they will. But those who do that have to accept responsibility for what gets built in that way.

Of what do we build our lives? Do we build them of commitments to great purposes, of high values, of deep appreciation of beauty and goodness, of integrity and of discipline and of love? Or do we try to build them of the things that magazine advertisements promote?

Of what do we build our churches? Are they built of strong beliefs in eternal truths and of deep commitments to the loving purpose of God for the salvation of the world? Or are they built of the comfortable little services designed to serve its own members and, perhaps, to attract some of the desirable outsiders into membership?

And of what do we build our world? Do we build it of commitments to justice and well-being for all people? Or do we build it of competitions to see who can most effectively exploit others and prosper from it — or out of balances of military power that are designed to oppress and to destroy?

When we get honest, we have to admit that all of us are built of some good stuff and of some stuff that is not good. A song from the '60s described the lives and the houses that people were building as "little boxes made of ticky-tacky." Most of us have incorporated a certain amount of ticky-tacky into our structures — but we are likely not to realize it until judgment day comes.

Paul says we will be rewarded for what we have built and built well. Then what is the reward? The reward for building a good life is the good life itself. What we claim to have built is really God's gift to us. A life built of great commitments and high values and of love will be life in its fullness and there is nothing better that we could ask for in this life. It is not the wealth or the status symbols or the accumulations of pleasure that really make a life, it is the deep wholeness and humanity. No matter how much of those other things a person has or doesn't have, it is the quality of the life in the center of the circumstances that is the reward.

And the reward for building a church and a world that live up to their highest purposes is that we get to enjoy the benefits of such a church and such a world. We get to enjoy the service of a church that puts us in touch with the living God and enables us to live the good lives God wants for us. The reward of living in a world that is committed to justice and well-being for all is that we get to live in safety and in a life-enriching harmony with all other people. That, too, is the gift that God keeps wanting to give us.

To what extent are we enjoying that reward? To what extent are you enjoying the wages of work well done? We may not really know until some crisis makes it obvious. Paul introduces the idea of a judgment day into our thinking. "... the work of each builder will become visible, for the Day will disclose it, because it will be revealed with fire, and the fire will test what sort of work each has done" (1 Corinthians 3:13). Are we talking about the final judgment? Paul may have been. But judgment day can come right in the middle of life when something happens that puts our building to the test, something like a catastrophic illness, or a national crisis like the September 11 tragedy, or maybe some opportunity to do some great good that shows whether or not we are willing to rise to the challenge. Just as a hurricane or an earthquake can test the quality of a building's construction, so a crisis in our lives, or in the life of our church or nation, can show us how well we have built. If we have incorporated too much "ticky-tacky" into the construction, the structures may not be able to stand and serve. If we have built well, our reward will be that we will be able to cope and to keep on living a good quality of life in the midst of whatever circumstances may come along.

But Paul adds something very interesting. He says that even if the crisis proves the inadequacy of our building, it may still work for our salvation. It can show us what is important and what is not. The "fire" can act as a refiner's fire and cause us to rebuild and to rebuild better.

Let me tell you a story about a fire. A certain Christian man finally got that big promotion in his profession. He moved to a new city to assume the responsibilities of vice president of a major bank. He and his family were excited about building that fine new home that they had always dreamed of. They built it in an affluent suburb where all of the homes were fine. They brought into it all of the things that they had accumulated and treasured over the years and they carefully selected the new furniture and appliances that would make their home just right. The family was really beginning to enjoy their new home and their new situation in life. Everything looked just right — but no one could see the defective wiring that a careless workman had left as his contribution to their happiness. One night only a few months after moving into the house, the man had a dream that there was a fire in the attic. He woke up in a fright — and discovered that his dream was true. Quickly, he woke up his wife and children and got them out of the house as it burst into flames. As he stood and watched his dream house burn, neighbors came running up to him and asked if there was anything he wanted them to try to save. He shook his head and said, "No. My wife and children are safe and there's nothing else in the house that is worth the risk of life." Very quickly, the fire had caused him to put things into perspective. It would be unrealistic to say that they did not suffer some grief because of their loss. But they knew to be grateful that they still had everything that was really important. That was a kind of a salvation.

Many have gone through crisis experiences that helped them to realize that some of the things they thought were very important really weren't and some of the things they had neglected were the things that really made life worth living. That can indeed be an experience of salvation — and that, too, is a kind of reward.

But then Paul moves on to enlarge his metaphor and he has a surprise for us. He says, "Do you not know that you [you Christians, you churches] are God's temple and that God's Spirit dwells in you?" (1 Corinthians 3:16). If we can keep our lives from being cluttered up with things that distract us from what is important, the Spirit of God will teach us real wisdom and help us catch a new vision of things as they really are. One of the things we will be shown is that since you belong to Christ and Christ belongs to God and all things belong to God, then all things belong to you.

Now, there is a vision we may have a hard time catching. We are an awful lot like the Corinthians. They were so preoccupied with who has wisdom and who doesn't and who has wealth and who doesn't and who has status and who doesn't and which house church has the most attractive pastor and which has the truest doctrine that they were missing the magnificent vision of the whole that was there before them. We do that, too. We divide our lives up like we divide our property into little gated communities with guards at the gates or like pieces of turf with "keep out" signs on the fences. Then we exhaust ourselves with being defensive of what is ours and jealous of what is not. Paul says to forget that foolishness. Everything good is yours. Does that come as a surprise? Can you take it in?

Some of our songwriters have caught the vision. An old spiritual that came to us from a group of people who had nothing at all in this world said, "All around me looks so shine, asked the Lord if all was mine. Every time I feel the Spirit moving in my heart, I will pray." Another hymn describes the beauty that surrounds us when "morning has broken" and how that beauty takes on eternal significance. Then it says, "Mine is the sunlight! Mine is the morning born of the one light Eden saw play! Praise with elation, praise every morning, God's recreation of the new day!" You don't have to own a sunrise or a sunset to enjoy it. You just have to claim it and take it in before it slips away. It was put there for you. It is yours. God gave it to you.

You can feel the same way about the wisdom and the accomplishments and the goodness of other people. They are yours, too, because ultimately they are God's. In just that same way, every bit of the beauty and goodness and truth and nobility and aliveness and joy that are to be found in this world, in all of life, yes, and in death too, are yours. Don't try to own them in some way that hoards them and keeps them away from others. That won't work. That will spoil it. But simply move through life with arms and heart wide open to embrace and to share every good thing that is there for you. And when the time comes for you to leave this life, approach the great unknown beyond this life in the same way. Everything good is yours. God has freely given it to you. And that is your reward just for allowing the Spirit of God to show you that you are beloved children of God.

---

1. Jonathan Kozol, *Amazing Grace* (New York: Crown, 1995).

**Epiphany 8
Ordinary Time 8
1 Corinthians 4:1-5**

Dealing With Criticism

No one likes criticism. We all like to be liked. But the moment any person ventures out to offer any leadership, or to express any opinion that is not shared by everyone else, or even just to live in any unique or creative way, she or he is likely to be enveloped in a cloud of criticism. Most of us find that a very unhappy experience. After it has happened to us a few times, we are sorely tempted not ever to do or say anything again that would invite criticism. But that would not be the right thing to do. It would cause us to live lives that are both unhappy and indecisive. And, it would leave our critics free to run the world in their own way. If we are going to live satisfying and significant lives, we are going to have to learn to deal with criticism. We may be able to get some practical experience in that by following the example of Paul. He had lots of experience in dealing with criticism.

If we read widely in the writings of Paul, we will realize what a multifaceted person he was. His writings include profound theological reflections on the shape of reality and the way to fullness of life, practical advice about how to live a Christian life in the real world, directions on how to run a church, and expressions of the loving concern of a good pastor for his people. But we will also find quite a lot of argument intended to defend his authority as an apostle, to refute the arguments of those who disagreed with him, and to defend himself against his critics. That is the first thing we can learn from Paul about criticism: that it happens. It comes with being a decisive person. We may as well get ready for it. But we can learn more if we study Paul's response to his critics.

Actually, Paul's two letters to the Corinthians are full of conflict and defense against his critics. Paul handles much of this indirectly and diplomatically. Later in the correspondence, the conflict is more obvious — and sometimes it gets pretty rough. But, here in the fourth chapter of First Corinthians, Paul speaks directly to his critics about their criticism.

Paul explains the role he plays as he understands it. He plays the role of a servant of Christ. A servant has no authority of his own, but he may exercise a great deal of authority on behalf of the one whom he serves. He represents the risen Christ. And he understands himself as a steward, the trustee, the keeper of God's mysteries, that is the wisdom of God through which we are brought to salvation. He acknowledges that a servant has to be trustworthy. He has to live in such a way that both his master and others can trust him. Paul says that he has done his best to do that. That being the case, he feels that he has both the authority and the responsibility to explain the meaning of the wisdom of God and to give decisive leadership to the church. He has done that. Paul felt that the Corinthian church was in danger of getting off of the track and he felt that it was his responsibility to get it back on. No one ever accused Paul of being shy. Paul spoke out and acted decisively and now, almost 2,000 years later, the world is better off for it.

Paul found that the Corinthians were playing little games. They were all trying to increase their own status in the church and in the community by enhancing their own honor and by cutting others down. They had fallen into comparing their leaders, doing a critical analysis on each of them. That made finding fault into an art. And they were using their criticism as an excuse for not following their leaders.

For their own good, Paul felt that he had to assert himself. He told them that it was not their business to judge him. He was the servant of Christ and so it was Christ who should judge. He said that he had done his best to be trustworthy and that he did not know of anything wrong that he had done. Finally, he said that if he had done anything wrong, that would become apparent in the judgment when Christ will judge us all.

With Paul's experience in mind, let's think about how we ought to deal with criticism.

The first thing we need to do is to find our way into a vital relationship with God. God is that greater reality that is both in and beyond all other realities. God is ultimately the one who counts. It is your relationship with God that ultimately tells you who you are and how you fit into life. The good news of Jesus Christ tells us that God knows each of us, that God forgives our limitedness and wrongness and accepts us as we are, that God loves us, and that God has given us the status of children of God. That is who you are. Start there.

Now notice that the Christian gospel makes a distinction between being right and being okay. Most people are accustomed to thinking that you have to be right to be okay and that if you are okay, then you must be right. God takes a different approach to that. God tells us that we are okay simply because God loves us. Whether or not we are right about things is a separate matter and will be dealt with in a different way. If you can come to know yourself as God knows you, if you can learn to be honest about your limitations and still accept yourself and affirm yourself as you are, if you can know yourself as a child of God, then you will find yourself able to exercise a remarkable freedom when it comes to making decisions and taking necessary actions. There are two important reasons for that.

First, you will be able to disengage from the petty little contests that people get into when personalities rather than issues are in competition. If you know who you are, if you know that you are a child of God, then you will know that your status and your personhood are not in jeopardy. You don't have to prove anything or to win anything for yourself. You can stay focused on the issues and let people say what they will.

The second reason is that you need to be free to ask if you really are right. You need to be able to own your ambivalence, to listen to the sincere opinions of others, and to evaluate the evidence. If you should discover that you have been wrong, you will not be undone. You will still be a beloved child of God.

Once you have entrusted your ego to God's keeping, you can freely give attention to your purpose. Ask what it really is that God wants said or done. The answer to that question will come from two places at once.

It will come from your basic and growing understanding of the Christian gospel and of the purpose of God. You can access that through a daily study of the Christian scriptures and traditions and regular practice of worship and devotional life. We can't just arrogantly assume that we already know all that God knows. Understanding the purpose of God is something that must be sought humbly and diligently.

The other place from which the answer will come is a sensitivity to what is going on in your own life and in the lives of others and in the world around you. As these two come into dialogue within your consideration, you will find yourself becoming convinced that certain things need to be said or done. (You may also find yourself being convinced that some other things might just as well be left unsaid or undone.) But when you come to believe that some things need to be said or done for the good of your family, your church, your community, and your world, then do what you really believe God wants you to do.

It is always good to take a critical look at your convictions before you act on them. One good way of dealing with criticism is to be the first critic. Set your convictions in the context of the Christian faith as a whole and ask if it is really the right thing to do. Sometimes different aspects of the faith will argue with one another. Sometimes Christian compassion will argue with Christian conviction. Talk with others about your conviction. Listen appreciatively to those who disagree. Be honest with yourself about the fact that there are two sides to almost every significant question. Ask if you may be wrong. Be open to the answer that you might get. Ask yourself what is motivating you. Remember that we very seldom act out of pure motives. Ask yourself, "Is it the love that I have learned from God that is motivating me?" Sometimes even the right thing to do is the wrong thing to do until you can do it in love.

When it has become clear to you that, in spite of all arguments to the contrary, God really wants you to say or to do some particular thing that is needed to make a difference, go ahead and act decisively. You will be sorry if you do not. And, the processes by which human life and history are shaped will be impoverished by the lack of your decisive action.

Then be ready for the criticism. People who speak and act in a way that can make a difference will always have to endure criticism. There may be different kinds of criticism. There may be the constructive criticism that comes from the people who see the "down side" of your best actions, the negative aspects of what you propose that you should already have considered. There will be the honest criticism that comes from people who hold contrary opinions as conscientiously as you hold your convictions. There may be petty criticism from jealous people. And there may be vicious criticism that comes from people who believe that what you are saying or doing will somehow be to their disadvantage and will say or do any mean thing they can to discredit you, whether or not it is true. It is not always easy to know which kind of criticism you are receiving.

Some of the most heroic people, in this regard, are those people of high principles who go into politics in the hope of making a difference for the good of all people. They must know when they venture out into that commitment that they will have to endure enormous amounts of criticism. There will be the entirely legitimate criticism of their positions and proposals that will come from members of the other party or from people of equally high principles who have a different idea about how to solve the world's problems. They will know that, in order to be effective, they will have to make some political compromises and that they will have to support some proposals that are part good and part bad. Almost every decisive political action has a "down side" to it. They will have to endure criticism for this, even from their friends and from themselves. But, there are some political groups that have intentionally made a political strategy out of character assassination. They search out every little thing that anyone might not like about a person and publicize it and ridicule it at every opportunity — and they are good at making opportunities — and they don't mind manufacturing derogatory misinformation if they can't find anything else to criticize. This is the really vicious aspect of political life today. Then there are always petty people and "armchair quarterbacks" who enjoy cutting people down and who assume that anyone in politics is fair game. A person who goes into politics knows that he or she is going to have to cope with all of those kinds of criticism. But if people of good conscience and high principles don't pay the price of going into politics, they will abandon the formation of public policy and the making of history to people whose motives are less noble.

To some extent, the same things could be said about a person who goes into such fields as school administration, or law enforcement, or business administration, or even leadership in a civic club or the P.T.A. (It can be said of anyone who goes into the ministry, too.) Dealing with criticism is part of the price a person must pay for any kind of active citizenship and for any kind of decisive Christian discipleship.

When the criticism comes, remember that you are standing before God and not before the critics. You are acting in obedience to what you believe to be the will of God. You are acting out of motives that you believe God has generated with you. You will count on the judgment of God to determine whether you were right or wrong.

Deal as kindly as you can with your critics. Appreciate those who intend to offer constructive criticism. Respect those who honestly disagree. Be ready to do combat with those who are opposing you because of some vested interest of their own, but try not to be drawn into the combat in a way that will make you as mean as they are. If you do that, ultimately, you will lose and meanness will be the winner. Try not to be overcome by evil but overcome evil with good (Romans 12:21).

Be ready to pay the price for decisive action. On the night before he died, Jesus told his disciples many things to prepare them to carry on the work that they had begun together. Among those things was the warning that they would encounter opposition and hatred. He said, "If the world hates you, be aware that it hated me before it hated you. If you belonged to the world, the world would love you as its own. Because you do not belong to the world, but I have chosen you out of the world — therefore the world hates you" (John 15:18-19). Be ready for abuse. It comes with the territory.

Remember that unless some are willing to pay the price of taking decisive action, history will stagnate or be taken captive by those who are willing to pay the price. Unless we, who are committed to the loving purpose of God, are willing to pay the price of acting in the service of that purpose, then there will be those who will pay the price of acting in hate or in greed or even in indifference. It can be a lonely and uncertain and costly thing to speak up or to step out and to act decisively. But we have to believe that the ultimate judge of our actions is that one who presently stands shrouded in mystery — but who holds the future in divine hands. Stand before that judge and do what you believe is right.

**Transfiguration Of The Lord
(Last Sunday After Epiphany)
2 Peter 1:16-21**

Remembering Jesus

Christians share a memory — and a belief — that gives us a place to stand, a way of getting things into perspective, and an ability to cope no matter what is going on in the world around us.

We share the memory that once, a long time ago, there was a young teacher who was totally committed to the loving purpose of God for the world. He came healing the sick, feeding the hungry, and making other loving responses to human need. He came announcing a new possibility that God offers to the whole creation and teaching people how to live in that new possibility. He came calling others to join him in a life that is open to the saving work of God and committed to the loving purpose of God. When the powerful people of his day tried to turn him aside from his purpose, he chose to endure a cruel death on a cross rather than to abandon God's loving work. But God would not let it end that way. God raised Jesus up out of death and caused him to be with God and to share with God in everything that God does. We do remember Jesus, don't we? In spite of all of the difficulties related to passing the memory down through the generations for 2,000 years, we have a pretty good idea of what his life was like. We share that memory.

We also share a belief that makes that memory meaningful and important. It is the belief that the great eternal God, who made the heavens and the earth, was purposefully doing something very special through the life of Jesus, something to help us know God, something to help us and all people to enter into the new possibility that God opens to us.

We share that memory and that belief, don't we? That is what it means to be a Christian.

Late in the first century, or early in the second, the early church went through a time when some things were happening that threatened the church's integrity and its future. The apostles, who had held the church together, had all died. The Bible had not yet been put together in the form in which we now have it. Things were happening that put stress upon the life of the church, and lots of people were falling into confusion.

At that time, an unknown church leader undertook to call the church back to the faith that was taught by Peter and Paul and the other apostles. He wrote a letter to the churches in the name of Peter to say to the churches the things that he knew Peter would want them to hear. That was a widely used and perfectly accepted thing to do in those days. The book from which we read our scripture lesson was the result.

The writer of 2 Peter was going to have some important things to say to everyone and some harsh things to say to a few. But first, he called them to remember Jesus. He focused their attention on one particular event in the life of Jesus that gave a basis for the Christian belief about Jesus. It was an event that Peter had shared. Do you remember the story of the transfiguration?

One day, Jesus took Peter and James and John with him up onto a high mountain to pray. While they were praying, the disciples saw Jesus change. His face and his garments glowed. And they saw Moses and Elijah, two of the great leaders of God's chosen people from the past, talking with Jesus. Then, while Peter was stammering and trying to think of the right thing to say, a bright cloud enveloped them and they heard the voice of God saying to them, "This is my Son, the Beloved; with him I am well pleased; listen to him!" (Matthew 17:1-8). If the disciples still had any notion that Jesus was just another teacher or just another revolutionary leader, like others only better, the vision changed all of that. Because of the vision, the disciples knew that, in Jesus, something entirely new and different was happening — and that it was the doing of God.

The writer of 2 Peter reminded the early church of that memory because things were going on that made them need that recollection. Sometimes things go on in our world and in our lives that make us need that memory, too.

Sometimes things don't work out like we expect them to. Through most of the early years of the life of the church, the Christians had expected Jesus to come again soon, on a day of judgment and salvation, to bring his work to completion. They had organized a lot of their thinking and actions around that expectation. But years after the apostles had all died, Jesus had still not come back. Things were not working out as they had expected.

We have some similar experiences, don't we? Things don't always work out as we had expected. No one ever told us that, if we believe the gospel and live Christian lives, everything will work out well for us. But sometimes we let ourselves believe that. It seems to us that, if God is a loving God, good things ought to happen in our world. Good things do happen, but bad things happen, too, things like natural disasters, and acts of terrorism, and wars that cause enormous amounts of suffering. It seems to us that, if God is a loving God, he ought to be able to keep things like that from happening. Things don't always work out like we had expected them to.

And it seems to us that, if we do our best to live Christian lives and to treat others fairly and to raise our children in Christian homes, things ought to go well for us. And many things do go better for us than they might have if we had lived otherwise. But we soon find that a fickle economy can take away the job and the savings from a Christian as easily as they can from other people — perhaps more easily. Even though we do our best to bring our children up in the Christian faith, sometimes during adolescence they can still get into the wrong crowds and start using drugs and get swept away into a life that we don't want for them. Yes, and some of us have found that good Christians can get cancer or Alzheimer's disease just as other people can. Things don't always work out like we expect them to. Sometimes experiences like those can shake the foundations of our lives and make us ask questions about our faith.

In those times, we need to remember Jesus. We need to remember how he sought out the people who were distressed and hurting and how he reached out to them in love. And, we need to remember that it was God who was at work in the things that Jesus did and that God is still reaching out to those who are hurting.

The people who lived in those later days of the early church sometimes had to cope with confusion in their understanding of the Christian faith. By that time, all of the letters of Paul had been written and maybe one of the gospels, but they had not yet been put together in the form of a Bible as we know it and sound Christian doctrine had not yet been well defined. When the writer of 2 Peter spoke of the scriptures, he was talking about what we call the Old Testament. Even the most sincere Christians had differences of opinion. And there were some who were intentionally attacking the Christian faith. Some were misinterpreting Paul's teachings about Christian freedom to say that there is no moral law. Some were saying that, since judgment day had not come, there was no judgment. Some, under the influence of the "Epicurean" philosophers, were attacking the scriptures and calling them mere myths. They were not using the word "myth" like some of our modern theologians do. Some modern theologians use the word to describe a story or a tradition that is the bearer of eternal meaning. Those ancient critics simply meant that the scriptures were a bunch of fairy tales that someone had made up and that they were not true. That was causing a lot of the early Christians to question what they thought.

That happens to us today, too, doesn't it? There are a lot of different and sometimes conflicting opinions about important matters even among sincere Christians — and they are not always respectful of one another as they argue. We have seen theological differences divide families and churches and communities. People from other religions and people with no religion at all sometimes call important Christian beliefs and practices into question. As a defense against the harm that religious conflicts can do, our culture has developed a secular approach to life that virtually forbids any public discussion of religion and that indirectly suggests that there is something wrong with religion as a whole. In that kind of a situation, many people have become very confused about what to believe. Some have been led to give up on religious faith all together.

When we find ourselves in that kind of a situation, we need to remember Jesus again. The story of Jesus puts us in touch with the most profound aspects of the truth about God and puts them before us in a form that we can understand. It puts the truth about God before us in the form of the story of someone like ourselves, a man, Jesus of Nazareth. We believe that it was God who chose to be made known to us in that way.

Another sad thing happened in the early church during the time when 2 Peter was being written. Some who called themselves Christians were not living up to their faith. Some were just being lax in their practice of their religion, demonstrating that it really wasn't very important to them. Others were going along with some of the popular social practices of their day that involved idolatry and immorality. In fact, some of the supposedly sophisticated interpretations of the Christian faith that were emerging were just excuses for moral laxity. Christians need to be able to believe in one another as well as in God. When people saw professing Christians not living up to their faith, they sometimes experienced bitter and destructive disillusionment.

Unfortunately, we have had that experience, too, haven't we? Newspapers seem to take special delight in making headlines of the moral and ethical failures of high profile evangelists and church leaders. Those failures are deeply disappointing to people who need to believe in their church. It is also disappointing to see a church or a church-related institution get so caught up in the pursuit of institutional success that it forgets its primary function. Almost every one of us knows someone who talks loudly about his or her religion and is anxious to push it on you, but who really does not practice what he or she preaches. Disillusioned people are always eager to point their fingers at the hypocrisy of the religious. That is hard for us to deal with. We need something we can believe in, something with integrity that we can trust.

When we need something we can believe in, we need to reclaim our memory of Jesus. There is the story of someone like ourselves who gave up his life rather than give up the integrity of his faith. And God was doing something special through Jesus.

Lots of things can happen in our lives that can confuse us and bewilder us and cause us not to know how to go on. Lots of pressures and forces swirl around us like the currents of a rapid river that threaten to knock us off our feet and to sweep us away. There are no easy answers or simple solutions to all of these things.

But when we find ourselves up against things that confuse and threaten, we will do well to reclaim the memory that all Christians share, the memory that the writer of 2 Peter shared with the bewildered believers in his day, the memory of Jesus. No, this is not an invitation to be irresponsible and to stop thinking about the things that challenge us in life. It is not a promise that "remembering Jesus" will work like a magic word and make all of your problems go away. This is rather an invitation to remember that, at one time in history, God did something very special through a young teacher named Jesus.

It is not enough just to remember that there was a Jesus. We need to remember the story of Jesus, what he did, what he said, what happened concerning him. If, to be honest, you really don't know the story, or if it has been a long time since you read it, you would do well to read it again. Each of the first four books of the New Testament — Matthew, Mark, Luke, and John — tell the story. They are not hard to read or to understand and you can read one of them in just a few hours. Read the story again and remember that God was doing something special through Jesus to help us know God.

No, remembering Jesus won't make all of the problems go away. But it will give you a place to stand while you deal with them. It will help you to get everything into perspective so that you can discover what is true and important and good and what isn't. It will help you to get in touch with God so that there will be a spiritual dimension to your life. It will give you something to believe in. And it will put you in touch with a source of enablement as you cope with the problems that arise in life.

The writer of 2 Peter reminded the people of the early church — and us — of something that must always have been a life-shaping memory for the Apostle Peter himself. He reminded us of Jesus — and of what God said about Jesus, "This is my Son, my Beloved; with whom I am well pleased" (2 Peter 1:17). "Listen to him!"

Sermons On The Second Readings

For Sundays In Lent and Easter

Temptation Of The Palms

Richard W. Ferris

*Dedicated to my wife, Emily,
whose unconditional love for me
and support of my ministry have
helped me to rise above all obstacles.*

Preface

I preach with what I have, words. I offer the hope, compassion, and love of a God whom I have known since I was a small child; a God who has seen me through the best and the worst of times; a God who came to my world in the form of someone like me.

I communicate with words. Inflection changes, volume goes up and down, an eyebrow might rise now and again ... but it comes down to the words that I speak ... and the way in which I speak them. I have always believed that a child can judge the true sincerity of an adult better than another adult. So it is the adults who need our special treatment.

Speak from the heart. Be yourself, not somebody else. Don't turn on the preacher mode with the preacher voice and the ecclesiastical language. Speak from the heart the words of your people, the words your people use and understand. And then, most importantly, they will hear you.

I preach with what I have, words. I don't use projectors or sound effects, although it might come to that one day. I don't put paint on my face as yet, though it might be nice to disguise who I am at times. I preach through who I am, for it is who God has made me. I like to have fun; I like to laugh. Even more than that, I like to make others laugh.

I share these words and thoughts with you in the hope that you can pass them on to others, through your words and who you are.

R. W. F.

Foreword

Richard Ferris offers remarkably clear and direct sermons bearing the vitality of the message that is central to Christian faith as the way of the cross and the way of the Savior who suffers, dies, and yet triumphs over the powers of sin and death.

A sermon that serves as a transparent medium for the Christian message is indeed a precious jewel. Great theologians who have penned long and complicated volumes rightly have thought of the sermons they wrote and delivered as the highest point of their work for the church. Paul Tillich and Karl Barth are great examples of authors of heavy theological studies who were able to do more for fellow Christians in sermons than in their abstract doctrinal treatises. In this set of sermons for the Lenten season we find another masterly guide to the depths of Christian life as it leads from Ash Wednesday right through to the joys of the Easter morning.

> Dr. Gene R. Thursby
> Department of Religion
> University of Florida

**Ash Wednesday
2 Corinthians 5:20b—6:10**

A Christian's Resumé

It's time to update your resumé!

If you're a part of the workforce of the early twenty-first century, that's a common-sounding statement. Job security is almost nonexistent. Competitive wages might mean a couple dollars above minimum wage. Advancement could very well propose that for your good efforts you would be awarded more work for the same salary. Benefits rarely include 100 percent paid insurance and retirement fund, but rather offer you both at cost to be deducted from your paycheck.

With those kinds of incentives, most people with jobs always have their eyes open to other opportunities. A favorite pastime for many is searching the employment ads in the Sunday newspaper. Keeping one's resumé up-to-date is a high priority on people's lists of things-to-do.

Go to the library or a bookstore and you can find volumes on "how to" write the perfect resumé. Go on the Internet and find free advice and subscribe to websites that will help you piece together what you need to tell a prospective employer in order to get the best job and highest paying position that's available to you. They will tell you what to say and what not to say. You can find out how to put your skills and work history in an order that will be most attractive. You will even discover those little things you might not have thought of that will make you a potential candidate over others.

It's all about salesmanship. It's about presentation. It's about being like that barker at a local carnival who is able to attract the most people into the tent because of his or her ability to say the right things in the most appealing way.

And ... it's all perspective. You have to try to second-guess what it is the employer is looking for. Will they care that you grew up on a farm and have a strong work ethic? Or will they be more interested in your cosmopolitan life that has molded your creative talents since leaving the farm? Will they care that you were president of your senior class and yearbook editor, or is the fact that you sold subscriptions door-to-door more important?

In the text from 2 Corinthians, the Apostle Paul presents a resumé of sorts that is written from the perspective of God's point of view. Paul includes many descriptions in his resumé that would not impress most prospective employers. Today's resumé experts would probably have a field day with Paul's resumé, using it as an example of what not to include. But again, I suggest it's all a matter of perspective, of point of view. It's all in whom you are trying to impress.

There was a women's tournament at the golf club, and the turnout was so great the women had to use the men's locker room as well as their own. Naturally, on that day the room was off-limits to men. But eight-year-old Joey didn't realize that. When he walked innocently into the men's locker room, he was greeted with shrieks as the women grabbed for cover. "What's the matter," Joey asked, "haven't you ever seen a little boy before?"

Paul says to the Corinthians, "What's the matter, haven't you ever seen a real Christian before?" Paul sees having gone through great endurance while suffering afflictions, hardships, calamities, beatings, imprisonments, riots, labors, sleepless nights, and hunger as things for which to be commended. He would proudly present these before God and fellow believers as signs of his devotion and undying zeal for the ministry of Jesus Christ. Unfortunately, if you put that on your employment resumé, I doubt very much that you would be put at the front of the line. Those are not the types of things employers want to see in your job history. Even more disappointing, those are not the things most congregations want to see in the history of their minister or even their members.

What good church folk want to see is that next part of Paul's resumé. That part that includes purity, knowledge, patience, kindness, holiness of spirit, genuine love, truthful speech, and the power of God. That's what churches want — not only in their pastors, but also in the members of their congregations. That's what we want to see in everyone else, of course, but we know that we can't quite include that in our own resumés, at least not as something that is true about ourselves all of the time.

But people are reading our "living resumés" all of the time. People, who know that we are Christians, are watching us. They are waiting for the mistake! And Paul recognizes this fact when he says: "We are putting no obstacle in anyone's way, so that no fault may be found with our ministry" (2 Corinthians 6:3).

A small boy was closely watching a neighboring pastor build a wooden trellis to support a climbing vine in his garden. The boy did not say a word the entire time that he watched. Pleased at the thought that his work was being admired, the pastor finally said to the boy, "Well, son, trying to pick up some pointers on gardening?"

"No," the boy replied, "I'm just waiting to hear what a preacher says when he hits his thumb with a hammer."

Like it or not, our resumés are being read by everyone who meets us. If they know we are Christians, then they read them accordingly. If they don't know we are Christians, then our resumés are failing us. As followers of Christ and believers in salvation through faith in grace, we know that our failures will not condemn us. For we have been forgiven. But keep in mind, our failures might just end up condemning someone else — someone who has read our resumés through the way that we live, and has come away disillusioned with Christianity.

On the other hand, when it comes right down to it, most people don't care about those shortcomings and failures. Most people have their own agendas, and it takes a lot to rattle them. If anything, it might help them relate to us if they know we don't have a perfectly-written resumé.

In a recreation room of a California retirement home, four ladies were playing bridge and chatting. An elderly gentleman wandered into the room. He was a newcomer and they all perked up.

One of the ladies said, "Hello, there. You're new here, aren't you?" The man smiled and said that he had just moved in that morning.

Another lady asked, "Where did you live before you came here?" He replied, "I was just released from San Quentin, where I spent the last twenty years."

The third lady nosed in and asked, "Oh, really, and what were you in for?" The man quietly announced that he had murdered his wife.

The fourth lady sat up quickly, smiled brightly, and boldly asked, "Oh, then you're single?"

In his resumé, it's obvious that Paul cannot leave well enough alone. He's not afraid to hold anything back. After listing all of those wonderful attributes of his life as a Christian, he then dives back into the whole perspective issue. Because he knows people are watching and making judgments upon his life, he makes it very clear that there are two points of view when it comes to assessing his life. There is the point of view of the world, as represented in those who do not believe in Jesus' saving grace. And there is the point of view of God, who now judges Paul's life through what Jesus has accomplished.

As Paul puts it, he is looked upon "in honor, and in dishonor; in ill repute and good repute." He says that as Christians we are "treated as imposters, and yet are true; as unknown and yet are well known; as dying and see — we are alive; as punished, and yet not killed; as sorrowful, yet always rejoicing; as poor, yet making many rich; as having nothing, and yet possessing everything!" (2 Corinthians 6:9-10).

A mother came to President Abraham Lincoln seeking the pardon of her son, who was under sentence of death. The result of her pleading was that Lincoln issued a pardon. After leaving him, as she passed through a corridor, she exclaimed to the man who accompanied her, "I knew it was a lie!" The man then asked her, "What do you refer to?" She replied with passion in her voice, "Why, they told me he was an ugly-looking man, but he is the handsomest man I ever saw in my life."

From what point of view do we approach God? As scared little creatures about to stand before a harsh judge who will punish us for all the wrong that we have done? Or from the perspective of guilty children pardoned by a loving and gracious parent? What do our resumés say about us? Or can we even think of enough to put down on a piece of paper that describes the characteristics of our lives that make us, as Christians, different from those who do not believe?

A man asked God how long a million years was to him. God replied, "It's just like a single second of your time, my child." So the man asked, "And what about a million dollars?" The Lord replied, "To me, it's just like a single penny." So the man gathered up his courage and asked, "Well, Lord, could I have one of your pennies?" God smiled upon the man and said, "Certainly, my child, in just a second."

We can continue to view our lives only from the perspective of the world, and our resumés will be written with a single slant: to live up to the expectations of others. That's important so that we don't become stumbling blocks to others. Realistically, we know that we will never measure up to those standards. You can't please all of the people all of the time.

If we view our lives from God's perspective, then there's room for error. God looks at our world and us differently than we do. While God knows the importance of living a life in the shadow of Jesus Christ, he was wise enough to know that Jesus had to come into the world so that we might live eternally. He knows that as high as we set our standards, as complete as our resumé may seem, we will always come up short. As our Creator, he knows that "from dust we were made, and to dust we shall return."

There was an old minister who survived the great Johnstown flood. He loved to tell the story over and over in great detail. Everywhere he went he would spend all his time talking about this great, historic event in his life. One day he died and went to heaven. On his very first day all the saints gathered together to share their life experiences. You might say they were reading their resumés to one another. The old minister got all excited and ran to Peter, who was in charge of the meeting, and asked if he might tell the exciting story of his survival from the Johnstown flood. Peter hesitated for a moment and then said, "Yes, you may share that story. But you might want to remember that Noah will be in the audience tonight."

During this Lenten season, let's update our resumés. Let's add those elements of our lives that are missing. We can include those skills and characteristics that humbly will lead others to Christ. But let's not try to impress anyone with our work history. The only One we need to impress already knows it. And he sees our lives from the other side of the cross.

Lent 1
Romans 5:12-19

Adam's Legacy

In the musical *Fiddler on the Roof*, Tevye is the Jewish father of five girls living in a Russian village who finds himself going through a period that is continually challenging his traditions. First, his oldest daughter, Tzeitel does not want to accept the man picked for her by the village matchmaker. But Tevye has already struck up a deal with this man to marry his daughter. And so Tevye goes through a mental wrestling match with himself that goes something like this: "On the one hand ... I'm the papa, and I'm supposed to decide on the daughter's husband. But on the other hand ... she doesn't love the man that I've arranged for her to marry." So on and on he goes, with "on the one hand this" and "on the other hand that" until he comes to a conclusion that "they love each other." Ultimately Tzeitel is engaged and married to Motel the Tailor, her choice for a husband.

Then, just when Tevye thinks things have settled down, his second daughter, Hodel, along with Perchik, a modern-thinking student from Kiev, announce that they have become engaged. This comes without any discussion with her father. Tevye replies, "Oh, so now the daughter is telling the papa that she is engaged. What has happened to tradition?" Here we go again! Tevye starts on the one hand and then the other hand, until he convinces himself that maybe it's not all bad, because after all, "they love each other."

The straw that breaks the camel's back comes when Chava, the third daughter, confides to her father that she is in love with Fyedka, a Russian villager, who is not of the Jewish faith. As hard as he tries with his "on the one hand, but on the other hand," Tevye cannot accept his daughter marrying someone outside the faith. At this point, tradition has to stand. He cannot give in to any more reform. So when Chava defies him and marries Fyedka anyway, he announces that Chava no longer exists. In Tevye's mind, he now has only four daughters.

Tevye's struggles with tradition, and with his changing, modern world, exemplify the obstacles that exist between the old and the new, and the changes that have to take place to be able to let go of the old and embrace the new.

Saint Paul talks about the old and the new in this section from Romans. On the one hand is Adam, the first man created, who introduced sin and death into the world. On the other hand is Jesus, who, though sinless himself, was able to sacrifice his life for the lives of all those who have sinned.

I can just hear Tevye going back and forth on this one: "On the one hand, God created Adam. And Adam was created in the image of God. And God said it was good. On the other hand, Adam disobeyed God. And everyone since Adam has had a difficult time keeping God's Law. So, on the one hand, it was Adam who first sinned, but on the other hand, we've been doing it ever since."

However, it was God who gave Adam a mind with which to make a choice. Of course, on the other hand, having created Adam in his own image, Adam could have chosen to obey God. On the other hand, since Adam, sin has been a tradition for all humans. But on the other hand, God demands obedience. It would be hard for even Tevye to come up with a suitable resolution to this dilemma. But God has a solution.

Now, on the one hand, Adam, who represents us all, being the first created in the form that we exist, has carried a bad reputation throughout history. Granted, he knew what God told him, but he had no experience from which to draw. He was the first sinner, so there was no record of sin. We, on the other hand, have all chosen sin over God at some point in our lives. We have a whole history of sin and consequences to draw from when we make our decisions to sin. On the other hand, Jesus also represents us all and has shown us that we can choose right over wrong, good over evil, God's way over our own way. As Tevye might say, "What's a papa to do?" On the one hand, God loves us. On the other hand, God hates sin. What *is* a papa to do?

The pastor of a small, country church moved to the pulpit at the appropriate time for the sermon. "Before the sermon," he announced, "I'd like to introduce a guest minister who is with us today." The pastor told the congregation that the guest was one of his dearest childhood friends and that he wanted him to greet the church and share whatever he wanted.

With that, an elderly man stepped up to the pulpit and began to speak. "A father, his son, and a friend of his son were sailing off the Pacific coast," he began, "when a fast-approaching storm blocked any attempt to get back to the shore. The waves were so high that, even though the father was an experienced sailor, he could not keep the boat upright and the three were swept into the ocean as the boat capsized."

The old man hesitated for a moment, making eye contact with two teenagers who were, for the first time since the service began, looking somewhat interested in what was being said. He continued his story, "Grabbing a rescue line, the father had to make the most excruciating decision of his life: Which boy would he save with the lifeline? Would he throw the line to his son, whom he loved beyond comparison, or would he throw it to the other boy? He only had seconds to make the decision and knew that he most likely could not save them both. The father knew that his son was a Christian. He also knew that his son's friend was not. The agony of his decision could not be matched by the torrent of waves.

"As the father yelled out, 'I love you, son!' he threw out the lifeline to his son's friend. By the time the father had pulled the boy back to the capsized boat, his son had disappeared beneath the raging swells into the black of night. His body was never recovered."

By this time, the two teenagers were sitting up straight in the pew, anxiously waiting for the next words to come out of the old minister's mouth. "The father," he continued, "knew his son would step into eternity with Jesus. But he could not bear the thought of his son's friend dying without knowing Jesus as his Savior. So, he sacrificed his own son to save the son's friend."

The old minister paused and looked over those seated before him. Then he continued, "How great is the love of God that he should do the same for us. Our Heavenly Father sacrificed his only begotten son so that we could be saved. If you do not yet know him, I urge you to accept his offer to rescue you and take hold of the lifeline he is throwing out to you today."

The old man turned and sat back down in his chair as silence filled the room. The pastor again walked slowly to the pulpit and delivered a brief sermon with an invitation at the end. But no one responded to the appeal, and soon, the service ended and everyone was leaving the church.

Immediately, the two teenagers were at the old man's side. "That was a nice story," one of the boys said politely, "but I don't think it was very realistic for a father to give up his only son's life with just a hope that the other boy would become a Christian."

"Well, you've got a point there," the old man replied, glancing down at his worn Bible. Then a peaceful smile broke out on his narrow face. "It sure isn't very realistic, is it?" he said to the boys. "But I'm standing here today to tell you that story gives me a glimpse of what it must have been like for God to give up his Son for you and me. All in the name of hope.

"You see — I was that father and your pastor is my son's friend."

What's a papa to do? On the one hand, God loved his only begotten son. On the other hand, God loves us. But God, being God, can't live with our sinfulness. Somebody had to pay the price for our sins. Somebody had to redeem us from the clutches of death. Otherwise, we would spend eternity separated from God. God chose salvation for all of his creation over the suffering of his own son. That's what a good papa does. He takes care of all his children, no matter what the cost.

Professor Lowell of Harvard University was speaking to a gathering on Columbus Day. He told the crowd that there were three profound things about Christopher Columbus' discovery of America. First, when he left Spain he didn't know where he was going. Second, when he arrived in the New World he didn't know where he was. Third, when he returned to King Ferdinand in Spain he didn't know where he had been. Someone later added to Professor Lowell's speculation: "And he did it all on borrowed money!"

First, when we started our journey in this life, we didn't know where we were going. Most of our lives, we don't know where we are. And when we return to where we started, we won't know where we have been. But we'll have made the whole trip on borrowed money, the body and blood of Jesus Christ!

On the one hand, Adam left a legacy of sin and death, born from Adam's disobedience. On the other hand, Adam left a legacy of Jesus Christ, born from his own offspring. On the one hand, we are children of Adam's legacy of sin. But ... on the other hand, the hand marked by the nail of the cross, we are the children of Adam's legacy in Jesus Christ. And it is that legacy that will last forever and ever.

Lent 2
Romans 4:1-5, 13-17

Abraham Believed God

Abraham believed God. What more powerful statement of faith can there be than those three simple words? Abraham believed God. Let's make a very important distinction about this statement. It doesn't say that Abraham believed *in* God. It says, "Abraham believed God," and because of his belief in what God said, Abraham was credited with righteousness. It wasn't just that Abraham believed "in God" as in the belief that "God exists," or that some superhuman being created the universe. Abraham believed what God had to say the way one friend believes another. That seems to be a very important consideration when it comes to the way God interacts with us.

One summer in the village of Crete, the drought of the past winter threatened the crops. The priest in the local church told his congregation: "The only thing that will save us is for us to offer a special litany of rain. Therefore, I ask that you go back to your homes, fast during the week, and believe that the rains will come. Then return next Sunday for the litany of rain." The villagers listened to him and fasted during the week as he had told them. On Sunday morning, they returned to the church. But as soon as the priest saw the people filing into the church, he was furious. "Go away," he shouted to them. "I will not do the litany. You do not believe."

"But, Father," they protested, "we fasted just like you told us and we came back today believing as you asked us. Why are you being so harsh to us?"

"Believe, you say?" the priest questioned. "And where are your umbrellas?"

And where are *your* umbrellas? My guess is that if the local weather forecasters predict rain, you will be prepared with your umbrellas. But if God tells you to that his son will return to earth as the sovereign judge of all and you need to get this urgent message out to others, you would probably question its relevance to your life. You would think to yourself, "I believe it, but it hasn't happened in 2,000 years. I doubt it will happen in my lifetime."

If God told Abraham it was going to rain in the middle of the desert, Abraham would run for cover. When God told old man Abraham that he was going to become a father, even in his old age, Abraham began to build a cradle and get a nursery put together. When God told Abraham that he would be the "father of many nations" and his offspring would be too numerous to count, Abraham began to divvy up his land mentally. When God told Abraham to pick up everything and move to a new home, Abraham wasted no time in packing his belongings and following God's command. Abraham believed God. Abraham responded to God because Abraham believed God.

Even when God told Abraham to sacrifice his son, Isaac, upon an altar in the mountains, Abraham believed that it was the right thing to do. And he believed he had to do it because God told him to do it. Only when an angel of God stopped him and gave him a way out did Abraham change his course of action. That, too, was because Abraham believed God.

And what did Abraham's belief get him? Initially, it brought ridicule. Even his wife Sarah laughed at him. The very thought of a ninety-year-old woman and a man on the brink of the century mark having their first child together was just too much. But God showed them both it was not a laughing matter.

Abraham's belief brought him challenge and turmoil. He had to walk the streets of Sodom and Gomorrah searching in vain for enough righteous people to save the cities. Because he believed God, he found himself in a situation where he had to lie about his wife and say that she was his sister in order to save his life. Even though Abraham believed God, he didn't always trust God's wisdom. Even though he believed God, he didn't always want to hear what God said. He didn't always want to hear that God demanded righteousness from his people. But he was more than ready to believe that through the covenant God made with Abraham, people could be credited with righteousness through their faith.

What did Abraham's belief get him? Ultimately it got him salvation.

Look at what others believed. Noah believed God when he said there was going to be a great flood. He didn't just get down on his knees and pray for deliverance, he built an ark. Moses believed God wanted his people, the Israelites, to be free from Egyptian captivity. He didn't hide in the wilderness and wait to join the great exodus, he went back to the pharaoh, risking his life, and demanded, "Let my people go." A young child named David believed God when he told him he could defeat the giant Philistine named Goliath. Armed only with a slingshot, he headed into battle and won. John the Baptist believed God when he told him that the Messiah was in the world. He preached repentance of sins to a wicked world and thousands turned to God. Jesus believed God when he stood in front of Pontius Pilate and said nothing in his own defense. Jesus believed God as he carried his own cross along the path to Calvary. The disciples of Jesus believed God when their resurrected leader told them to go into all nations, baptizing and making disciples of all peoples.

They all believed God. It wasn't always easy to follow through on their belief, but they all believed. Noah had to watch the destruction of humankind. Moses had to take the harsh judgment of his people as he led them for forty years. Then he had to stay behind as they crossed over into the Promised Land. David became a great king of God's people, but the road to greatness was paved with treacherous curves. John the Baptist before Jesus, and the disciples after Jesus, all sacrificed their lives for believing God. Jesus, himself, believed God even as he hung up on the cross and gave up his life.

Many great people believed God. They went beyond "believing in" God, to "believing" God. Believing, however, didn't always mean that they blindly ran into something. Sometimes they hesitated. Sometimes, it took a little convincing on God's part. The prophet, Jonah, for example, didn't want to believe God. He didn't like the outcome that God had planned. But in the end, with the help of a great fish, Jonah's belief won out and God's plan was carried through.

Are we so different? We believe God. We believe that Jesus came into the world to die for our sins. We believe in the promise of Jesus, and we put our faith in that promise. And yet we still hold back when it comes to putting that faith to the test in our day-to-day living. We don't always want to do what we know God is telling us to do. When we look at a lifetime, we can accept the concept of God's grace by putting our faith in Jesus for eternal life. But when it comes to putting that same confidence in Jesus to see us through the rigors of the next day, we become anxious and we hesitate to trust him completely. What we need to learn is that eternity starts today. Jesus' saving grace is just as applicable for getting us through income tax time as it is for getting us through the gates of heaven.

The age-old debate always involves whether one believes in God or not. Is there a God, or isn't there a God? And for many people it is enough that they believe in God. They never quite get beyond belief in God to where they are able to believe what God says. For them, simply putting their trust in the fact that God exists is enough. Believing "in God" becomes the basis for their concept of salvation. With this type of thinking which is prevalent in our world, it doesn't really matter what you believe about God, as long as you believe in some kind of god. But Abraham believed God, and through his belief he was given righteousness. The kind of righteousness God demands of his creation.

Imagine, if you will, a tightrope stretched across the street between two tall buildings (you might insert the names of two well-known buildings in your town or city, or you might name some high spot with which your people are familiar). That's a pretty good drop. A man stands at one end of the wire and announces his intent to walk across the wire from one side to the other. A crowd gathers to watch because what he intends to do is dangerous, not to mention, a bit strange. The tightrope walker asks the crowd if they believe he can make it across. They respond that they believe he can do it in order to encourage him to take the risk. Carefully, very slowly, he teeters his way across, almost falling, but not quite; then dances on the wire proving that the crowd was right to believe him. Reaching the other side, he holds up a wheelbarrow and again asks the crowd if they believe he can push it across the wire ahead of him. Some nod their agreement that they believe; others shrug their shoulders in a "not too sure" response. The tightrope walker then singles out a man who had nodded and points to him. "Sir," he asks, "do you believe I can make it?" The man responds, "I sure do." The tightrope walker says to the man, "Then prove your faith by riding in the wheelbarrow."

Jesus has promised to guide our lives over the dangerous courses it will lead us. Would you ride in the wheelbarrow if Jesus were pushing it?

Some things have to be believed to be seen! If we don't believe the powerful words God has spoken to us, we will never see the marvelous things God can accomplish.

Because Abraham believed God, he was credited with righteousness. It was his belief, and the faith he demonstrated in that belief, that made him righteous before God. Not his works, not his attempts at impressing God, but only by following through on believing what God told him.

In his letter to the Romans, Saint Paul says that if we work for wages, then we expect to get paid; we expect something to be due us. It's the old adage: A day's pay for a day's work. But if we don't do the work, and still get paid, then it's a gift. It's something we get undeserved. That's called grace.

Abraham and all the others were credited with righteousness as a gift. It came not through anything they had done, but only through what they believed. And they believed God when he said, "My grace is sufficient."

The God "who gives life to the dead and calls into existence the things that do not exist" has told us that his promise comes to us by faith, that we might rely solely on the grace of God for our salvation. And that grace is guaranteed to all Abraham's offspring.

God is offering us a gift. He truly offers it with no strings attached. It sounds way too good to be true.
Believe it.
Abraham did.
Because God said it.

Lent 3
Romans 5:1-11

Access Denied

We live in a world of secret passages. We need keys, and perhaps more than one, to get behind locked doors. We need photo ID's to get past security guards. We need passwords to access computer files. We need PIN numbers to get money out of our own bank account or to charge groceries on our bankcards. Some buildings are so sophisticated that you have to use your handprint to get clearance to enter into secured rooms.

Just try to get past security without the right password and the computer screen will begin flashing the words: "Access Denied." No matter where we go today, whether it's online or on board a 747 airliner, we have to have the right information to gain access. If we don't know the secret password, or we don't have the proper identification as a cleared, non-risk person, we will be denied access.

In this fifth chapter of Paul's letter to the Romans, Saint Paul writes that through Jesus Christ "we have obtained access to this grace in which we stand." To follow the train of thought with which I began, Jesus is the password to grace. Jesus is the key to gain the righteousness we so desire. It is the nail-scarred hand of Jesus that can be put in place of our own hand that will open the door to eternal life.

Through Jesus Christ we have access to the grace of God.

After the revival service had ended in a small, coal-mining town, a man came up to the preacher and said that he would give anything to believe that God would forgive sins. But he insisted, "I cannot believe God will forgive me if I just turn to him. It's too cheap."

The preacher thought for a minute, and then began to question the man. "You were working in the mine today, right?"

"Yes," the man replied. "Just like every other day."

"How did you get out of the pit?" the preacher asked.

"The same way I usually do; I got into the cage and was pulled to the top."

"How much did you pay to come out of the pit?" the preacher inquired.

"I didn't pay anything," the man said, beginning to look a little puzzled.

"Weren't you afraid to trust yourself to that cage? Wasn't it too cheap to risk your life to?"

"Oh, no! It was cheap for me, but it cost the company a lot of money to sink that shaft."

"And there you have it, my son," the preacher smiled. "God paid an infinite price for our salvation. It does not come inexpensive to the one who has paid, no matter how cheap it might seem to us. And it comes to us only by our faith, not by anything we might try to do to repay the cost."

Paul says that we have obtained access to God's grace. And yet, everywhere we look, into the lives and faces of Christians, into the mirror in our own home, we see the flashing message: "Access Denied." Why is that? If access has already been gained, why does it appear to be denied? What is it that denies us access?

Is it the lack of an historical past such as the Jewish people have? Do we, as Gentiles, not have the connection with Abraham that our Jewish brothers and sisters have? Is that what's denying us access?

Is it not having a tradition of adhering to the laws that stands in the way of obtaining the grace of God? Perhaps, like the coal miner in the story, we have a hard time believing that grace can come to us so easily if we have not paid some kind of price for it. Therefore, we have to create some kind of an obstacle course of demands that we have to follow in order to achieve the right to God's grace. And what we actually do when we approach God's grace in that way is to cheapen it even more. The ultimate price has already been paid, and it's offered to us as a gift from God. Then we turn around and "slap God in the face" by saying, "God, I want somehow to repay you for your gift."

We are denied access to God's grace only by our refusal to accept it. And I say "only" because that's the only way that we are denied. God will not deny us. Jesus Christ will not deny us. Not even the church will deny us. *Only*, we, ourselves, can deny ourselves the grace of God. Only *you* can deny yourself access to the grace of God.

So if you see that "Access Denied" sign flashing when you approach God, back off, and look within yourself ... because that's where it's coming from.

Paul tells the Christians in Rome that we "have peace with God through our Lord Jesus Christ." We have obtained access to grace and that should bring with it not only a sense of peace, but also the assurance that all is right with God. He goes on to give a kind of formula that leads a follower of Christ to that peace. He says that "suffering produces endurance, and endurance produces character, and character produces hope, and hope does not disappoint" (Romans 5:4-5).

Henry Wadsworth Longfellow said, "If we could read the secret history of our enemies, we would find in each man's life sorrow and suffering enough to disarm all hostility." Suffering can lead to war, or it can lead to peace, both in the world around us, and within us. When we allow our own suffering to dictate our anger and frustration with life, then it destroys us. It steals life from us, and it robs us of the joy our Creator intended for us.

Jesus endured his suffering without losing faith in his Father. It was not suffering that he brought upon himself, but suffering that was heaped upon him for doing his Father's work. His endurance of the suffering made it possible for him to live at peace with himself while, at the same time, accomplishing the work that had been set before him.

A man was confined to his bed due to a lingering illness. His grandson brought him a cocoon of a beautiful species of butterfly as a get well gift. Having placed it on his windowsill, the man watched as the butterfly began its struggle to emerge from the cocoon. It was a long, hard battle with nature. As the hours went by, the struggling insect seemed to make almost no progress.

Finally, the human observer, thinking that "the powers that be" had erred, took a pair of scissors and snipped the opening larger. The butterfly crawled out, almost effortlessly, but that's all it ever did. The pressure of the struggle was intended to push colorful, life-giving juices back into the wings, but the man in his attempted mercy prevented this from happening. The insect was never able to do anything but crawl. Instead of flying on rainbow wings above the beautiful gardens, it was condemned to spend its brief life crawling in the dust.

Suffering produces endurance; endurance produces character.

When he was seven years old, his family was forced out of their home on a legal technicality, and he had to work to help support them. At age nine, his mother died. At 22, he lost his job as a store clerk. He wanted to go to law school, but his education wasn't good enough. At 23, he went into debt to become a partner in a small store. At 26, his business partner died, leaving him a huge debt that took years to repay. At 28, after courting a girl for four years, he asked her to marry him. She said no. Now endurance is endurance, but you'd think this guy would know when to give up. But he didn't.

At 37, after two defeats, he was elected to Congress. Two years later, he tried for re-election and was defeated again. At 41, his four-year-old son died. At 45, he ran for the Senate and ... he lost. At 47, he failed as candidate for vice-president of the United States. At 49, he ran for the Senate again, and lost. At 51, he was elected president of the United States. His name, of course, was Abraham Lincoln, a man many consider the greatest leader this country ever had.

Suffering produces endurance; endurance produces character, and character produces hope.

A biology examination was being held in little Judy's class at school and the question was asked: "Upon what do hibernating animals subsist during the winter?" Judy thought for a few minutes and then wrote: "All winter long hibernating animals subsist on the hope of a coming spring."

Is it food and water that keep us going? Is it mental stimulation that helps us endure the long winters of life? Is it a sense of purpose that makes us wake up each day and face the challenges? Sure, we can say, "Yes," to all three questions. But beneath all of them is hope. Hope for something better than the suffering we've known. Hope for something easier than the endurance we've had to experience. Hope for integrity that goes beyond our flawed character. There is always the hope that we will become better people.

Thornton Wilder said that "hope is a projection of the imagination; so is despair." We can choose what we want to project. If we choose to deny ourselves access to God's grace, then we can project despair. But if we choose to access God's grace by using the password "Jesus Christ," then we project hope. And every aspect of our lives will proclaim that hope to the world. Through hope, we attain peace, and we are not disappointed.

The one-time Prime Minister of England, Ramsey McDonald, was discussing the possibility of lasting peace with another government official. The other man was an expert on foreign affairs and was quite unimpressed by the prime minister's idealistic viewpoint. He remarked cynically to McDonald, "The desire for peace does not necessarily ensure it." McDonald admitted, "Quite true. But neither does the desire for food satisfy your hunger, but at least it gets you started toward a restaurant."

Our desire for peace does not necessarily ensure it. But it gets us started toward Christ. Our access to the grace of God does not necessarily mean we will take it. But it's there, given to us through the sacrifice and death of Jesus.

We've been given the password, the key that unlocks the door. And now, as Saint Paul says, we can even boast about it. It's not a secret and it's not something we have to keep hidden. We boast not about ourselves, for we have done nothing to achieve this grace, this forgiveness of sins. But we boast of God who has succeeded in bringing it about through Jesus. He showed it to the world when on the third day, Jesus rose again from the dead. We can boast that Jesus was victorious.

Let us live in the peace of knowing what Jesus has done, and let our lives reflect the victory. Access is not denied, unless we deny it. The grace of God abounds and our sins have been forgiven. As we get ever closer to the cross in our Lenten walk, I pray that each of us will be so overwhelmed by the peace of God which passes all understanding that we can't help but keep our hearts and minds in Christ Jesus. And I pray that this will happen in such a way that others will see and will access that grace for themselves.

Lent 4
Ephesians 5:8-14

Light Is As Light Does

If you saw the movie, *Forrest Gump* a few years back, you will remember how Forrest always had a quote from his mama to sum up just about any situation that a person might find himself or herself in. And if Forrest were to comment on this text from Ephesians, he might have this to say: "It's like my mama always used to say, 'Light is as light does.' "

Light is as light does. And what light does is shine out of the darkness. What light does is to make darkness disappear. Light and darkness cannot exist in the same space, because anytime light shows up, it pushes the darkness away. Darkness can exist on the edge of light, but it can never invade the space light has claimed.

Our lives seem to be filled with gray areas. Areas that are not fully illuminated nor are they fully darkened. Yet, while we try to convince ourselves that these gray areas exist to give us choices, we know deep down inside that the right choices always lead to the light, not the darkness. From inside those gray areas we can see that the right choices are not hidden from us, but are in plain view.

The Ephesians text tells us: "Sleeper, awake! Rise from the dead, and Christ will shine on you." Those gray areas are described as sleep from which we can awake, or even death, from which we can rise. And when we escape those gray areas, Christ will shine on us. Not only will he shine on us, he will shine out from us.

As Christians, we believe Jesus is the light of the world. He illuminates darkness so that in his light all secrets and hidden evils are revealed. If we choose to live in the light of Jesus, all that is dark within our lives is revealed and nothing is hidden from him, or from the rest of the world.

Light is as light does. What is it about light that makes it better than darkness? The obvious answer is that you can see light. Not only can you see light, but light also makes all things in its path visible so that you don't stumble into things. Light has a presence that makes it known to you. You can't miss light when it's around although you may not consciously think about it. But take it away, turn it off, cover it up, and you miss it immediately.

Darkness, on the other hand, is the absence of light. Darkness is void of light.

When we think of it in those terms, and believe that Jesus is the Light of the world, it is then we can say that Jesus is something you can see, while evil is hidden. Jesus makes everything else visible, while evil blocks things out. Evil is the absence of Jesus. Evil is void of everything that Jesus has come to represent to people.

Light is as light does. Light promotes growth. Darkness leads to death.

A woman was working in her garden and came upon a large, green, healthy-looking squash plant, and she began to admire it. The stems appeared to be strong, and the leaves were large. She envisioned the beautiful squash that this plant would one day produce. Oh, that every plant in her garden could be as productive as this squash plant.

A few days later she noticed that the plant was terribly wilted. There were no signs of any damage, nor were any of the plants around it in this condition. She couldn't figure out what had happened and she tried to give it extra care to nurse it back to health. But in a couple more days, it was completely dead. She pulled the plant up and examined its roots. There she discovered that a bore worm, which could not be seen from the outside, had eaten the heart out of the stem of the plant.

That's how our dark, hidden sins work on us. Like the bore worm, hidden sins can eat away at the heart of our Christian experience and leave us spiritually dead. When left unexposed to the light, sin continues to do its dirty work: obstructing our lives, destroying the true joy of life, and separating us from a loving God.

Light is as light does. A lighted path is easy to follow. We stumble in the darkness.

A family had gone to the movies, and on the way in, the young man of the family stopped by the refreshment stand to pick up some popcorn. By the time he got into the theater, the lights were already dim. He scanned the theater and couldn't find his family. People watched him pace up and down the aisle, searching the crowd in the near-darkness. As the lights began to go down even further, he stopped and asked out loud, "Does anyone recognize me?"

Is the path to our church, to the Christian life, well lit so that people can recognize it? As people come into our church, and into our lives, they are looking for family and companionship. People want to recognize the aisle that leads to the altar of God and they want to be recognized. They want to know God and they want to be known by him. People need to fit in and have a place among others. Like a lighthouse on the shores of the ocean, light can lead people to safe harbor or it can warn them of dangerous waters.

Are you a light that others can see in the darkness? Are you easily identifiable as a follower of Jesus so that people recognize our church as a safe place to be? Are we, as a congregation, a string of lights that shine out of this building and into our community? Can we lead people to the safety of Jesus and away from the dangers of sin?

Light is as light does. When the power gets low, or the connection is faulty, a light might begin to grow dim. And when the power source is completely severed, the light goes out completely, and that is darkness.

Just before the beginning of the Sunday service at a large Episcopal church in New York City, a man wearing a large hat was discovered sitting in the front row. An usher moved to his pew, leaned in, and discreetly asked him to remove his hat. The man replied that he would not. The head usher then was summoned, made the same request, and received the same answer. About that time the president of the women of the parish arrived and was asked to assist. She had the same dismal result. Finally, with only two minutes remaining before the opening hymn, the senior warden of the parish was also asked to intercede. He tiptoed up beside the man and tried to seize the hat, but the man was able to dodge his attempts to grab the hat. By now, there was no time for further confrontation.

As the opening hymn began and the procession entered the church, the man stood, removed his hat, and did not put it on again.

At the conclusion of the service, the four frustrated people waited for the man at the rear of the church. The senior warden approached him and said, "Sir, about the hat: perhaps you don't understand, but in the Episcopal church men do not wear hats at worship."

The man replied, "Oh, but I do understand. I've been Episcopalian all my life. As a matter of fact, I've been coming to this church regularly for two years and I've never met a soul. But this morning I've met an usher, the head usher, the president of the church women, and the senior warden."

What does it take to get your light turned on? What does it take to get your attention? Do you run around with your lights on dim most of the time so that people won't notice you? God is our power source. The Holy Spirit living within us gives off a light that people cannot miss. Are we sometimes too busy going about with church work that we forget to do the work of the church? It doesn't matter how well we have down the routine of running a church, if we are not a running church. We can master the budget, the music, the worship, the fellowship groups, the Sunday school curriculum, and all sorts of committees, but if we are not running our light outside the church building, then it is all for nothing.

Light is as light does. And light cannot help but to shine outward. You cannot hide your light under a bushel basket and expect it to be seen by others and attract attention. A light that is hidden is darkness and does not do anyone any good.

Light is as light does. And ultimately light will show the flaws and imperfections of all those around us. Our heroes get brought down, our highest government officials have a dark side, our best friends surprise us, and our parents are really human after all. And, oh, how we love to jump on the sins of others.

There was a young priest who was going to the confessional booth for the first time. He went with another priest, his senior. After a day of hearing confessions he was approached by the older pastor who offered some advice: "You know, I think that when a person finishes with a confession, you should say something on the order of, 'I agree it is terrible what you have done, and I would encourage you to stay away from that kind of behavior from now on ...' instead of saying, 'WOW!' "

Saint Paul tells us, "For it is shameful even to mention what such people do secretly; but everything exposed by the light becomes visible, for everything that becomes visible is light" (Ephesians 5:12-13). Sins are revealed not to be talked about or to become the basis for gossip, not to be pitted one against another to show that I am less of a sinner than you, but sins are revealed so that they might be forgiven and corrected. Sins are revealed so that what is done in the darkness might be overcome by what is done in the light. We are not to attack our brothers and sisters for their sinfulness, but are to admonish them concerning the dangers of being drawn to the darkness.

Light is as light does. We are children of light who walk in the light. And while this passage tells us more about what life in the light is not than what life in the light is, like a parent pleading to his children, Saint Paul challenges us to discover that for ourselves. "Try to find out what is pleasing to the Lord," he says. We know that the light pleases God. So if we live in the light of Jesus, we will reveal all those things that are pleasing to the Lord. Conversely, we can avoid those things that are covered by darkness.

On that first Easter, God broke through the darkness once and for all. The darkness of the tomb of death was exposed when Jesus rolled away the stone. His light now shines throughout the world.

It's like my Father in heaven always says, "Light is as light does." You who are light ... be light. Do what light does. And you will no longer live in darkness.

Lent 5
Romans 8:6-11

Enjoy The Scenery

Some of us can remember the days before interstate highways and massive traffic slowdowns when a leisurely drive to a relative's house was as much about scenery as it was about getting places. Who cared if the highway weaved around curves and some hills were steeper than others? It was fun to see fields with cattle and sheep, and sometimes even a white hillside where turkeys and chickens roamed freely behind a fence.

Those were days when you could load up the station wagon and start out on the trip of a lifetime. Regardless of where you were starting from, the adventure would undoubtedly lead to parts of the country that you had only seen in books and magazines. From the east, west, north, or south, from the central plains, wherever it was you called home, there was a lot to be seen beyond your immediate area.

Just map out your itinerary to include places that you have always wanted to see and those that any traveling partners would enjoy. Drive through the cornfields of Indiana and Illinois, and the wheat of the Dakotas, Kansas, and Nebraska. Swing by that "new" arch structure called the Gateway to the West in St. Louis. They say you can even go up inside and view the whole city.

You can drive along the beaches of either coast, or into the mountains that spread throughout our country. You can enjoy the forests of evergreen or walk among the petrified trees of long ago. Sit on the banks of the Mississippi and you can almost see Tom Sawyer floating by on a raft. Climb the steps in Mesa Verde National Park and you sense the presence of the cliff dwellers who built their homes in the Colorado mountainside. On another mountainside in South Dakota, you can marvel at the danger and skill it took to carve the faces of four American presidents.

Using a little imagination, you can see Charles Blondin walking across the gorge just down from Niagara Falls. And it takes no imagination, just wonderment, to appreciate the color and beauty of the Grand Canyon.

All those places are still there, and you can still see them and enjoy them, but traveling has changed. If you still choose to travel any great distance by car instead of flying, most travel is done on interstate highways. And unless you can count seeing the World's Largest Buffalo along I-94 in Jamestown, North Dakota, or other tall, man-made structures, you don't see a lot. To get to those gems of scenery, you have to take a side trip. The old highway system went this way and that, connecting one small place to another, regardless of the hills that had to be climbed or the curves that had to be maneuvered. Interstate highways try to be the shortest distance between two points. They are straighter, less hilly, and, if necessary to accomplish their goal, will go right through the side of a mountain or under a water source.

But the highways are not the only things that have changed. People have changed as well. The simple wonders that surround us become hidden from our view by all of our modern necessities that we carry with us. We feel like we're interrupting something if we try to point out some beautiful scenic spot when the kids are listening to their CDs and the adults are watching a movie. Headphones in place, eyes closed, it's like: "Don't bother me with stuff outside. Just tell me how long before we get there."

We have become so disoriented that we confuse the distractions in our lives with the realities. What we might perceive as distractions are actually the realities. To a young person riding in a car, the beautiful scenery is a distraction to concentrating on the music. To a caring and concerned onlooker, the music is the distraction to the world.

Has our focus in life become "just getting there" instead of living it as we go along? Are we able to enjoy the scenery along the way or do we shut it out because we don't have the time to deal with it? Do we live only in the flesh, or do we allow God's Spirit to dwell in us?

The Greeks had a unique race in the ancient Olympic games. The winner was not the runner who finished first. It was the runner who finished with his torch still lit. In our journey through life, we have to pay attention to the fire, to make sure that it stays lit, and not just focus on the finish line. If we reach the finish, but our flame has already burned out, then we have not won the race.

To live in the Spirit enables the flame of life to keep on burning. To live in the flesh takes fuel from our flame, and eventually it burns out. As Christians we admit that the journey is just as important as the destination. Yet, even Christians are overcome by the distractions of the flesh, which not only attempt to put out the flame of the Spirit, but also try to block the road to our destination.

New York was playing the Milwaukee Braves in the World Series when Yogi Berra was the catcher for the Yankees. Hank Aaron was the chief power hitter for Milwaukee. As usual, Yogi was engaged in his ceaseless chatter, intended to pep up his teammates on the one hand and distract the Milwaukee batters on the other. As Aaron came to the plate, Yogi tried to distract him by saying, "Henry, you're holding the bat wrong. You're supposed to hold it so you can read the trademark." Aaron didn't say anything, but when the next pitch came he hit it into the left-field bleachers. After rounding the bases and tagging up at home plate, Aaron looked at Yogi Berra and said, "I didn't come up here to read."

Hank Aaron would not be distracted. He kept his mind, and his spirit, if you will, focused on the road ahead. And choosing that path led around the bases, time and time again. When Hank hit it out of the park, he didn't have to run those bases, he could walk them, enjoy them at his own pace, knowing he had accomplished what he set out to do.

That's how we should walk through life: enjoying the scenery as we go. We were not born into this world just to read about it or see it portrayed on television and in movies. We don't need headphones to hear it. We came to experience it.

Soviet leader Nikita Khrushchev used to tell of a time when the Soviet Union was plagued with a wave of petty theft. To overcome the problem, authorities placed guards around the factories. At one lumberyard in Leningrad, the guard knew the workers in the factory very well. The first evening, out came Pyotr Petrovich with a wheelbarrow and, on the wheelbarrow, a great bulky sack with a suspicious-looking object inside.

"All right, Petrovich," the guard said, "what have you got there?"

"Oh, just some sawdust and shavings," Petrovich replied.

"Come on," the guard said, "I wasn't born yesterday. Tip it out."

Petrovich did as the guard demanded and out came nothing but sawdust and shavings. So he was allowed to put it all back again and go home. When the same thing happened every night of the week, the guard became frustrated. Finally, his curiosity overcame his frustration. "Petrovich," he said, "I know you. Tell me what you're smuggling out of here, and I'll let you go."

"Wheelbarrows, my friend," said Petrovich. "Wheelbarrows."

Sometimes the distractions in life veil our eyes to what is going on right in front of us: relationships fall apart, families break up, our work suffers, we fail to help those who need our help, and we forget the mission of the church.

Any of us more than forty years old can probably remember where we were when we first heard of President Kennedy's assassination in 1963.

British novelist David Lodge, in the introduction to one of his books, tells that he was in a theater watching the performance of a satirical revue he had helped write. In one sketch, a character was being interviewed. He listened to a transistor radio to show his indifference to the interview. The actor playing the part always tuned in to a real broadcast. Suddenly the announcement that President Kennedy had been shot came over the air. The actor quickly switched off the radio, but it was too late. Reality had interrupted the performance.

We worship ... we pray ... we read the Bible. But we do it casually. We don't always believe in the reality in which we're involved. We perform in front of others. But we don't really expect anything significant to happen. Then, when we least expect it, God breaks through. His presence overtakes us, and we remember that living in his Spirit is the reality. Everything else is just a distraction.

We were born into this world in the flesh. Through the baptism of Christ, we are reborn in the Spirit. As spiritual beings, the flesh becomes a distraction. But in Christ, it is a distraction that we can live with.

Enjoy the scenery in your journey through life. Don't be distracted by those things that would tempt you to believe anything other than that God's kingdom is a wonderful place filled with beautiful sights and lovely creatures.

Though we exist in the flesh, we live in the Spirit. Even as we live with the pain and discomfort our broken bodies might afford us, we walk in the Spirit of a new and better place. For it is only in the weakness of the flesh that we ultimately find our strength in the Spirit.

As we continue our journey toward Easter, may God grant you the ability to see all that he has laid out before you.

Passion/Palm Sunday
Philippians 2:5-11

Temptation Of The Palms

A couple of years ago a popular slang expression came out that said: "Give it up." To show you that like someone who is being introduced or a piece of music that's about to be played, the person making the introduction will indubitably instruct you to "Give it up for...." And you applaud. You scream and yell and jump up and down. You do whatever it takes to show that you really are excited to see this person or hear this particular song. Go ahead; give it up.

If that phrase was around a couple of thousand years ago in Jerusalem, someone might well have instructed the crowd to "give it up for Jesus" as he rode into town on the back of that donkey. Along with waving palm branches and throwing down garments, the hosannas and alleluias of the assembled admirers could definitely have been construed as "giving it up for Jesus."

After all, this was an exciting time. Jesus of Nazareth was an exciting guy. He had the spunk to stand up to the self-righteous Pharisees. He made the little people feel just as important as the powerful and wealthy. He spoke with such authority that even the Roman soldiers seemed to listen to him. He befriended everybody, saint and sinner alike. And those stories about him!

It was said that he healed the sick. That he gave sight to the blind. That he could touch someone's crippled limb and make it healthy. There were even stories of how he made dead people come back to life.

Some people went so far as to say that Jesus was the promised Messiah — the long-awaited Savior of the people; the one who would lead Israel back to the greatness it had known under kings such as David and Solomon.

So why not "give it up" for Jesus? If all this was true — the stories, the speculation, the miraculous abilities — then Jesus deserved complete devotion and loyalty. This was Jesus' day, and this crowd was Jesus' greatest fan club. Jesus deserved a welcome fit for a king, and more. For Jesus was truly sent by God. Or, so it seemed ... for the moment.

And this is precisely the temptation that Jesus faced on that day: to be who the people wanted him to be and not be who he really was. The temptation to give in to the desires of the crowd; to be worshiped and lifted up as a great charismatic leader; to fulfill the political agenda that others had in mind; to free the people from the Romans, not from their own sinfulness. The temptation was there to exploit his equality with God.

It was at this very point in his ministry, and in his life, that Jesus had to "give it up" for the people. He had to empty himself and become their servant, not their king. He had to humble himself completely, and walk through the next six days not only as one of them, but as one who would be thoroughly humiliated, condemned, and executed as a criminal. Jesus the Messiah, the Son of God, handled like a piece of human garbage, so the powers that be might prove him weak and ineffective.

None of us go to a parade to give it up. None of us really go to see anyone famous or notorious to give it up. We go to receive. We stand in line and pay our money to be entertained. We wait in a crowd for hours just to get a glimpse of some celebrity, and if we're lucky, an autograph or some other piece of memorabilia we can take home with us. We want to get something for our efforts.

Those people standing along the roadside on Palm Sunday were willing to give it up for Jesus, only if they got something in return. They would cheer Jesus on as long as he took them where they wanted to go. They would support Jesus as long as he fulfilled the role they had picked out for him. But let Jesus waver from the path they wanted him to walk down, and suddenly he was walking alone.

We human beings are a fickle lot. We listen to speakers to hear what they have to say to us, not about anybody else. We want politicians to tell us things that are going to make our lives better, not necessarily things that will improve the world. We want instructors to teach us things we want to learn, not necessarily things they want to teach us. We want preachers to tell us we're doing good things and that we're headed in the right direction that will ultimately get us to heaven. We don't necessarily want to hear the truth. If a speaker doesn't have something to say to us, something that will directly affect our lives in the way we want them affected, we tune them out.

As a speaker, Jesus was no exception. As long as he kept the people entertained, they were happy. As long as he promised them a better life, they were interested. As long as it appeared he might be the one to set them free from the dreadful Romans who occupied their land, they followed him. But as soon as he was tested, and failed their test, he was abandoned.

How many times have we said, "Jesus could have ..."? How many times have we asked, "Why didn't Jesus...?" We think that if we were writing the script, we could have done a much better job. That's what some of Jesus' contemporary temporary followers thought, too. One of them even tried to rewrite the ending by forcing Jesus' hand. But it didn't work.

Jesus didn't give in to the temptation of the palms. He didn't budge an inch off the course his Father had set for him. Yes, he could have. He could have done a lot of things, and in our imaginations we can conjure up all kinds of different endings to Jesus' mission and ministry.

He could have taken the throne that the Palm Sunday crowd wanted to put him on. He could have led Israel to worldly dominance by crushing the Roman Empire with the mighty hand of God. He could have healed the nation of pestilence and disease. He could have fed all the hungry of the world with a bumper crop of manna from heaven like Israel had never seen before. He could have eradicated evil from the face of the earth and set up his kingdom right then and there.

He could have. He could have. We know he really could have. But he didn't. He didn't because he was Jesus. And that wasn't what Jesus was about. That was what those people were about.

They celebrated him one day and condemned him the next. That's what we're about. We're like that when we try to make Jesus into something that he was never meant to be. We're like that when we still try to tempt Jesus by waving the palms and carrying a banner that makes Jesus out to be a leader who exemplifies our politics and our expectations for the future.

Jesus was never what people expected him to be. Jesus was always obedient. But he wasn't obedient to the passing whims and zealous aspirations of people. He was obedient to his Father in heaven, even to the point of death ... death on a cross.

In our human fickleness, we are also controlling. We have even been taught that we should control our own destinies. Hidden behind the Palm Sunday crowd's exuberance, were a controlling people. They were a people willing to manipulate the events at hand in order to determine a future that would be beneficial to them.

Is that any different than what we do today? Individuals use other individuals just to get what they want. Governments use other governments and even their own citizens to bring about the ends they desire. And we have adopted the philosophy that the ends do indeed justify the means, as long as the ends are in our favor.

Jesus didn't give in to that philosophy ... or did he? For Jesus, the means to the end that he wanted to achieve was the path to Calvary; a road less traveled. For Jesus, it was a trail of complete self-denial and sacrifice. To us, it was a mysterious walk that took Jesus from the adulation of the crowds to the glorification of God.

When you look at it that way, perhaps the temptation of the palms was not that great. If you have a choice between being revered by people or applauded by God, which would you choose? Of course the choice is not that easy if you consider that the cross stood between you and the glory that would come from God.

Jesus resisted the temptation of Palm Sunday. And because he was able to overcome any inkling to give in to his ego, he was able to fulfill his purpose on earth. As a lamb sacrificed on the altar, Jesus was given over to the enemy and died for our sins — crucified for us that we might have everlasting life.

And God exalted him. God, not the people in the crowd, gave him a name that is above every other name. He made it so that at the name of Jesus, every knee should bend, not just on earth, but under the earth and in heaven as well; and every tongue should confess that Jesus is Lord.

We have to be careful not to be lured in by the temptation of palms. We have to be cautious not to jump on every bandwagon and cheerleading squad that puts Jesus up on a pedestal and hails him as the driving force behind whatever cause they have determined him to be "for" or "against."

Jesus' ministry was a demanding ministry. His mission was an urgent mission. He could not be sidetracked by every diversion that he faced. He had to keep focused, always, on the ultimate goal. He came into our world for one purpose. He achieved that purpose by giving it up, giving it all up, for us. "Though he was in the form of God, he did not regard equality with God something to be exploited." Instead, he emptied himself.

Let's do "give it up" for Jesus. And the way to do that is not by being his cheering section, not by lining the streets and getting caught up in crowd hysteria. To give it up for Jesus, we have to focus on the same urgent mission that Jesus came to accomplish: the salvation of all humankind. Starting with our own circle of family and friends, and venturing out into the world around us, we give it up for Jesus by professing the name that causes every knee to bow and every tongue to confess — and by living a life that screams and shouts the name of Jesus in every kind act we do, and every caring word we speak.

We give it up for Jesus ... by giving up "ourselves."

Good Friday
Hebrews 10:16-25

After Good Friday

Obsolete. Superceded. Null and void.

Those are all words that could be used in a court of law to describe legal contracts or agreements that are no longer in effect. Stipulations become obsolete with the passing of time or when two partners break off their partnership, whether it's a business or a marriage. Procedures can be superceded by new practices when old stipulations become obsolete. Whole contracts can become null and void when one side or the other fails to live up to the agreement.

Now the happiest resolution to a contract dispute comes when one side offers the other a better deal. Take a professional athlete for example. If a team owner says, "Let's forget about the three-year, $10 million deal we have going. I want to offer you a seven-year, $50 million contract." That's a better offer. It assures the athlete four more years of guaranteed salary, and about $28 million dollars more than the rate he's now receiving. And it assures the team owner that the athlete will play on his team for four years more than he's now obligated.

Of course in our modern world, a lot can change in three years, and the athlete might want to hold out to see if a better offer comes by. Another team could offer him more money with more incentives. On the other hand, the athlete could permanently injure himself and not get as good an offer as he has now. Contracts can be risky.

God, however, doesn't make contracts. He makes covenants. Covenants are not based on material property or services rendered;

they are based on trust. Covenants are based on relationships. Covenants are promises that are made voluntarily and accepted of one's own accord.

Down through history God has made covenants with his people. God made a covenant with the first people in the Garden of Eden when he told Adam and Eve they could live there forever as long as they obeyed him. Of course, the first two people with whom God ever made a deal broke that first covenant. And thus began a history of disobedience.

God made a covenant with Noah after God flooded the earth. He told Noah that he would never again destroy the earth by flooding. As a sign of this covenant, he put the rainbow in the sky, to remind Noah and his ancestors of his promise. Noah accepted God's promise.

God made a covenant with Abraham. He promised Abraham that he would be the father of many nations, that his offspring would be more numerous than the stars in the heavens and the sands of the seashore. All this he promised to a man who should have been a great-grandfather by this time, and who, as yet, had no children with his wife Sarah. But God promised, and Abraham believed, and a covenant was made. God made his stipulations to Abraham and gave circumcision as a sign of his covenant.

God gave Moses some stipulations of this covenant that he made with Abraham and we call them the Ten Commandments. He told Moses and the Israelites to obey and that he would be their God and that they would be his people. As an added incentive, God would continue to lead them safely away from the Egyptians and into the Promised Land. We know that these people were a stubborn people and that it took forty years to get there, but God was true to his promise.

Down through the years there was give and take, laws to obey, and directions to follow. The people were to do their part, and God would provide salvation and protection, and establish them as a great nation. The people made sacrifices as ordered. They followed rituals as directed. They negotiated with God to have a king appointed. They fought wars and lost lives under the banner of the Most High. Israel was the nation of God and God was source of their strength.

But the covenant was weakened time and time again. Not by God, he held up his part of the agreement. It was the people who came up short, over and over again. They disobeyed his commandments. They strayed from their loyalty to him. They worshiped other gods in the forms of materialism, greed, power, and lust. It became apparent that something had to be done to rectify the situation. So God made a better offer.

Now we don't know for sure, but we can assume that God in all of his wisdom knew from the start what would happen. And so, he had a back-up plan: Jesus. A new covenant that would end all covenants. A covenant between the Creator and the creation that would cover everything once and for all, and that would supercede all former covenants making them obsolete and null and void.

After Good Friday, things were changed forever. After Good Friday, God had spoken. After Good Friday, all else was forgotten, including the sins of the world. For on Good Friday, the final sacrifice was made, and nothing more could be done to reconcile people with their God. Easter was the day that the victorious court verdict of "Not Guilty" was pronounced upon all humankind, but it was on Good Friday that the deciding evidence was laid to rest.

Somebody had to do it, and Jesus was that someone.

In olden days, during the dark winters of a frozen Alaska, food was often scarce. A young man would venture out, armed only with a pointed stick and a compassion for his starving Eskimo village. He would wander about in the darkness, anticipating an attack of a polar bear. Having no natural fear of humans, a polar bear would stalk and eat a man. When a bear would attack, the Eskimo hunter would wave his hands and spear to anger his attacker and make the bear rise up on his hind legs to over ten feet in height. Then, with the spear braced to his foot, the hunter would aim for the heart as the weight of the bear came down upon his spear. With heart pierced, the bear might live long enough to maim or kill this noble hunter. Loving family and friends would then follow his tracks out of the village and find food for their survival. They also found evidence of profound courage and sacrifice.

Early Christian missionaries to the Eskimos proclaimed that Jesus Christ is the "Good Hunter" who lays down his life for the world. It was an illustration they could understand, and one that can remind us why Jesus did what he did. Because of God's love and compassion for us, Jesus became the New Covenant he would make with his people. A covenant that transcends all times and all places, and puts every living being in a new relationship with God.

There was a little girl whose parents had lived in a miserable marriage and finally ended it in a divorce. Having felt they had nothing in common except for their affection for the child, they broke their covenant. One day the girl was seriously injured when she was struck by bus as she raced into the street while playing. Taken to the hospital, she was examined by the doctors but was found to be beyond human aid. The parents were given the sad news and stood silently, one on either side of the bed, looking down helplessly at their only child. As they stood there, the girl's eyes suddenly opened and seeing her parents she tried to smile. Then drawing one arm from under the sheet, she held it out in the direction of her father. "Daddy," she said, "give me your hand." Turning to her mother, she stretched out her other arm. "Mommy," she said, "give me your hand." Then with a final effort of her faltering strength, she drew them together.

This is a picture of what Christ did on the cross. Our Savior took the hand of sinful, hateful humanity and placed it in the loving hand of God. Jesus became the New Covenant, making it possible for us to be reconciled to God. Jesus broke down the barrier that existed under the old covenant. He restored the broken fellowship caused by sin and turning our backs on God.

The little girl died with a vision of her parents together. But what would happen after that would take an effort on the part of the parents. Jesus died to bring God and us together again, but even under the New Covenant we have to make the effort to keep the relationship going.

A New Covenant has been created between God and his people. In this covenant, the laws are not written on tablets of stone, but in the hearts and minds of the believers. God promises this in the New Covenant: "I will remember their sins and their lawless deeds no more. Where there is forgiveness of these, there is no longer any offering for sin." No more sacrifices necessary.

The New Covenant is an "after Good Friday" covenant. It is sealed with the blood of Christ and therefore nothing more needs to be added. Only our commitment is to believe it.

A little boy came to the Washington Monument and noticed a guard standing by. The boy looked up at the guard and said, "I want to buy it." The guard stooped down and asked, "How much do you have?" The boy reached into his pocket and pulled out a quarter. The guard said, "That's not enough." The boy replied, "I thought you would say that." So he pulled out nine cents more. The guard looked down at the boy and said, "You need to understand three things. First, 34 cents is not enough. In fact, $34 million is not enough to buy the Washington Monument. Second, the Washington Monument is not for sale. And third, if you are an American citizen, the Washington Monument already belongs to you."

We need to understand three things about what happened on Good Friday and the covenant of forgiveness that came out of it. First, we cannot earn God's forgiveness. Second, it's not for sale. And third, if we believe that Christ died for us on that cross, then we already have his forgiveness.

Isn't it wonderful to be living after Good Friday? Isn't it great to be reconciled to God? Isn't it assuring to know that forgiveness and salvation are ours, that the ultimate sacrifice has been made, and that through the New Covenant of Jesus Christ, nothing more is needed?

Then go ... Good Friday has passed and Easter has established the New Covenant. Live in an Easter world, free from the bonds of sin, and the grip of death. Live with the knowledge of a risen Lord, and an ever-loving God. But always remember, without the payment made on Good Friday, there would be no after.

Easter
Colossians 3:1-4

Taking You Up With Him

"If I go down, I'm taking you down with me." We've all heard that line. It's been used in movies and on television shows. We've seen it written in books and even in real-life news articles. Maybe we've even had it said directly to us. Somebody is in big trouble, and they are not going to face the punishment without involving someone else in their suffering.

Sometimes there's even a line that follows: "That's not just a threat; it's a promise," just to let us know that they are not bluffing. If they are going to bear the guilt, they are not going to bear it alone.

It's human nature not to want to take the blame for something, even if we are guilty of a wrongdoing. And at precisely such moments of confrontation, of being caught, we turn to our natural defenses. The number one of which is passing the buck.

All we have to do to find historical evidence of this type of vengeful practice is go to the beginning of the book we turn to for our religious background, the Bible. In the third chapter of Genesis, when God asked Adam if he did indeed disobey and eat the fruit he was told not to eat, Adam said, "Well ... yeah, but, it was that woman you gave to me who handed me the fruit and told me to eat it." Adam is implying that he would have never done it on his own. In essence, Adam is saying, "If I'm going down, I'm taking Eve with me."

Anyone who has ever spent time with children, whether their own or someone else's, has seen this tendency of the first man come all the way down through history to the present time. "It wasn't my fault. It was my sister. I didn't do it. It was my brother. Julie pushed her down, not me. I did it, but Billy made me do it."

We place the blame elsewhere. We don't want to face the punishment. That's what appears to be human nature. But to accept blame willingly or even take on the guilt of others — that's not our standard operating procedure. That's alien to our nature.

So when Jesus of Nazareth comes along and accepts not only the blame for the things we have done, but also for the things we have left undone, it's hard for us to comprehend. It goes against human nature. Instead of what we are used to hearing from other people, instead of being treated the way we have come to expect other people to treat us, Jesus says, "When I go up, I'm taking you with me." Then he adds, "That's not a threat; that's a promise." And when Jesus makes a promise, you can count on it.

Perhaps you've used those words yourself. Again, talking to children we will often use the threat/promise approach. "If you don't finish your homework, I'm going to ground you for a week." "If you touch those cookies in the cookie jar, you are going to bed without any television." "If you don't sit still during church, I'm going to spank you when we get home." (Oh, that last one is always a good one to make small children feel good about going to worship!) And we will often add those words that provide the finishing touch, "That's not just a threat; that's a promise."

Unfortunately, the church has taken the threat/promise approach far too often in its history. The church says to us, "If you don't change your ways now, you are going to hell." "If you are not actively involved in the worship and ministry of this congregation, you are not a Christian." "If your lifestyle does not conform to the standards we have set, you are outside the Kingdom of God."

But Jesus did not die on that cross to "take us down" *with* him. He died on the cross to go down *for* us. He went down in our place. We will all admit that, in the eyes of justice, we should have been on that cross. If the guilty are punished for their sins, then we deserve the punishment. If an eternity with God is dependent upon our worthiness to stand in the presence of God, then we are unworthy.

Jesus went down. He didn't take anyone with him. Not the soldiers who drove the nails into his hands. Not the crowd who gave him up and jeered at him. Not Pilate who washed his hands. Not even Judas who betrayed him.

He went down without a fight. He went down without a complaint. Jesus didn't whine or place the blame on anyone. Jesus went down and didn't take anyone down with him. But when he came up, he offered to take everyone along — even those who took him down.

That's what Easter is about. It's not just an empty tomb announcing that Jesus defeated death. It's not about Jesus showing the world he couldn't be put out of business. It's not even that Jesus wanted to give his followers proof of who he was. None of that mattered if people didn't understand the significance of the resurrection for their lives. Jesus already knew what he was capable of doing and he never felt compelled to give demonstrations. But if people didn't personally connect with Jesus' death and resurrection in their own lives, then none of what happened on Good Friday and Easter morning accomplished its intent.

Before his death on the cross, Jesus told his disciples that he was going to prepare a place for them. He shared with his followers the teachings of a better life here on earth. And he promised them that wherever they went and whatever they would be doing in the future, he would be with them.

That was his promise. He did not threaten them. He promised. And to this day, he has kept his promise, among his new disciples, you and me, and all who continue to put their trust and hope in him.

The resurrection finalized our ultimate connection to Jesus Christ. Because he went down for us, he came up with us, and takes us along with him. He has taken our lives with him to the next step. Through resurrection, our lives have been "kicked up a notch." We're not on the same level anymore. It's impossible for us to be connected with the resurrected Lord and still consider ourselves bottom-dwellers.

On Easter, we're used to hearing the story of Easter. We expect to hear how Jesus died, was buried, and especially the ending where he rose again from the grave. On this Easter, from what Saint Paul has written to us in his letter to the Colossians, we are also hearing how intimately our lives as Christians are tied into Jesus' resurrection. We have been raised with him to a new level of life. That's not some future event. That's now, here, where we are and as we live. And Paul tells us to seek and to love things that are above. He implores us to focus, to set our minds on those things, things at a higher level of existence, because that is where Christ has taken us.

Our lives have been changed, not because of anything in particular we have done or are doing, but our lives have been changed because Jesus has changed them. And because we are eternally connected to his life, we have the power to change the lives of others. When others view us in our "resurrected" lives, they are able to see Jesus.

Joey was six years old and wanted to meet God. He knew it was a long trip to where God lived, so he packed his suitcase with his mom's chocolate chip cookies and a couple of small cans of orange juice as he started his journey. He hadn't gone very far from home when he met an old man sitting in a park just staring at some birds playing in the fountain. Joey sat down next to him and opened his suitcase. He was about to take a drink from his orange juice when he noticed that the man looked a little hungry, so he offered him one of his freshly-baked cookies. The man gratefully accepted it and smiled at him. His smile was so pleasant that the boy wanted to see it again, so he offered him his other orange juice. Again, the old man smiled at him. Joey was delighted! The two sat there together all afternoon eating and smiling, but they never said a word. It began to get dark out and Joey realized how tired he was and he got up to leave, but before he had gone more than a few steps, he turned around, ran back to his new friend, and gave him a hug. The man gave him his biggest smile ever.

When Joey got home a short time later, his mother was surprised by the look of joy on his face. She asked him, "Joey, what did you do today that made you so happy?" Joey replied, "I had lunch with God." And before his mother could respond, he added, "You know what? He's got the most beautiful smile I've ever seen!"

Meanwhile, the old man, also radiant with joy, returned to his home. His son was puzzled by the look of peace on his father's face and he asked, "Dad, what did you do today that made you so happy?" He replied, "I ate cookies in the park with God." And, before his son could respond, he added, "You know, he's much younger than I expected."

The world can be a scary, sad, and lonely place in which to live. We might not always like what life dishes out. We might not always like the trials and tribulations that we have to face. Sometimes we get tired and worn out. Sometimes it seems like we've been robbed of all hope. We often question the meaning and purpose of life itself.

That's why God has given us each other in communion with Christ Jesus. Together, we can see above the pain, the hatred, the mistrust, and the violence that goes on all around us. Together, we can reach up to find the strength to endure and the spirit to persevere. Together, we can find the joy in living that God intended for us.

Together, Jesus has taken us all to another level. Not down, but up. Life is good, when we connect with Jesus. Life is joyous, when we keep focused on things above. Life is about being taken up with Jesus. Meaning in life, fulfillment in life, and happiness in life come from those simple things that Jesus taught. Like sharing cookies and juice with God and having his arms wrapped around us in an eternal hug.

Easter 2
1 Peter 1:3-9

Living Hope

A middle-aged man was on a Caribbean cruise enjoying his first real vacation in years. On the first day out to sea he noticed an attractive woman about his age who smiled at him in a friendly way as he passed her on the deck. This pleased the man greatly. That night he managed to get seated at the same table with her for dinner. As the conversation developed, he commented that he had seen her on the deck that day and he had appreciated her friendly smile. When she heard this, she smiled and commented, "Well, the reason I smiled was that when I saw you I was immediately struck by your strong resemblance to my third husband."

At this he perked up his ears and said, "Oh, how many times have you been married?"

She looked down at her plate, smiled modestly, and answered, "Twice."

Hope is the sustainer of life. It's the motivator to action. It's the promise of tomorrow.

In the 1960s, Cleveland, Ohio, became the butt of many jokes nationwide. In the same way that smog was used to get a laugh in talking about Los Angeles, mention of the Cuyahoga River flowing through Cleveland and into Lake Erie was sure to get a rise out of people. What was so funny? Well, who had ever heard of a river catching fire? It's a ridiculous concept. And yet time and time again the polluted Cuyahoga was shut down to water traffic due to chemical fires that were starting up all over the river because of the unprotected dumping of hazardous wastes. Pictures appeared in newspapers and magazines. Television newscasts documented this unprecedented phenomenon. And the city of Cleveland had to face up to its neglect of the local environment.

The Cuyahoga River was burning, and Lake Erie was declared to be dying. Just put up the tombstone marker and move on to other things.

Today, the river is no longer burning, and Lake Erie has been resurrected. I don't know that I would go so far as to take a drink out of the Cuyahoga River, but I would not hesitate to take a swim in Lake Erie. What was seemingly dead is now very much alive. What was an abomination is now, once again, a productive member of our ecosystem.

We have been quick to write an obituary for our world. If day-to-day pollution doesn't do it, we find other ways to kill ourselves off. The threat of nuclear war has for years inspired science fiction writers to imagine the end times and to write of human self-destruction and the elimination of all life on earth. And if not the end of life, they would speculate on the mutation of living creatures into some sort of monsters that will inherit the earth.

Global warming due to our usage of fossil fuels is currently a major issue. We're putting a hole in the protective layers of atmosphere that protect the earth and we're told that we could be headed for another episode like Noah and the flood as the polar icecaps melt away. Overpopulation and too little food and living space continue to scare us. Worldwide diseases, some of which we thought we conquered, and new ones that keep springing up, threaten to overtake us. Terrorism across the globe has us fearing that life may never be as good as it once was.

The Cuyahoga River was never completely dead. Lake Erie did not die. And as long as there is life still flowing through the system, there is hope of reawakening, resurgence, and resurrection.

We need the vision to see beyond what might appear to be there in front of us, to be able to see what could, quite possibly, be there. As Robert Kennedy often said about himself, "Some people see things as they are and ask why? I dream things that never were, and ask why not?"

Several years ago a teacher assigned to visit children in a large city hospital received a routine call requesting that she visit a particular child. She took the boy's name and room number and was given instructions by the teacher. "We're studying nouns and adverbs in his class now. I'd be grateful if you could help him with his homework so he doesn't fall behind the others." It wasn't until the visiting teacher got outside the boy's room that she realized it was located in the hospital's burn unit. No one had prepared her to find a young boy horribly burned and in great pain. She felt that she couldn't just turn and walk out, so she awkwardly stammered, "I'm the hospital teacher, and your teacher sent me to help you with nouns and adverbs."

The next morning a nurse on the burn unit asked her, "What did you do to that boy?" Before she could finish the profusion of apologies that immediately came out of her mouth, the nurse interrupted her: "You don't understand. We've been very worried about him, but ever since you were here yesterday, his whole attitude has changed. He's fighting back, responding to treatment. It's as though suddenly he's decided to live." The boy later explained that he had completely given up hope until he saw that teacher. It all changed when he came to a simple realization. With joyful tears he expressed it this way: "They wouldn't send a teacher to work on nouns and adverbs with a dying boy, would they?"

Hope is taken from us when those things that contribute to living are taken from us. We can be discouraged, we can be desolate, we can be knocked down, but that doesn't mean we have lost hope. As long as we have a breath of life left in us, we have a living hope. And as long as we have our assignment for tomorrow, we continue to believe that tomorrow is a possibility.

Go to any rehabilitation hospital and you will find people with all sorts of needs and ailments. When people enter a hospital like that, they find out quickly that they have to work to get better. A stay in a rehab hospital is not an easy vacation. Patients learn a lot about themselves that they didn't know they were capable of doing. They find hope. As long as possibilities exist for them, there is hope. Even people who "are dying" are helped to live. That is the epitome of hope.

Peter's letter to the "exiles in Dispersion," as he calls them, is a letter of hope and encouragement to the young church as they were facing desperate times. He reminds these Christians that through the resurrection we have been given new birth in a living hope. Jesus was not dead, but living. Despite all appearances, Jesus is alive, and as long as he is alive, we live in the same hope. We live not only in the hope of a resurrection from the dead, but resurrection in our living as well.

Although these people that Peter was addressing had not seen Jesus, they loved him. And although they did not see him during this time of great trial and tribulation, they believed in him. That is living hope. It is hope that cannot be restrained by worldly powers. It is hope that cannot be thwarted by things of the past. It is hope that cannot be extinguished by fears that some great calamity might lie ahead. Living hope does not die. And for the followers of Jesus, not even physical death of the body will destroy our hope.

None of us walked the earth with Jesus, as did Peter, Andrew, James, John, and the rest. And yet we love him. None of us can see Jesus now, not like Mary and the other women saw him after the resurrection. He doesn't appear to us like he did to Paul on the road to Damascus. Yet we believe in him. And we believe that even though we suffer the trials of this life, we will one day rejoice in all things. We believe that through this enduring faith in Jesus Christ, the outcome will indeed be the salvation of our souls.

We're not the kind of people who would buy a pig in a poke. Could you imagine buying a car without taking it on a test drive, much less without seeing it? Would you move to a house in a city where you've never been without checking it out and carefully selecting just the right house? Would you marry someone without seeing him or her first? Not on your life!

And yet we put our living hope in someone we've never seen. We put our complete trust in a notion that says this man Jesus died on a cross for our sins and that God is able to forgive us everything because of him. We believe that because of him, God is able to overlook our shortcomings and promise us eternal life. That because of Jesus, we live our lives differently, never losing hope for a better tomorrow and living today with appreciation for what it brings.

There's a story of the long and rough Atlantic crossing, when passenger ships were still prevalent, in which a seasick passenger was leaning over the rail of an ocean liner and turned several shades of green. A steward came along and tried to cheer him up by saying, "Don't be discouraged, sir! You know, no one's ever died of seasickness yet." The nauseous passenger looked up at the steward with a deadly glance and replied: "Oh, please, don't say that! It's only the hope of dying that's kept me alive this long."

Sometimes it appears that Christians live, only to die. Yet we profess that Jesus died, that we might live. Is life, as God created it, ever so bad that only the hope of dying can keep us alive? I hope not.

The text from Peter tells us that we will be tested, and tested by fire at that. But the testing always ends, and the results are praise and glory and honor. That's called ... life. Everybody goes through it, and everybody has to endure. You start here, and you end up over there. You sometimes walk through the valleys to get there; sometimes there are mountains to climb. In Christ, however, the ending is always the same, regardless of what it took to get there. That's living hope. There's always a possibility. There's always help along the way. There's always the strength to reach where you're heading.

The Cuyahoga River never lost living hope and it changed. Lake Erie never lost living hope and it changed. The world has not lost living hope and it changes. Where there is life, there is hope. In living hope, there are always possibilities. There is always regeneration and rebirth. Jesus is alive, and in the living Jesus, we find living hope.

Let us live not to die. Rather, let us live ... to hope.

Easter 3
1 Peter 1:17-23

Because

A group of kindergarten children visited the local police station and were given a tour by one of the police officers. While there, they got to look at some wanted posters of notorious fugitives. One child pointed to a picture and asked the officer if it really was a picture of the wanted person. The policeman guide answered that indeed it was.

Then the youngster inquired, "Well, if that's him, why didn't you keep him when you took his picture?"

We've all been there. On the other side of a "why" question.

"Why do I have to eat my broccoli?"

"Because it's good for you."

"Why is it good for me? I like chocolate better. Isn't chocolate good for me?"

"It's good for you because it has all kinds of good things in it to make you big and strong."

"Why does it have good things in it and chocolate doesn't?"

"Because that's just the way it is. God made broccoli to have important vitamins and all kinds of good things in it that makes your body grow healthy."

"If God made it so good for us, then why didn't God make it taste as good as chocolate?"

You try everything within your power to keep up. You try to answer each question. You go through that whole chain of "why" questions until you reach a point where there is nothing left to say but ... what?

"Because."

"But Mommy, *why* do I have to go to bed?"

"Because!" No need to qualify that answer. No need to tack on "I said so" or "Your daddy will answer that when he comes up here and you don't really want to hear his answer." Just a simple, "because."

A friend of mine has a son who was the master of the "why" question. He would question everything, and unless you could come up with a reasonable answer, it was unacceptable to him. Some of his teachers loved that about him. For others, that characteristic drove them up a wall. If a teacher gave him an assignment, even at an early age, it had to be justified, or he would not do it. It had to make sense to him, or he would have no part of it. If he was told to do fifty math problems for homework and they were all simple addition, he might do ten. "Why do the others?" he would ask. "They are just busywork." If given an assignment to conjugate verbs, or diagram sentences, he might do half of them. As he would say: "To do more is just busywork."

Busywork — this boy had no patience for busywork. Even if you explained that the practice was to help him learn and understand for the long run, he would come back and say he could do it in less time, with less work, and understand it just as well and for just as long. Of course, because of this attitude, his grades were usually less than what the other students received, and then he would have to engage in extra credit activities that he never equated with busywork.

We live in a world that has been influenced completely by the scientific method. That is the method of questioning everything in order to find answers as to why things are as they are. Why do things happen this way? Why do people behave the way they do? Why does this person grow up to be a physician who saves hundreds of lives and his brother becomes a murderer? Why do followers of Jesus still fall into sin? We want to be able to explain everything, and sometimes we just can't. Sometimes our audience isn't ready to hear what we have to say, and sometimes we don't really have satisfactory answers to all the questions about God and creation.

A colleague of mine once told me a story about how her six-year-old daughter had come to her with the question: "Where do babies come from?"

This woman admitted that her heart began to pound and her palms got sweaty, but she knew that the time had come to have "the talk" with her young daughter. So she cleared her throat, took a couple of deep breaths, and began to tell her daughter about how a man and woman fall in love. She described how men and women have different bodies and how God created them to work together to create babies. She went into detail about eggs and sperm and how through this miraculous event, a baby starts growing inside the mother.

The woman concluded her explanation after about fifteen minutes and then smiled at her daughter and gave her a big hug. When she released her, her daughter said as though completing the original question, "Oh, because Julie said that babies came from storks and I said that babies come from hospitals. So which one of us is right?"

Why do you love someone? Layer by layer you try to get to the bottom of that question until you reach the point ... because. Just because.

Scripture tells us "We love, because God first loved us." Our love, then, is simply a reflection of God's love. Or, at least, it should be. And yet we know that when we examine our motives, even in loving someone, we often find there is more involved than: "We love, because God first loved us." We love, because we find some sort of fulfillment in loving and being loved. We love because we have been taught that loving is the right thing to do. We love — there we go again, trying to explain why we love, using the scientific method of stating a problem, putting forth a hypothesis, testing it, and then coming up with a conclusion.

But is "because" the real answer to "why do we love?"

Why do you strive to live a good and holy life? Is it "because"? Because God expects it of you? Because if you don't you will be punished and you fear living eternally separated from God? Is it because that's the way you were brought up? Why do you, assuming that you do, live a good and holy life?

Someone once said that the answer to "why" is not "because." Rather, the definitive answer to "why" is "why not?"

The answer, "because God wants us to," is the wrong answer. Now, it's the right answer, but it's the wrong answer. Does that make sense? God wants us to live a good and holy life. God wants us to love one another. Those are both accurate statements. But the right answer as to why we live good and holy lives is because *we* want to.

In other words, "Why not?" God has done this for us, so why not do that for God? God has set us free to live as we please, so why not live to please God?

We don't say, "Why not?" in a flippant and arrogant manner as though it isn't any big deal. We can say, "Why not?" because it's still our choice. Not just because God says so, but also because we choose so!

There was a couple who made a sizable contribution to the church to honor the memory of their son who lost his life in the war. When the announcement was made of the generous donation, a woman sitting in the congregation whispered to her husband, "Let's give the same amount for our boy!" Her husband said, "What are you talking about? Our son wasn't killed."

"That's just the point," she said. "Let's give it as an expression of our gratitude to God for sparing his life!"

Why not? We live good and holy lives not because God told us to, not because our parents told us to, not because the church tells us to. We live good and holy lives as an expression of our gratitude to God.

God has already given us approval through Jesus Christ. We are free to live accordingly. God saved us and we can now live as saved people. How we live as saved people depends on how we understand what it means to be saved. If we believe that our salvation is dependent upon the things we do, then we are not living as saved people, rather we are living as people attempting to be saved.

If we believe that our salvation is dependent upon the blood of Jesus Christ, then all that we can do to "live as a saved person" is to show our gratitude toward God. And the text from 1 Peter implores us to do so by "loving one another deeply from the heart."

Two friends were camping in the forest and were standing by their tent on the first morning sharing some coffee. Suddenly, they spotted a grizzly bear heading for them at full speed. Quickly, the one man reached down and grabbed his running shoes and started putting them on. The other man looked at him and said, "What are you doing? Do you think you can outrun that grizzly bear?" Jumping up and beginning to take off, the first man replied, "No, and I don't need to. All I need to do is outrun you!"

Many people go through life doing only what they feel they need to do. If going to church and giving a little money is all they feel they need to do in order to stay ahead of God, then that's what they do. If making a good living and supporting their family is all they feel they need to do, then that's what they do. If saying a quick prayer before meals and reading a few verses from the Bible is all they feel they need to do, then that's what they do. They do it because that's what they feel they need to do. They figure that's the least that God expects from them, and the least is good enough. "And besides," they figure, "just look at our friends and neighbors. They don't do half the good that we do."

Those are "because" kinds of answers. When we live our lives trying to fill in all those explanations that go with "because," we find ourselves fruitless and ineffective in our efforts.

But when we live our lives as kind of a "why not?" answer, we begin to approach God's intent for us. Why not love our neighbors? Why not do good things for people as a reaction to God's goodness towards us? Why not live as though Jesus saved me and has given me the freedom to show my gratitude and joy without any requirements or strings attached?

You can live your life "because" and continue to fill in the reasons for the rest of your life. Or *why not* just live? Live each day in gratitude for everything you have, and will have, eternally. Live as though you have a God who has taken care of all the big problems and who has given you the means to deal with the small ones. Live with the love that has been showered upon you in this life and will follow you into eternity.

Just live life as the gift that God has given you. And why not?

Easter 4
1 Peter 2:19-25

Sheep That Count

Once upon a time there was a lamb named Edgar. Edgar lived with his family and friends in a large flock that roamed the countryside under the leadership of a kind and protective shepherd. Edgar followed his mother, along with the others, from one grazing spot to another, and seemed perfectly content with his life. He would play games with the other lambs, chase butterflies in the meadows, and nuzzle up close to his mother for afternoon naps in the sun. Like all the other sheep in his flock, he went wherever the shepherd led and would get his soft, thick hair cut on schedule.

One day, during a game of hide and seek, Edgar was hiding in some tall grass near the tree line to a neighboring woods. From out of nowhere he heard a voice calling to him, "Hey, Edgar."

Edgar turned to see a handsome fox peering out from behind one of the trees. He had never seen a fox before, so he didn't know that he was supposed to be afraid and run from it. "Who are you? And how did you know my name?"

"Everyone calls me Destiny. And I guess you could say I'm sort of your destiny. I know all the lambs in your flock by name. That's part of my work on earth, to get to know you all."

"You look different. Are you a sheep?"

"Not really. I could have been a sheep, I suppose, but I chose to be who I am. And you can be like me if you choose to get out from under the oppression of that shepherd."

Destiny then began to teach Edgar about the world outside his flock. He told of all the wonderful creatures that roamed the woods and of the many things that Edgar had yet to experience. He had definitely gotten Edgar's attention.

"Now, Edgar, don't tell your mother or the other grown-up sheep about me. They won't like it that I'm sharing secrets with you that they don't want you to know about. Why, some of the things I've told you, they have never heard because they refuse to listen. They just want to live in bondage to that stupid human being, walking around eating grass and giving up their coats for him every time he takes a notion. But you, Edgar, you are different. You have a mind of your own. I like that about you."

So Edgar went back to the flock, thinking about all the things he learned from Destiny. And like Destiny told him, he spoke not a word of it to his mother. He did tell many of the other lambs, trying to convince them that there was more to life than following the flock. Some took an interest, others warned him not to think like that. But it seemed that the more the others condemned his new way of "free-thinking," the more he knew that he must be right.

"It's time we leave this flock, and venture out on our own," he told those who would still listen to radical ideas. "Do you want to spend the rest of your lives going nowhere; wandering from field to field; always going where you are led; never making a decision for yourself bigger than which clump of grass you will bite off or beside which rock you will sleep? It's time to make a choice."

The others seemed tempted, but they would not change their ways. Edgar kept visiting with Destiny on the sly, always careful that none of the adults would see him, and especially careful not to get caught by the shepherd.

Destiny continued to tell Edgar about the outside world. He made it sound so exciting that Edgar became more and more rebellious. He refused to eat with the rest of the flock, always going just a little further outside the circle. He continually had to be chased back by the shepherd. Edger grew tired of the scolding he received for his insubordination.

"What's gotten into you, Edgar?" his mother asked. "You were always a perfect child. You never talked back and you always listened. You were one of the shepherd's favorites. Now, you do nothing but cause him grief. What's going on?"

"I want to get out of this flock, Mother!" Edgar shouted. "I want to see what's out there in the rest of the world. I want to think for myself, make my own choices. I'm sick and tired of following someone else's footsteps all the time."

Edgar's mother didn't understand this talk, or where it had come from. All she knew how to do was what she had always done. And that was to follow the shepherd, stay in the flock, and be kept safe and healthy. That seemed like quite enough for her. She told her son what all the elders had always said to her, "The grass may look greener over there somewhere, but without the shepherd, its taste will seem quite bitter."

But Edgar knew he had to taste that grass over there and beyond. He knew there must be a better life outside the flock, and he would not be happy until he found out.

Finally, one day, Edgar took up Destiny's offer to come and see his den. He had told Edgar how nice it is not to have to sleep outside and to be protected from the hot sun and the rain and the blowing wind. Edgar could not wait to see this wonderful place. So he carefully sneaked away from the flock and the watchful eye of his shepherd.

Edgar never returned to his flock. Of course, he never got to see the rest of the world either, not even the inside of Destiny's den. Destiny had played a mean trick on Edgar, and Edgar became Destiny's victim.

But the other lambs that coveted Edgar's freedom didn't know what really happened. They had visions of Edgar out in the world on one adventure after another, and a few of them followed Edgar's Destiny.

We don't always want to follow our shepherd. It's tempting to want to go it on our own. But the price of leaving the flock — is it ever worth it?

There's an old Texas story that goes like this: A new school marm in a prairie schoolhouse asked a little boy, "If there were twelve sheep in a field and one jumped over the fence, how many would be left?"

The pupil said, "None."

The teacher said, "You don't know arithmetic, do you?"

"No, ma'am, but I know sheep."

The shepherd knows his sheep. Jesus knows his followers. God knows his children.

Peter is writing to Christians during a time when being a follower of Jesus was not a very pleasant nor always positive experience. Throw in the fact that Peter's audience for this particular text included slaves, and you can understand why the writer felt especially compelled to offer words of support and encouragement.

Peter doesn't tell them to find a way out of their rut. He doesn't instruct them on how to rebel against slavery and fight for freedom. Instead, he tells them that Jesus is to be their example in all things. That, even in their present circumstance, Jesus is their strength and assurance. And, like Jesus, they should seek God's approval in what they do and keep that as their major priority in this life.

Jesus suffered though he himself did nothing wrong. Jesus was treated unjustly, and yet he did not speak out against his enemies. When he was attacked, he responded in love and not in retaliation. Like a shepherd who leads sheep to nourishment and safety, Jesus is an example to us in our day-to-day struggles with the reality of our world. As Jesus chose to accept the abuse of the world in order to save the world, we follow in those steps today. And we have to admit that there are sometimes more important issues than our comfort, our lifestyle, and even our health. We have to choose our fights carefully and always weigh in the balance the good of the outcome we are trying to achieve.

Now, for a reality check, and without rationalizing what I just said, I have to add that not all selflessness is admirable, and not all self-defense is bad. I do have problems condoning some situations of oppression for the sake of the gospel. A child does not have to tolerate an abusive parent. No one needs to live in constant danger in fearing his or her spouse. And if our neighbor attacks us and physically threatens our life and the lives of our loved ones, then there is a "time for war and a time for peace." But we should not look for excuses simply to get out of a tolerable, but unpleasant situation.

When the world looks at us, the sheep of his fold, they see Jesus. We are the living remnant of the Christ who came into this world to save it. And although Peter is not condoning slavery or any other oppressive lifestyle, he is telling us that with Jesus as our example, we are to take certain misery and hardship upon our shoulders and represent Jesus in everything that we say and do. It's not always easy, and it's certainly not always what we want to do, but that is the life we have been called to live and the witness we are to bear.

There is a legend that recounts the return of Jesus to glory after his time on earth. Even in heaven he bore the marks of his earthly pilgrimage with a cruel cross and shameful death. The angel Gabriel approached him and said, "Master, you must have suffered terribly for people down there." Jesus replied that he did. Gabriel continued: "And do they know and appreciate how much you loved them and what you did for them?"

Jesus replied, "Oh, no! Not yet. Right now only a handful of people in Palestine know."

Gabriel was puzzled. He asked, "Then what have you done to let everyone know about your love for them?"

Jesus said, "I've asked Peter, James, and John and a few more friends to tell others about me. Those who are told in turn will tell others about me and so on and so on. My story will be spread to the farthest reaches of the globe. Ultimately, all of humankind will have heard about my life and what I have done."

Gabriel frowned and looked rather skeptical. He well knew what poor stuff people were made of. He said, "Yes, but what if Peter and James and John grow weary? What if the people who come after them forget? What if way down in the twenty-first century people just don't tell others about you? Haven't you made other plans?"

And Jesus answered, "I haven't made any other plans. I'm counting on them."

Jesus still seeks sheep he can count on. He wants sheep that will follow their shepherd anywhere. He needs sheep who will go into the thickets and swamps of the meadows, and to the top of every mountain and bottom of every valley. Twenty-one centuries later, he's still counting on you and me. His early disciples chose Jesus' priorities and devoted their lives to reaching the world. Christ counted on them and they delivered. Can he continue to count on us?

Easter 5
1 Peter 2:2-10

The Church That Jesus Built

In the Old Testament, kings believed that God gave them direction in their dreams. If they wanted to know what they were supposed to do in their administration, they would try to receive a direct word from God in their dreams. If they weren't getting any messages in their dreams while lying in their own beds, then they would sleep in the Temple, where they believed it would work better.

And thus we have the origin of the time-honored tradition of sleeping in church. I wanted to point that out at the beginning of the message so that those who would appreciate it the most would have a chance to hear it.

Brick and mortar. Lumber and nails. Arches, rafters, and flying buttresses. Rock and concrete. When you build a church, what are the elements you want to include? Does it have to have a steeple? Must you have a bell in a bell tower? Do you install a baptistery, or does your particular brand of Christianity prefer a baptismal font? Do you install pews, or use removable chairs to give your building more versatility?

When Jesus built his church, he didn't consider any of these components. When Jesus built his church, he started with a very small, but firm foundation. Upon that foundation, he built a structure that has been rocked and windblown, shaken and flooded, even attacked by numerous enemies, and yet has withstood and survived down through the ages.

During a Sunday school class for seven-year-olds, one little boy suddenly exclaimed to his teacher, "Can we hurry up? This is boring!" Immediately the little girl to his left gave him a sharp elbow to the side and rebuked him. "Shut up. It's supposed to be boring!"

What is this church of Jesus Christ supposed to be? Are we simply in a "church building" that has become stiff and boring, weathered by the years and near extinction? Or are we a "building church," with veins full of life and the empowered goals of still wanting to reach the heavens? The church that Jesus built was a living church, alive with the "living stones" that were its building materials. Living stones that had as their cornerstone the very stone that the builders of the world had rejected. Though rejected by mortals, God previously chose this cornerstone, so that it would become the foundation for his building on earth.

Jesus had faith in his construction ability. Though he had the whole world from which to choose, he selected very simple material: a few fishermen, a tax collector, and some others of seemingly simple means and position. There were no kings in his foundation. He didn't use any successful business personalities in his first floor. And he completed the first stage of his structure without the help of aggressive marketers and developers.

Jesus just used stones, a variety of living stones. He used stones that would weather the cause. Stones that would not crumble under the weight that would be built upon them. The building material that Jesus chose was well suited for the building he intended to construct. For the church that Jesus was building was to be a living, breathing construction of dynamic proportions. One that would outlast the ancient structures of Jesus' time that still stand today. The church of Jesus Christ was built to last an eternity.

We still get hung up on the "church building." Is it meeting our needs? Do we need to make major repairs rather than just continued maintenance? Should we add-on or rebuild? Should we renovate our sanctuary and modernize to fit the times?

Jesus is more concerned with building the church than the church building. "If you build it, they will come." Ever since that line emerged from the movie *Field of Dreams* we have been using it to describe everything from a shopping mall to a major league baseball stadium. But the truth remains whether it's a church building or a baseball stadium: just building it is not enough. It's how you build it. If you don't build the baseball team to go with the stadium, people will not come, not in the way the owners want them to come. And if you build a fabulous church building, but do not build the church in proportion to it, you end up with a fabulous, empty church building.

A certain church was having air-conditioning installed in the sanctuary and so the pastor was meeting with the contractor. The man asked the pastor a number of questions about the seating capacity, square footage, usual attendance, and so on, all the while taking notes. Then in the midst of his calculations, the contractor suddenly crumpled up the paper he was figuring on and started over.

"What's wrong?" asked the pastor.

"I was figuring for a theater instead of a church," replied the contractor.

"What's the difference? Wouldn't they be the same?"

"No, not really," answered the contractor. "You see, in a theater with all that's going on up on the screen, there are certain biological changes that take place: heart rates are elevated, blood pressure increases, and body temperatures begin to climb. In other words, there is a greater need for the cooling process when people get excited. On the other hand, in the church ... well, you know."

Can living stones create a dead structure? Jesus built his church with living stones. In today's text, Peter calls us "a chosen race, a royal priesthood, a holy nation, God's own people." He goes on to say that because we are as such, we can proclaim to the world "the mighty acts of him" who called us "out of darkness into his marvelous light." We don't read anything here that talks about a sleeping church, or a stagnant church, or a church built with inanimate materials that are held together with mortar or nails. The church that Jesus built was built with carefully chosen building materials that, like the material of no other building, are alive and vibrant and continue to build themselves. Materials that will not become brittle and break apart, but that will continue to breathe new life into the church.

We are "a chosen race, a royal priesthood, a holy nation." Before Jesus, we were nothing. Nothing held us together. We were not a people; we were only individuals inhabiting the same world. Jesus changed our world, and that's exciting. Jesus made us into God's people by making us into his church. Jesus pulled us together and united us into something special.

On September 11, 2001, we learned something new about tall buildings. We learned that no matter how well built they might appear, no matter how carefully the architect might have constructed the building with the proper materials, no matter if all natural disasters were considered, two monumental buildings were able to collapse. They were actually made to tumble from the top down, not being able to sustain their own weight. In a matter of seconds, what had taken years to build was a pile of rubble of gigantic proportions. We witnessed something we believed to be impossible.

Can one person change the world forever? With the billions of people who now inhabit the earth, a statement like that seems trivial. Of course one person can have an impact. One person can cause a degree of good or a degree of bad. But one person is not going to make much difference in the whole scheme of things.

Yet we believe that one person has changed the world. That the organization of people started by one man over 2,000 years ago is still changing the world from day to day. That a small nucleus of people living in an ancient time has grown into the great body we call the church, and that it will continue to grow in unity, from now until the time that its founder returns to this world. We believe that no power on earth can cause this church to crumble, because Jesus is the cornerstone. And Jesus will hold it together.

We are not about a church building; we are about "church building."

A pastor of a small southern church was on his way home when he met an acquaintance from town who was not a member of his church. After chatting a while, the man asked how many members the pastor had in his church. The pastor responded, "Fifty active members." The friend said, "My, that certainly speaks well for you." But the preacher responded, "Well, I wouldn't exactly say that. All fifty are active — but 25 are actively working for me and the other 25 are actively working against me!"

When we work together, we build up the Body of Christ. When we work against each other, we work to tear it down. Jesus' original disciples didn't always agree on everything, but they knew how to work together in spite of their disagreements. They were able to build upon what Jesus had started. They found ways to do it together by sharing the responsibilities of church building.

Jesus knew he couldn't do it alone. He knew he needed others to help him. The job of building his church would be turned over to those who would follow him. Now, it is in our hands. How shall we build our church? Will we build with brick and mortar, or with living stones? Are you willing to get your hands dirty? Are you willing to exercise your spiritual muscles? Are you willing to hold the light so that others can see in the darkness?

Haven't you ever just needed someone to hold the light for you while you were doing something? Or maybe it's always been your job to hold the light so someone else can see to get a job done. Whether it's down in the basement or under the hood of a car, sometimes it's just too much of a job for one person to do alone. Jesus wasn't afraid to ask for help. He still isn't. He's asking us now, seeking our assistance in building his church, a light in the darkness of the world, a beacon in the middle of a stormy sea. And we are all he's got.

A little boy was watching his father fry some eggs for the family breakfast and said he had a joke. "Dad, how can you eat an egg without cracking the shell?"

His father thought about it for several moments then finally concluded, "I don't know how. How do you eat an egg without cracking the shell?"

The little boy replied, "Have someone else crack it for you."

Sometimes people in the church want the benefits the church has to offer without sharing the responsibilities. We all want revival as long as someone else does the praying. We all want more people in the pews as long as someone else does the inviting. We all want to see the church built up with more programs as long as someone else does the work.

If you want to eat eggs, you're going to have to break some shells. And if you want to build a church, you're going to have become a part of the construction crew.

Easter 6
1 Peter 3:13-22

King Of The Mountain

In a large stone cathedral in Europe there was a grand, magnificent pipe organ. On a particular Saturday afternoon, the sexton was making one final check of the choir and organ loft high in the balcony at the back of the church. As he was making his inspection, he was startled to hear footsteps echoing up the stone stairway behind him. He thought the doors were all locked and that no one else was in the church. He turned to see a man in slightly tattered traveling clothes coming toward him.

"Excuse me, sir," the stranger said. "I have come from quite a distance to see the great organ in this cathedral. Would you mind opening the console so that I might get a closer look at it?"

The custodian at first refused, but the stranger seemed so eager and insistent that he finally gave in. "May I sit on the bench?" This time the sexton met the stranger's request with an absolute refusal.

"What if the organist came in and found you sitting there? I would probably lose my job!" But again the stranger was so persistent that the cathedral custodian gave in. "But only for a moment," he added.

The custodian noticed that the stranger seemed to be very much at home on the organ bench, so he was not completely surprised when the man asked him if he might be permitted to play the organ. "No! Definitely not!" said the sexton. "No one is allowed to play it except the cathedral organist." The stranger's face fell, and his deep disappointment was obvious. He reminded the custodian how far he had come and assured him that no damage would be done.

The sexton looked around at the empty church. He was sure there was no one else around even to hear what was going on. So finally, the sexton softened once again and told the stranger he could play the instrument, but only a few notes and then he would have to leave. Overjoyed, the stranger pulled out some stops and began to play. Suddenly the cathedral was filled with the most beautiful music the custodian had ever heard in all the years he had spent in this cathedral. The music seemed to transport him heavenward.

In what seemed like all too short a time, the shabby stranger stopped playing and slid off the organ bench. As he started to walk away and down the stairway, the custodian cried, "Wait! That was the most beautiful music I have ever heard in the cathedral. Who are you?"

The stranger turned for just a moment as he replied, "Mendelssohn." The man was none other than Felix Mendelssohn, one of the greatest organists and composers of the nineteenth century. We hear his music at Christmas when we sing, "Hark! The Herald Angels Sing," and at weddings when the bride comes down the aisle.

The cathedral sexton was alone now in that great stone edifice with the beautiful organ music still ringing in his ears. "Just think," he thought to himself, "I almost kept the master from playing his music in my cathedral."

How often do we keep the Master from playing his beautiful music in our cathedrals? Do we keep Jesus from working his wonders in our lives almost daily just because we refuse to allow him entrance into our hearts?

There's a childhood game that some of you may have played that in today's world would probably not be politically correct. It's call "king of the hill" or, taken to the next level, "king of the mountain." The object of the game is quite simple. You stand on top of a hill, a mound of dirt or gravel, or anything that is elevated from the ground around it, and you throw, push, or bump everyone else off. The longer you can stay there without getting pushed off yourself, the more powerful you prove to be.

There can be several approaches to this game in order for it not to become too boring with the biggest kid always on top, always the "king." Sometimes two players will team up and throw everyone else off and then take turns being "king of the mountain." Sometimes it's all in the footwear, depending on the "mountain" you're trying to hold, and the most gripping shoes or boots will help you hold your ground. Sometimes you might just hit the ground and wrap your arms around the "big guy" while you wait for others to attack and throw him off while you are keeping him off balance. Then you jump up and push your rescuers off along with him.

It's not a game for the kind-hearted or for those with a strong ethical belief in friendship. When you play "king of the mountain," it's every person for himself or herself. You want to stay on top for as long as you can, and that means keeping everyone else off.

In the text from 1 Peter chapter 3, the fifteenth verse says, "In your hearts sanctify Christ as Lord." I get a visual picture of a game of "king of the mountain" going on inside of each one of us. Jesus tries to stay on the throne of our lives, but there is always somebody else trying to throw him off the mountain. There is always something else trying to take his place in our hearts. We might *say* that Jesus is on top, our number one priority, but then we knock him off on a daily basis, allowing the lordship of a variety of things to take over our lives. And so it becomes a daily battle: a struggle to be the "king" of our own mountain.

Peter's message to Christians is to "not be intimidated" by the world around us. We are "not to fear" what others fear, but are to be ready at all times "to defend" the hope that we live in. Our outward actions, what we do and what we say, begin inside of us and develop in our hearts. If we hold Jesus in high esteem on the inside, it will show on the outside.

Time and time again, throughout the New Testament, it seems as though followers of Jesus are called upon to live a life that does not conform to the surrounding cultural norms. We are asked to keep Jesus and his example in his rightful place and not to let anything take his place on the top of the mountain in our hearts. When we do that, it forces us to do things that go against the grain of our society. We do not seek what we feel we deserve, but what we believe God wants for others.

Family is a God-given gift to each of us, but family should not push Jesus off the throne of our hearts. Patriotism is fine and honorable, but love of country cannot overshadow the love of Jesus Christ. It's nice to have nice things: a house, a car, furnishings, and toys for our leisure time. But I don't read anywhere in scripture that these are to be priorities in the life of a Christian. Material possessions should not take the place of Jesus in our hearts. We all like to have friends and to be popular with others. So, we often give in to the requests and lifestyles of our friends. But when we put our friends on top of the mountain, there's no room for Jesus and we have to push him off once again.

There are all kinds of things that interfere with Christ's lordship in our lives, and those things can change depending on the stage of our lives we are in. Sex, addictions, greed, hatred, anger, relationships, jobs, ambition, and the list goes on and on. Sometimes the lord of our life can change on a daily basis. Jesus might be there for a while, but like an ongoing game of "king of the mountain," he is pushed from dominance to allow some other lord to take over.

Peter tells us that through baptism we are saved — saved in the same way that the waters of the flood saved Noah and his family. The same waters that destroyed all the rest were used to save those eight people. He says that baptism is not the same as cleaning dirt from the body, but rather an appeal to God for a good conscience through the resurrection of Jesus Christ.

Martin Luther made reference to his baptism each morning as he would remember who was the Lord of his life and who had saved him. He made the sign of the cross on his forehead as a reminder that he was marked with the cross of Christ forever. So even though he believed he was saved by Jesus' death on the cross, he knew that each day was a new day and that there were other lords in the world fighting for the throne in his heart.

And so it is with us. Though the battle was fought years ago on that hill outside of Jerusalem, and won by Jesus of Nazareth when he became the "King of the mountain" once and for all, the little skirmishes still go on in our lives each day. Other lords still fight the fight for our souls and try to push Jesus off the mountain of our lives.

There's an old story about two men who met on the street. One said to the other, "Have you heard about Harry? He embezzled the company out of half a million dollars."

The second man said, "That's terrible. I never did trust Harry."

The first man said, "Not only that, he left town and took Tom's wife with him."

The second man said, "That's awful; Harry has always been a no-good scoundrel."

The first man said, "Not only that, he stole a car to make his getaway."

The second man said, "That's scandalous; I always did think Harry had a bad streak in him."

The first man said, "Not only that, they think he was drunk when he pulled out of town."

The second man said, "Harry's no good all right. But what really bothers me is, who's going to teach his Sunday school class this week?"

We are inundated with rivals to Jesus each and every day. We need to be renewed in our faith, and in our hope, and in our baptism ... each day. We need to allow Jesus back where he rightfully belongs, on the throne of our lives to be Lord and Savior over us. When Jesus is on the throne, it shows in every area of our lives: in how we speak to others, in how we act toward others, and in how we live our lives privately. Everything about us points to Jesus, the Lord of our life.

According to an old legend, a man became lost in his travels and wandered into a bed of quicksand. Confucius saw the man's predicament and said, "It is evident that men should stay out of places like this." Next, Buddha observed the situation and said, "Let that man's plight be a lesson to the rest of the world." Then Muhammad came by and said to the sinking man, "Alas, it is the will of God." Finally Jesus appeared. "Take my hand, brother," he said, "and I will save you."

Do you really want anyone but the Master sitting upon the throne of your life? Like the sexton in my opening story, how close do we come to sending him away without giving him the chance to play beautiful music in our cathedrals? Now some of us cannot make music of any kind, and others of us can play chopsticks, if we're lucky. But none of us can duplicate the works of the Master, nor can we find substitutes to take his place.

There is only room for one King of the Mountain. And that means all of the others must be pushed off. Who, in your life, will stand alone at the top?

Ascension Of The Lord
Ephesians 1:15-23

The Eyes Of Your Heart

John Edward believes that people don't just die, but that they "cross over."

That's nothing earth shattering to Christians because we believe that, too. We believe Jesus taught it and promised it. We believe scripture tells us that is what happens to us when we die. Before Jesus left his disciples he told them he was going to his Father's house to prepare a room for them. He told the thief on the cross, "Today you will be with me in paradise." When Peter asked Jesus where he was going, Jesus told him, "Where I am going, you cannot follow me now; but you will follow me later."

The biggest difference between John Edward and most Christians is that John Edward believes that those who have crossed over still communicate with us. John Edward is a medium who has his own television show in which he professes to communicate with the loved ones of his studio audience. He also holds private readings that cost in the neighborhood of $300 and has a waiting list of up to three years in advance. Needless to say, there are a lot of people who believe in crossing over and, in particular, in John Edward's ability to patch them through to their deceased loved ones. He is quite convincing.

To his credit, at the end of every program, he states that it is not necessary to have a medium present in order to hear from those who have passed, if only we would pay attention. He believes that people on the other side are constantly communicating with us, but that we just don't pick up on it. And he emphasizes communicating with loved ones while they are still with us, giving the impression that if we do, this line of communication will remain open after they have gone.

Truth is, we crazy Christians do talk to dead people. Well, maybe they are not really dead, but they have crossed over. We do it through prayer, and maybe John Edward is right when it comes to our listening skills. When we pray, we probably do more talking than listening.

What better example of "crossing over" is there than that of Jesus? Jesus, in his resurrected body, left the disciples in one, dramatic moment. Ascending to his new home with his Father in heaven, Jesus is taken up in a cloud while angels inform the disciples that one day he will return in the same manner.

Jesus crossed over. After his death and resurrection, the disciples viewed Jesus with the eyes of their hearts. They saw him in a new way, with a new kind of body and a new spirituality. He represented what they would become. And he was telling them that it was the way of God, and that it was good. To borrow a word from John Edward, Jesus "validated" what the disciples believed, and what we would believe these many centuries later. That Jesus was indeed the Son of God, and that there is life after death, in another place, and Jesus is there waiting for us.

Some years ago, Columbia University had a great football coach by the name of Lou Little. One day Lou had a boy try out for the varsity team who wasn't really very good. But Lou noticed that there was something unique about him. While he wasn't nearly good enough to make the team, he had such irrepressible spirit and contagious enthusiasm that Lou thought, *"This boy would be a great inspiration on the bench. He'll never be able to play, but I'll leave him on the team to encourage the others."*

As the season went on, Lou began to develop a tremendous admiration and love for this boy. One of the things that especially impressed him was the manner in which the boy obviously cared for his father. Whenever the father would come for a visit to the campus, the boy and his father would always be seen walking together, arm in arm, a visible indication of the exceptional bond of love that existed between them. They were seen every Sunday going to and from the university chapel. It was clear that theirs was a deep and mutually shared Christian faith.

Then, one day, Coach Little received a phone call. He was told that the boy's father had just died, and he was asked if he would please inform the boy of his father's death. With a heavy heart, Lou went to the boy and told him what had happened. The boy immediately left for home.

A few days later after his father's funeral, the boy returned to campus, just two days before the biggest game of the season. Lou welcomed the boy back and asked, "Is there anything I can do for you? Anything at all?" And to the coach's astonishment, the boy said, "Let me start the game on Saturday." Lou was completely taken by surprise. He thought to himself, *"I can't let him start. He's not good enough."* But he remembered his promise to help and said, "All right, you can start the game." But again, he thought, *"I'll leave him in the game for a few plays and then take him out."*

The day of the game arrived. To everyone's surprise the coach started this boy who had never played in a game all season. But imagine even the coach's surprise when, on the very first play from scrimmage, that boy was the one who single-handedly made a tackle that threw the opposing team for a loss. The boy went on to play inspired football play after play. In fact, he played so exceptionally that the coach left him in for the entire game. The boy eventually led his team to victory and was voted the outstanding player of the game.

After the game, Lou approached the boy and said, "Son, what got into you today?" The boy replied, "You remember when my father would visit me here at school and we would spend a lot of time together walking arm in arm around the campus? My father and I shared a secret that nobody around here knew anything about. You see, my father was blind ... and today was the first time he ever saw me play."

When the eyes of our hearts are enlightened, we are able to play over our heads in the game of life and see the purposes and power and love of God. This boy knew that his father had crossed over to a better place. A place where everyone is able to see with the eyes of their hearts, and no longer need to see with the eyes in their heads.

In today's text, Saint Paul tells us three things we can know by seeing through the eyes of our hearts: first, "the hope to which he has called" us; second, "the riches of his glorious inheritance among the saints," and third, "the immeasurable greatness of his power." Hope, inheritance, and power. Three important gifts that Jesus left with us when he "crossed over."

1. *The hope to which we have been called.* A sorcerer had fallen out of favor with the court, and the king sentenced him to death. On the day of the planned execution, the sorcerer told the king that if he would allow him to live for one year, the king could become famous around the world, because the sorcerer would make the king's horse talk. If the sorcerer failed, the king could then kill him. The king thought about it and agreed. The sorcerer was spared for one year and thrown into the dungeon.

A duke, who was friendly to the sorcerer, sneaked down to the dungeon and said: "You are indeed a fool. Both you and I know that you do not have the power to make animals speak. Now you will surely die."

The sorcerer answered him: "But, I have a year. Many things can happen in a year. The king might die. Or I might die. And who knows? In a year perhaps the horse might talk."

By Jesus' sacrifice, we have been spared and given hope. We don't know the number of days we have left on this earth before we ourselves "cross over." Whatever that number might be, it is a gift, a pardon. We live in the hope of the cross, and living like that, we have nothing to lose. Living or dying, we have hope. Hope for today, and for tomorrow. Hope for here, and hope for there, with Jesus, on the other side. We can see it with the eyes of our heart.

When we focus on the things that we can see with our eyes, we sometimes want to give up. When we feel only through our body, the pain is sometimes too great for us. When we think only with our minds, the thoughts can be defeating. But when we look with our hearts, there is always hope. In our hearts we can see that "maybe in a year the horse will talk."

2. *The riches of his glorious inheritance among the saints.* What person has not dreamed at one time or another about some long-lost wealthy relative dying and leaving them a fortune? We've probably all had those thoughts, and we've mentally spent that money. Yet we have already been named in a will that makes us all rich, and most of the time we don't even think about it.

If we look at life through the eyes of our hearts, things look different. What makes a person successful, what makes a person wealthy, even what makes a person healthy, looks different through the eyes of the heart. The worst disability in the world is not the loss of sight, or the use of your legs, or any debilitating disease. The worst disability is when your heart becomes blinded, and you can no longer see the riches that God has heaped upon you.

We are all wealthy people because we have inherited the riches that our brother Jesus has left to us. They are not the kinds of riches you can invest in the stock market or have insured by Lloyd's of London. They are riches that can only be seen through the eyes of your heart. They come in the form of blessings. They are blessings seen in the love of another person. Blessings that flow from the support of a circle of friends called the church. Blessings that will come to pass in an eternal life with a loving and compassionate God who will take care of all our needs forever and ever. We are wealthy people.

3. *The immeasurable greatness of his power.* We are an intelligent life form, we human beings. We know that there is a time and place for everything, and that everything has its limits. Yet space seems to be limitless. The universe has no definition. And we foolish Christians come along and confess to believing that God created it all. God has no limits. God's power is immeasurable.

Then, in the vastness of this concept of an almighty, limitless God, we believe that he cares about what happens to one little being on one little planet in one little solar system in one little galaxy. Yep, that's right. That's what we believe. And that's the core of Christianity. This great and powerful God who created all that exists, farther than the eye can see (unless it's the eye of your heart, that is), still cares about you. He cares about little ol' you. You may feel like one speck of dandruff on the shoulder of the universe, one unique snowflake in the midst of a snowstorm, or one little hair on the head of humanity. God, the powerful, cares about what happens to you and me.

And so he sent his Son, Jesus, into our little world to live as we do. Jesus, just as powerful and just as almighty, sent here to try to teach us something about his wonder. Jesus, sent here to live and to die so that one day we might be able to join him in another place. Jesus, just passing through to show us that there is more than meets the eye, even the eye of your heart.

In the 1800s there was a renowned Polish rabbi named Hofetz Chaim. An American tourist visited him and was astonished to see that the rabbi's home was only a simple room filled with books, with only a table and cot to live on. The tourist asked, "Rabbi, where is your furniture?" Hofetz Chaim replied, "Where is yours?"

The puzzled American asked, "Mine? But I'm only a visitor here. I'm only passing through." The rabbi replied, "So am I."

As you pass through, I pray that you might see a lot with the eyes of your heart. And that you will know the hope to which he has called us, the riches of his glorious inheritance among the saints and the immeasurable greatness of his power.

Easter 7
1 Peter 4:12-14; 5:6-11

A Holy-wood Ending

A couple from Minneapolis decided to go to Florida for a long weekend to thaw out during one particularly icy winter. Because both had jobs, they had difficulty coordinating their travel schedules. It was decided that the husband would fly to Florida on a Thursday, and his wife would follow him the next day. Upon arriving, as planned the husband checked into a hotel. He settled into his room and decided to open his laptop computer and send his wife e-mail back in Minneapolis. However, he accidentally left off one letter in her address, and sent the e-mail without realizing his error.

In Houston, a widow had just returned from her husband's funeral. He was a minister of many years who had been "called home to glory" following a heart attack. The widow checked her e-mail, expecting messages from relatives and friends. Upon reading the first message, she fainted and fell to the floor. The widow's son rushed into the room, found his mother on the floor, and saw the computer screen that read:

To: My Loving Wife
From: Your Departed Husband
Subject: I've Arrived!!

I've just arrived and have been checked in. I see that everything has been prepared for your arrival tomorrow. Looking forward to seeing you then! Hope your journey is as uneventful as mine was.

P.S. Sure is hot down here!

We all want to be "called home to glory" some day, but the key to our thoughts on "gloryland" is that it will happen in due time. It's like the words from country singer Joe Diffie's song, "Prop Me Up Beside The Jukebox When I'm Gone," in which he beseeches, "Lord, I want to go to heaven, but I don't want to go tonight." There are times we all want an end to our sufferings and our pain, from our loneliness and desperation, but we don't want a permanent end, at least not too quickly.

A couple of years ago actor and director Woody Allen released a film titled *A Hollywood Ending*. We've heard those words for years now describing everything from marriages to business endeavors. In the old sense of the meaning, "a Hollywood ending" meant "they lived happily ever after." It meant the guy got the girl. It meant the good guys won, and the bad guys were deservedly punished. It meant they saved grandma's house from the evil banker who demanded little Nell's hand in marriage if they couldn't come up with the money. A "Hollywood ending" meant that the doctors were able to come up with a cure for the incurable disease and save the lead actor's life.

That wasn't always true in every movie. Some directors would stray from the predictable ending even in the early years of movies. But in what we call the "golden years of cinema" people went to the movies to forget about their day-to-day problems. People used to go to the local theater to lose themselves in a fantasy world that would either scare their worries away or make them feel good about their own hum-drum lives.

Things have changed. Today, "a Hollywood ending" isn't so predictable. Whether it's on the big screen, or our favorite television shows, the good guys don't always win. The guy doesn't always get the girl. Grandma's house has been torn down and a gambling casino has been built on the property. And even with our high-tech medicine, more people die in Hollywood productions today than in yesteryear. Movies and television programs are more about picking up the pieces and moving on than about living happily ever after. In other words, what we see on the screen tends more to reflect real life than to take us safely away from our own misery.

There was a time when we were somewhat buffered from the suffering of the world. We had our own problems, felt our own pain, and perhaps that of our close friends and neighbors. But we were protected from the disasters and oppression that went on in other parts of the world. That's not to say that was good, especially when innocent millions were led to their deaths in Europe during the 1930s and '40s as well as in other places at other times. But it was safe for us. We were distanced from the suffering and could pretend it didn't exist even if we were somewhat aware of it.

Now we are deluged with images and stories from around the world. Not a day goes by that we don't hear of struggles and violence, of disasters and disease, of people whose lives have been destroyed and loved ones taken away. The more modern and sophisticated we've become, the more that suffering and pain have been brought into our lives on a daily basis.

We don't like to suffer. We don't like to see the suffering of others. We strive to alleviate suffering from the world. So why does Peter tell us in this text to "rejoice insofar as we are sharing Christ's suffering"? Why does he make it sound as though suffering, and specifically the suffering of Christ, is such a good thing? If we read the conclusion of that thirteenth verse we get an answer. It says: "so that you may also be glad and shout for joy when his glory is revealed."

So it's not the plot that brings rejoicing. It's not the period of great suffering of Christ, that with which we are to identify, that brings smiles to the faces and joy to the heart. It is the surprise ending. Like the old "Hollywood ending" in which all the major players lived happily ever after, the "holy-wood ending" in which the cross becomes the emblem or our salvation, is a happy ending. It's a glorious ending in which we are glorified because Jesus is glorified. It's an ending that keeps on going and continues adding new characters to the script because it's not really an ending, but the beginning of the sequel.

There's an old Chinese proverb that says: "If you wish to be happy for one hour, get intoxicated. If you wish to be happy for three days, get married. If you wish to be happy for eight days, kill your pig and eat it. If you wish to be happy forever, learn to fish."

We spend our lives looking for the happy ending. But we're still in the midst of the story, so the ending is yet out of reach. Jesus taught his disciples how to fish. It wasn't exactly the kind of fishing that the Chinese proverb was referring to, but it was Jesus' version of fishing. "I will make you fishers of people," Jesus told his disciples. He didn't even tell them that they would be successful, he just said to do it. He didn't say they would live without problems. He didn't say they would enjoy great happiness. In fact, they suffered, and we believe that most of them lost their lives doing just what Jesus had instructed them to do. So why did they endure the suffering of Christ? They followed his script because they believed in the ending.

A gardener took great pride in caring for his lawn. But one year it grew full of dandelions. He tried every method and product on the market to get rid of them, but nothing worked. Exasperated, he wrote to the Department of Agriculture explaining all that he had done. "What shall I try next?" he wrote. The reply came back, "Try getting used to them."

We try to regain our health and youthful vigor rather than accepting that we are growing older and making the best of what we have left. We dream of winning the lottery and never again having to worry about finances, instead of just planning to live within our means and enjoying it. We want God to take away all the suffering and pain that we endure, and we don't want to wait until we live in glory with Christ in eternity. We want it now.

A fortune-teller studied the hand of a young man and said, "You will be poor and very unhappy until you are 37 years old."

The young man responded, "Well, after that, what will happen? Will I be rich and happy?"

The fortune-teller said, "No, you'll still be poor, but you'll be used to it after that."

Peter tells us that we will be exalted "in due time." He describes our time of suffering with Christ as "a little while." Following that "little while" he says that the God of all grace will "restore, support, strengthen, and establish" us.

Are you one of those people who has to skip to the end of a novel shortly after starting it just to see how it ends? Do you rent movies and fast-forward to the end before you've watched the whole movie just to decide if it's worth watching the whole thing? If you're like that, then have I got good news for you! You don't have to read your daily horoscope. You don't have to go to a fortune-teller. You don't even have to go to John Edward and receive messages from people who have already "crossed over." The ending has already been revealed, and it's a glorious ending. Even if the final chapters are filled with suffering and pain, the ending is a "holy-wood ending." You will triumph with Jesus. You will rejoice with the angels. You will live with God in a painless world free of suffering and torment. That's how it's all been written, and the author is an undisputed authority on life.

A man had just had his annual physical exam and was waiting for the doctor's initial report. After a few minutes the doctor came in carrying the man's charts and said: "There's no reason why you can't live a completely normal life ... as long as you don't try to enjoy it."

If we believe the story of Jesus, and the ending that God wrote, then there is no reason why we cannot even rejoice in our sufferings. When we are able to accept illness and injury, hardship and struggle, contempt and injustice, and even the death of those we love, all as a part of our life with Jesus, then and only then can we learn to live in joy and happiness. Because there will always be suffering and pain. We cannot escape it. There will always be those elements of life that will beat down upon us and try to make us forget that Jesus ever lived. There will always be those times of weakness when we will question God's wisdom and his love for us.

But the "holy-wood ending" is still intact. Jesus died, taking the suffering of the world upon his shoulders as he hung on that wooden cross. In three days he had arisen to glory. In just three days he was back on top. And he invites us all to join him ... in the end.

The plot thickens. Sometimes the movie drags on with parts we would rather see edited out. But in the end, what was lost is restored. In the end, the suffering has ended, the pain has vanished, and the weak are made strong. In the end, God has established his kingdom, and, as trite as it may sound, we all will live happily ever after.

Sermons On The Second Readings

For Sundays After Pentecost (First Third)

The Gifted

William G. Carter

Pentecost
1 Corinthians 12:3b-13

The Gifted

If you ask me, a sermon should say only one thing. Some of us grew up listening to sermons with three points, and wondered, "What's the point?" The business of worship, the activity of preaching, is too important to be pointless. Each sermon needs to make a statement, to declare one thing that is vital for our faith, our hope, and our life, in the world.

So lest you miss it this morning, there's only one thing I want to say today. This sermon has one point to make, one claim that I want to lay upon our lives. Have a pencil? Ready to write this down? Here is the central message of this sermon: *The only church worth having, the only church worth belonging to, is a charismatic church.*

I trust this statement does not upset you. I am not going to apologize for it. While I have not said it publicly, I have deeply held the conviction for some time. *The only church worth having, the only church worth belonging to, is a charismatic church.*

No doubt some people have been confused when I have said that in the past. A few years ago, I was shopping in a religious bookstore. Another customer learned from a sales clerk that I was a pastor. She said, "I'm new in the area. I'm looking for a church. But it has to be a charismatic church."

I said, "You ought to come and worship with us. We have a charismatic church."

She took a second look at me and said, "You can't be serious."

"Oh, yes, I'm quite serious."

She said, "Do you have faith healings?"

"We probably do, but we don't make a big deal out of it. After all, it's a charismatic church."

She said, "I'm not sure I understand. Do people stand up in worship services and speak in tongues?"

"No," I said, "most of our members would find that intrusive. Sometimes at a congregational meeting, our church treasurer says some things that nobody else can understand. But she's not speaking in tongues; she's just explaining the budget."

She said, "I thought you said it was a charismatic church."

I said, "It is."

"Then do you have any strange manifestations of the Holy Spirit?"

I said, "We have a few quirky church members, if that's what you mean."

"I thought you said you were part of a Pentecostal church."

I said, "No, no, we're not Pentecostal. We're Presbyterian."

She said, "Well, if you're not a Pentecostal, you certainly can't be a charismatic!" Then she stomped away in a huff. Well, what does she know? It doesn't stop me from making the one claim that I want to make this morning, namely, that *the only true Christian church is a charismatic church.*

That doesn't mean everybody is going to understand what I mean. The other day I tried out my one-point sermon on somebody who dropped by the church office. He wanted to hear a preview for Sunday morning. Maybe he figured if I could sum up my sermon in a single line, he could turn off the alarm Sunday morning and stay in bed. In any case, I told him what I wanted to say. I said, "If the church is honest and true about what it takes to be a truly Christian church, it will say without reservation that it is charismatic."

He looked at me for a minute and raised one eyebrow. Then he said, "Oh, I get it. You don't mean charismatic-charismatic. You mean charisma-charismatic. What you're probably going to say is that a good church has to have charisma."

I said, "Not really."

"But it's true," he said. "If a church is going to grow and flourish, it has to have a certain charisma about it. It needs to appeal to people and win them over. A church needs charisma."

"No," I said, "that's not what I'm going to talk about."

"Maybe you should," he said. "After all, that's why a lot of people come to First Presbyterian Church. They like the pastors. They perceive a certain charm about the congregation. They recognize a certain sparkle, flash, and inspiration. It inspires confidence and certainty and pride. People look at our pastors and our church, and they see charisma."

"Ah, be quiet," I said. "That's not what I'm going to talk about."

No, today what I want to say is this: *that the church in its truest expression, the church at its best, is a charismatic church.*

I don't mean that in some spooky, ultra-spiritual sense. And I don't mean that in the sense of some appealing personal quality. No, I mean "charismatic" in the way that the Apostle Paul addresses that church in Corinth.

As you may remember, it was a troubled congregation. There were probably only fifty members in the church at Corinth, but they were at one another's throats. They were divided into political factions. They were debating sexual ethics. They were fighting about who should receive the Lord's Supper and who should not. They were suing one another in court. They were bowing before the shrines of their culture. They were defending their actions with indefensible slogans and bumper-sticker theology. To top it off, some of the church members insisted that they were more spiritual than some of the other members.

Paul addresses all of these problems in his letter. One of the final items on his list is the business of spiritual one-upmanship. That is what he begins to address in chapter 12. The Corinthians had no doubt that all kinds of wild, spiritual experiences were breaking out in their church. What they wanted to know is whether or not these experiences came from God. That's worth noting.

For instance, throughout history many cultures and religions have reported the experience of "speaking in tongues," or glossolalia. Among them are Hindus, Muslims, and followers of African folk religions. Speaking in ecstatic utterances is not a particularly Christian activity. It happens in many religions. Likewise, you can pick up the *National Enquirer* and read about faith healings, exorcisms, and miracles of various kinds. The question is not, "Do they happen, yes or no?" The question is, "Do they come from the Holy Spirit?"

Before Paul can answer, he realizes that he needs to change the terminology. The Corinthians wanted to know about "spiritual things." Paul speaks about "charisma," a Greek word that means "gift." The true church, says Paul, is a "charismatic" church, a gifted church. The word Paul uses is always plural: not merely "charisma," a single gift, but "charismata," a variety of gifts. No specific spiritual experience is better than all the rest. There is not one expression of the Spirit which is more charismatic than all the others. The Holy Spirit is more generous than any individual can know. The Spirit touches different people in different ways, creating all kinds of different experiences.

By this point, a dyed-in-the-wool Presbyterian like me may start to get a little nervous. I mean, what if these spiritual experiences get out of hand? Well, not to worry. After all, Paul is the one who coined the phrase, "Let all things be done decently and in order." (1 Corinthians 14:40 is a favorite verse of my very orderly denomination.) You see, Paul was the first Presbyterian, and he knows that if spiritual things get out of hand, the answer is not laying down a lot of rules and regulations. No, offer some substantive theology that lies at the core of our faith.

Paul can't deal with "spiritual experiences" without talking about "gifts of the Holy Spirit," the "charismata." And he can't talk about "gifts of the Holy Spirit" without talking about the Trinity. Do you remember what Paul says?

> *Now there are varieties of gifts, but the same* Spirit; *and there are varieties of services, but the same* Lord; *and there are varieties of activities, but it is the same* God *who activates all of them in everyone* (my emphases).   — 1 Corinthians 12:4

Spirit, Lord, and God: that's the Trinity. Of course, Paul has the order backwards. Usually we say God the Father, Christ the Lord, and God the Holy Spirit. But the apostle is beginning with his listeners. He takes seriously their experiences of the Spirit, as diverse and different as they might be.

Someone told me about his experience. "A few years ago," he said, "I suddenly discovered an ability that I never knew that I had. Somehow I was able to sense when people around me were in trouble. It came out of the blue. At first, it seemed like a heightened awareness of need. I'd notice a co-worker who seemed worried or a shipping clerk with a furrowed brow. In time, as I paid attention, I decided I could pray for those people, just a word or two, just something that let God knew I cared. Once in a while, I was put in a position to help in some tangible way."

Say what you want, but Paul would call that a gift of the Spirit, a charismatic gift of discernment. If I dare say so, most of us have more of these gifts than we realize or ever develop. We are God's gifted people, and there are varieties of gifts that come from the Holy Spirit. There are varieties of gifts....

But Paul doesn't stop there. He goes on to add, "There are varieties of service but the same Lord." The one way to tell whether a spiritual gift or experience has come from the Holy Spirit — and I mean the *only* way to tell — is whether that gift or experience is in service to Jesus the Lord. If it truly comes from God, then it continues in the life exemplified in Christ's incarnation: sharing his power, serving the needy, speaking his word, suffering in the shadow of the world's brokenness, and giving life as he gave his life. There is no true life of the Spirit apart from the life of Jesus.

I pause to warn us: When it comes to spiritual experiences, a lot of people like to get as mystical as possible and float above the world. They say things like, "Jesus is born within my heart," or "I listen to Jesus in my heart," or "My heart needs to be cleansed," or "My heart was strangely warmed," or "If you ask me how I know he lives, he lives within my heart." To put it in other words, "Faith is only a matter of the heart; forget about the world where the Word became flesh." Unfortunately there are some Christians who would like to be more spiritual than Jesus himself. This simply will not do. The life of the Spirit is rooted in the servant life of Christ.

But Paul doesn't stop there. He points to the source of the Spirit, to the Father of Jesus Christ, and says, "There are varieties of activities, but it is the same *God* who activates all of them in everyone." All things come from God. All things are activated and energized by God, and to God all things shall return.

Paul points us beyond our little bitty activities to the grand scheme of what God is doing in the world. We cannot talk about gifts of the Spirit without talking about serving Jesus Christ. And we cannot talk about serving Jesus Christ without contending with the God who has first called the world into being, and who will finally reclaim all things, in everyone. In the reign of God, there is no distinction between personal life and public life. There is no separation of "spiritual things" from the matters of this world, whether they be family life, local economy, national politics, or global suffering. God seeks to work in all things, making all things new, moving us to God's great, final day of redemption.

In the meantime, *we are a charismatic church.* If you ask me, that's the only church there is, because it means that we have been *gifted* by the Holy Spirit, to spread the *grace* of Jesus Christ, in the end that all things shall be caught up in the *glory* of God our Creator. The church which catches this vision is inspired by the Spirit to sing with Paul: "From God and through God and to God are all things. To God be glory forever."

Holy Trinity
2 Corinthians 13:11-13

A Name Not Taken In Vain

In the middle of March, 1961, a minister named Duffy splashed water on my head in the middle of a Sunday morning worship service. I was only one of a half dozen "Baby Boomers" whose parents had recently petitioned the Session for the sacrament of baptism. Having recently moved to a trailer park in Akron, Ohio, my parents thought the time seemed right to make their firstborn infant a Presbyterian.

The sacrament went rather easily. The only reported glitch was the last-minute discovery that my father had not, himself, ever been baptized. The minister discovered this fact somehow, probably to my parents' embarrassment. And so, about half an hour before the worship service, my dad got his forehead splashed in the pastor's study. "First things first," declared Reverend Duffy.

I have reflected frequently on that family legend, especially as the years have unfolded and I have grown in my understanding of Christian baptism. My parents were young and naive, relatively unschooled in the finer points of liturgical theology. For them, as for many, my baptism was a rite of passage. It signaled that they were offering me to the church, choosing to bring me up in a Christian denomination that they chose by marital compromise. They were promising me to the community of potluck suppers and flannel-board Bible stories. Since I turned out be something of a joiner, it was a community that I have never felt the desire to leave.

But they were doing something far more: They were giving me an identity. According to another family legend, they had squabbled over my name before I was born, and didn't settle on

William Glenn until I was a few days old. It took them over a year to offer me up for the sacrament of baptism. Whether they knew it or not, they declared that I was first, and foremost, a child of the God whose name is Trinity. Through Word and water, God announced a primary claim on my life. From that point on, every breath, deed, and thought has been a response to that name to which I belong.

Practically speaking, this is our first experience of the Trinity. In my case, it may have been precognitive. In my father's case, it may have been a post-adolescent lapse that needed to be completed. Either way, Christian baptism is the moment when God's name is imputed to us. The God who creates us is revealed as the personal God who adopts us into the holy family called *church*. As a single Parent, God devotes great resources to our welfare, surrounds us with unconditional and self-giving love, and always gives us plenty of freedom to respond to such gracious initiatives. Through faithful memory, I recall what was once said to me: "William Glenn Carter, I baptize you in the name of the Father, the Son, and the Holy Spirit." God so claimed me as a lifelong child of the covenant. As I have been instructed by the third commandment of Moses, I shall not take the name of God in vain. I take upon myself the name in single-hearted devotion, and therefore trust in the promised acquittal of grace.[1]

By taking the name of Trinity, we take upon ourselves the mantle of Christian theology, worship, and practice. Trinity is our Christian name of the God of Abram and Sarai. Through this Name, we have access to the promises of scripture. We are enrolled in the wide-sweeping story of biblical faith. The God who cuts a covenant with the matriarchs and patriarchs is the same Trinity who comes after us in the person and work of Jesus Christ. As we have seen in Jesus, this God is not bound by human limits or divine superiority. Rather, our God reveals love and purpose through the essential community of the Divine Being.

When Paul gives his blessing at the end of 2 Corinthians, he uses the words that we have come to know quite well. "The grace of the Lord Jesus Christ, the love of God, and the communion of the Holy Spirit be with all of you" (v. 13). He blesses us through a

God who is known in relationship. The love of God becomes real to us through the grace of Jesus Christ. Love and grace are expressed through the communal presence of the Holy Spirit.

Trinity is the name of the one God who lives in community, whose very essence is community. This God will never remain static, fixed, or speechless. As the Spirit glorifies the Son,[2] and as the Son reveals the Father,[3] the Father gives the life of eternity to the created order.[4]

The Christian life is life in the name of the Trinity. Christian community is where we listen to what we learn from the communal Trinity. Christian preaching dares to declare the word of the living Christ, and not merely the ancient aphorisms of the dead Jesus. We labor to speak a word that resonates with the redemptive purposes of God for the world. If the Triune God is essentially self-revealing, the people of God are called as witnesses to God's words and deeds. Christian faith always points beyond itself to the God who lives and speaks, for it is in the life and word of God that we find our origin, purpose, and destination.

I suppose this is why the preaching and teaching ministries of the church have become so dear to me, and probably why they demand so much of a minister's time and energy. I also suspect this is why I have come to believe that true pastoral care is more than a mere soul massage, and more like an invitation to claim God's presence and purpose for the world. Our prevailing North American culture has become far too insulated and self-absorbed for its own good, so much so, in fact, that it is hard for the holy God to get much of a hearing these days.

To crib the line from Jesus, Christian preaching will take what belongs to Christ and declare it.[5] Through our human words and humane deeds, we announce that God is truthful and gracious; righteous, yet available; powerful, while choosing to become vulnerable; and most of all, in spite of our sin, full of redeeming love.

In my first year as a pastor, I presided over a session meeting where a fight broke out. The fierce conflict, which lasted for 45 minutes, was precipitated by an announcement from the chairperson of the fellowship committee. He declared that fresh brewed coffee would no longer be served after worship. Instead we would have hot water, with our choice of tea bags or Folgers crystals. Since I was 26 years old and stupid, I thought the ensuing argument was about coffee, and tried to shut it down. Silly me! The elders tossed around that hot potato for three-quarters of an hour.

The real issue centered on the very nature of our life together as a community. Expediency was battling against intimacy. Since the chair of the committee was a lousy recruiter, he and his wife were often stuck in the church kitchen, rinsing out coffee grounds long after others had gone home. He wanted to leave church at the same time as everybody else, so he pushed for simpler refreshments for coffee hour.

"But you don't understand," exclaimed an exasperated opponent. "I come to worship to listen for God, and I go to coffee hour to talk to others." Naturally, for her, a community is enhanced by a stiff dose of brewed caffeine. It was a first reminder to me that the communal truth of the Trinity must be worked out in the life of a human community. The Word takes flesh, we say, and the all-too-human church is the Body of Christ.

The claims of the gospel must be embodied in a gathering of people, or else the gospel remains an abstract idea, high above everybody's heads. If a church is reticent to speak of God as Trinity, it cashes in a great resource for thinking about its very communal life. In the ancient understanding of the Triune God as a "circle dance," three divine persons constitute the unity of the one divine being.[6] The heart of the divine mystery is the experience and reality of fellowship. Whether people glimpse this fellowship in a Russian icon[7] or taste it in the reality of Eucharist or potluck supper, this communion is marked by complete and mutual participation, with shared power and purpose, all for the greater end of the redemption of the universe.

And so, the mysterious and distant doctrine of the Trinity gets me to look at our life as a congregation through new eyes. Week after week, I stand before people who are claimed by the name and do not take it in vain. They give generously, for it is God's nature to give to the world. They pray fervently, for they know that they are never abandoned or alone. They sing joyfully, for it is clear that the Triune God lives in security and joy. At its best, our life together is a reflection of God's life.

If grace, love, and communion can't be worked out here, among these people and in this place, I doubt they can be found anywhere else. And as we show one another grace, love, and communion, we participate in the very life of God. This is the life that can never, ever, die, for it is the life that brought back our Lord Jesus Christ from the dead.

---

1. Exodus 20:7 — "For the Lord will not acquit anyone who misuses his name."

2. John 16:12.

3. John 1:18; 14:7f.

4. John 17:1-3.

5. John 16:14.

6. Philip W. Butin, *The Trinity* (Louisville: Geneva Press, 2001), p. 64.

7. See Henri Nouwen's reflections in *Behold the Beauty of the Lord: Praying with Icons* (Notre Dame: Ave Maria Press, 1987) pp. 19-27.

Proper 4
Pentecost 2
Ordinary Time 9
Romans 1:16-17; 3:22b-28 (29-31)

No Shame

I am very taken by what Paul says. He claims, "I am not ashamed...." Most of us have known people, maybe a lot, maybe a few, and they are ashamed of something.

I struck up a conversation with a woman I had known for a couple of years. I thought I knew her fairly well. One day she blurted out that she had been married four times. I said, "You never mentioned it."

She said, "I guess I'm ashamed."

A man lost his job. That was hard enough. What made it more difficult is that he lost the job because he was caught taking a box of envelopes out of the office for personal use. He never mentioned it to anybody. He couldn't tell his family the real reason. He was ashamed.

There's a newlywed whose marriage is not going well. When he was a little boy some things happened that he never told anybody about. He shoved it down inside. Now he has a hard time getting close to his new wife. He wants to, but he can't. She said, "Let's go talk to a counselor about it," but he is afraid to go. He's ashamed.

There seems to be some shame around the church. Sometimes it keeps people out of church.

An older couple stopped going to church after their son committed suicide. The people in the congregation were very understanding when it happened, but there's no way they will go back there when so many people know their secret. They are ashamed.

A nominating committee asked a woman to serve as an elder in a church I used to serve. At first she said, "Yes," but then she dropped by for coffee to voice some second thoughts. "What if people find out about my daughter?" she asked. Her daughter is an exotic dancer who also had a problem with cocaine. "I've never been able to reach her since she was fifteen," her mom says. "I'm not sure the church would want a parent like me to serve," she said. I can hear the tremor in her voice.

Once in a while, one of our members may get in trouble with the law. It's right there, splashed across the paper, before they can defend themselves. It's embarrassing. Even if he is exonerated, he is afraid that everybody has an opinion about it. So he stays away on Sunday morning.

Other times, somebody may come down too hard and it bruises somebody's spirit. I have a friend in the ministry whose teenage daughter was attending a youth group meeting. They were talking about faith and doubt, and the girl got up the courage to tell the others about some of her doubts. The youth group advisor slammed down on her. "You're the minister's daughter," she said. "You ought to be ashamed of yourself." My friend said it took ten years before his daughter would even consider going back to a church.

It is painful to have shame rubbed in your face. But Paul says, "I'm not ashamed."

What a remarkable thing for him to say! The Apostle Paul grew up in a culture where shame was a way of creating order. It still happens in many corners of the Middle East. Woe to you, if you bring shame to your family! One of the members of our men's Bible study brought in a news clipping. It told of a woman in another culture who returned home after being abused by another man. What did her brothers do? Go after the abuser? Press charges against him? No, her brothers put her to death, announcing that her abuse had brought shame to her family.

All throughout the Jewish scriptures, the notion of shame is a very powerful force. I did a word search on my computer. The word "shame" shows up 174 times in the Old Testament. You can hear it repeated in passages like Psalm 25: "O my God, in you I trust; do not let me be put to shame" (v. 2). "Do not let those who wait for you be put to shame" (v. 3). "Let the treacherous be put to shame" (v. 3).

This was one of the ways that people worked out a theology of works. They believed that you had to be good. You had to maintain a good reputation. Your family needed to keep a good family name. And if there was ever a mistake, if there was a moral miscue, if there was an obvious and public sin, then the whole community descended on you and put you to shame.

As a Presbyterian, I admit there is some Puritan starch in my veins. Some of this shame business is in our background. In the early settlements of our country, you were mocked if you were a Sabbath-breaker. If you took a loaf of bread without paying for it, they put you in stocks for public display. Good Christians wagged their tongues and said, "For shame! For shame!"

Yet Paul says, "But I am not ashamed."

Paul, of all people. If anybody had anything to be ashamed about, it was the Apostle Paul. We know about his former life. He was the commander of the Jerusalem secret police. He is the man who dragged Christians out of their homes and demanded their death by stoning. I'm talking about Paul, or as we used to call him, Saul. He was no honey: pushy, arrogant, and always insisting on his own way. And that's how he acted *after* his conversion.

He says at one point in one of his letters, "I think all of you ought to stay single, just like me."

We were in a Bible study when somebody read those words. A woman spoke up and said, "Listen, Paul, you're going to have to stay single because I don't know anybody who could live with you."

Sometimes he says things that are an embarrassment to the church. Ever read his letter to the Galatians? He is furious with those Christians up in Turkey. They are up there in Asia Minor, debating the virtues of circumcision. Paul is furious with them. He calls them stupid and says, "You're bewitched." At one point, he gets so worked up that he says, "I wish those people who are upsetting you about circumcision would castrate themselves!" (Galatians 5:12). Now his angry outburst is a verse in our Bible.

When an apostle talks like that, he is an embarrassment. Paul ought to be ashamed of himself. Yet he says, "I am not ashamed."

Do you suppose he is one of these people who just puts it out there, and doesn't care what people think? You know the type. They shoot off their mouths, say whatever they want, and justify themselves by saying, "I'm only telling the truth." Certainly Paul has that capacity, just like the rest of us. You never know what he's going to say.

Sometimes he is able to be quite tender. He could be kind and gracious. He wrote to the Philippians, to a church he loved, and he said, "I have great affection for you from all the way down in my gut."

Paul could be crass. He could be tender. And he certainly could be honest.

He told the truth about his former life. "I used to hunt down Christians to destroy them," he confesses, "and now I am a Christian." How can anybody explain this — except by the power of God? Paul thought he knew what he was supposed to do with his life. Then he discovered he was wrong. That experience lies behind all of the theological language in the Roman letter.

"The gospel is the power of God for salvation to everyone who believes," he says. "I am not ashamed of the gospel, for it can take a wretched man like me and turn me in another direction. I am not ashamed of God's redemptive power."

The gospel has the authority to change our lives. It has the power to wipe away our shame. That is the essence of what the church has to say, and it's good news.

One of the problems, however, is that the news has been around so long that we have let it get rusty. We have turned the kingdom of God from a movement into an institution. For most of American history, the church has been a privileged institution in our culture. We have not had to fight for anything. We haven't felt the need to speak our message in compelling words. I'm afraid we have gotten a little flabby about our witness.

Not long ago we had two funerals in our sanctuary during the same week. Both were funerals for church members. At the first funeral, the funeral director pointed out three people who have never been in our church sanctuary. All three of them have lived in this community all their lives. All three asked the funeral director for directions to our church. Lifelong residents of our community, they didn't know where our building was located. Meanwhile here we sit, Sunday after Sunday, assuming people are going to drop in.

At the second funeral that week, we had at least fifteen people who used to attend our church but don't come anymore. In fact, most of them don't go to *any* church anymore. Some of them are still on our membership rolls. Most of them slipped out the side window and never came back. One man said he hadn't been here since the manse next door was torn down in 1992. He said, "I've thought about coming back a number of times, but I got into the habit of not coming, and now I feel ashamed."

I think we should respond to both of those situations with an honest look at our congregation and its message. First, we can never expect to have much of an impact if nobody knows where we are. Second, we can never expect to help people in the depths of their being if we don't help them counter the shame they carry with a dose of good news. It is really that simple, and it is really that difficult.

Years ago, something happened in one of the first churches I ever served. We had a nice little church. Every year, they put together a vacation Bible school. It was a great program, but nobody outside the church knew about it. The committee refused to advertise the program. They kept to the same teachers who taught the same things, and they did it really well. I said, "I'm only the pastor, but maybe we could let some people know about this."

"Oh, no," they said. "That's not necessary."

I tried to change their minds, but didn't get anywhere. One year, I took a big piece of orange poster board and wrote "Vacation Bible School." Adding the dates, times, and the church phone number, I put the sign out on the street corner. A couple of days later, the sign was gone.

The Sunday school superintendent took it down. "You don't get it," he said to me. "If we invite everybody, there's no telling who might come."

I said, "I thought that was the point."

He said, "We don't want just anybody to come. We want to keep it manageable. If anybody shows up, it could get out of hand."

I don't know why he was worried. In my kind of church, hardly anything ever gets out of hand. It sounded to me as if he was ashamed of what we were doing.

Here is something I want you to do. Think of the people with whom you spend the most time. Take a piece of paper and write down their names. With whom do you spend your time? List your friends, family members, co-workers, and neighbors. Then ask the question: Have you ever told them we're here? Do they have any idea how you're spending this hour? Would you ever invite them to come along with you next Sunday?

One year, our church sponsored a special day. We called it "Invite a Friend Sunday." The only people who brought a friend were the associate pastor and her husband, who invited their next-door neighbor. She belongs to a Lutheran church near her home, but she was here. Even I was ashamed that I didn't invite any of my neighbors. In fact, I am ashamed I don't even know most of my neighbors. Maybe I ought to cut back on the church work and do a little more of the Lord's work.

Paul reminds us that God has the power to transform every life. One way to say it is that God has the power to *take away our shame*. You know what the New Testament says?

> *The Father of Jesus is our Father, and Jesus is not ashamed to call us brothers and sisters.*
> — Hebrews 2:11

> *God has prepared a city for us, and God is not ashamed to be called their God.* — Hebrews 11:16

The Bible says Jesus is not ashamed of us. God is not ashamed of us. Where do church people get the crazy idea of wagging their fingers at the world and saying, "You ought to be ashamed"?

The good news of the gospel is that God deals with our shame. God sees those secrets that we don't want anybody to find out about us. God knows all those behaviors that we try to hide from other church people. God brings our dark secrets right out into the light where they can be seen, and then God cancels every one of them, and says, "No more damage!"

As it is written, "We look to Jesus, the pioneer and perfecter of our faith, who for the sake of the joy that was set before him endured the cross and disregarded its shame" (Hebrews 12:2). The old law was clear: *It is a shame to be sentenced to death and hung on a tree.* But that is the shame Jesus endured ... and he did it to take away our shame.

Despite whatever messages that parents or preachers told you, the gospel is not about shame. There is no shame in the gospel. It is not the church's job to reinforce the shame that has been dumped on us. What we do is point to the Christ who died a shameful death in order to take away all shame. Now we live in freedom. We belong to the daylight. Our mission is to invite others to share that freedom and join us in the daylight. We can do it because we're not ashamed.

Not long ago, I was talking with a man who sees the world in ways quite different from me. That's not a bad idea once in a while. All of us can get stuck in our little enclaves and rarely venture out of our comfortable circles. This was a person who has done great things to advance the gospel. He has his flaws. He has his troubles. But he keeps going. And he is effective.

I asked him, "What's your secret? How do you keep doing what you do?" He smiled. He took out a piece of paper from his wallet, unfolded it a few times, and gave it to me. This is what it said:

- I am a member of the fellowship of the unashamed.
- I have Holy Spirit power.
- I have stepped over the line.
- The decision has been made.
- I am his disciple.
- I won't look back, slow down, back away, or be still.
- My past is redeemed, my present makes sense, my future is secure.
- I am finished and done with low living, side walking, small planning, smooth knees, colorless dreams, same visions, mundane talking, chintzy giving, and puny goals.

- I no longer need preeminence, prosperity, promotions, positions, plaudits, or popularity.
- I don't have to be right, recognized, regarded, rewarded, or praised.
- I now live by grace, lean by faith, walk by patience, lift by prayer, and labor by power.
- My face is set, my gate is fast, my goal is heaven, my road is narrow, my way is rough, my companions few, my guide is reliable, my mission is clear.
- I cannot be bought, compromised, lured, manipulated, enticed, or bribed.
- I will not flinch in the face of sacrifice, hesitate in the presence of the adversary, negotiate at the table of the enemy, ponder at the pool of popularity, or meander in the maze of mediocrity.
- I won't give up, shut up, or let up until I've stayed up, prayed up, and preached up for the cause for Christ.
- I am his disciple.
- I must go until he comes, give until I drop, preach until all know, work until he stops me.
- When he comes back, I want him to recognize my face.
- For I have forgotten all that is in the past, I'm pressing on for the prize, the high calling of my Lord and Savior Jesus Christ.
- My colors are clear.
- I am his disciple.
- And I am not ashamed.[1]

That, my friends, is the great open secret of our salvation: "I am not ashamed of the gospel; it is the power of God for salvation to everyone who has faith" (Romans 1:16).

---

1. Original source unknown.

**Proper 5
Pentecost 3
Ordinary Time 10
Romans 4:13-25**

Uncle Abraham

I have good news for you this morning. None of you are good enough to be here.

Sorry about that. I thought I saw a few of you flinch. Maybe I need to be a bit more sensitive in how I begin. Let me try again.

I have good news for you this morning: God is not impressed with a person in this room.

By the look on some of your faces, I'm not sure that was any better way to start a sermon. Give me one more opportunity to get this sermon started. Here it goes.

I have good news for you this morning: Every single one of us is a complete and utter failure.

How am I doing so far? I thought so.

It is difficult to preach Paul's letter to the Romans. This document is heavy in all kinds of ways. It is a dense and demanding piece of correspondence.

Paul writes this letter to a congregation he did not start, to people whom he had never met. From the first sentence forward, he lays out chapter after chapter of his deepest theology. "The gospel is the power of God for the salvation of the world" (v. 16), he says in chapter 1. "It is possible for every creature in the creation to know God, and to love God" (v. 19). Yet this knowledge and love gets tangled up somehow. By the end of the first chapter Paul says, "All of us have a tendency to exchange the truth about God for a lie, we worship the creature rather than the Creator " (v. 25), and "we have no excuse" (v. 20).

In other words, none of you are good enough to be here. God is not impressed with a single person in this room. Every single one of us is a complete and utter failure.

Or as Paul puts it, "All have sinned and fall short of the glory of God" (Romans 3:23).

I will be the first to admit it: this is a lot to swallow before ten o'clock in the morning. It's heavy. Very heavy.

I have a friend named Dan. He recently retired as a minister. When Dan moved to Florida, he left behind with me a seventy-pound commentary on Romans. I think he did it out of self-defense. This is a heavy piece of scripture, in all kinds of ways.

When we hear Paul speak, this is the context for all that he has to say. If I did not know better, I would think Paul was simply going to tell us how bad we are. Yet as Paul begins his letter to the Romans, he issues a heavy indictment because that is the beginning of God's good news.

None of you are good enough to be here. Yet look around: you are here, because God has called you. God is not impressed with a single person in this room. Yet God loves us in spite of our spotty records of achievement. Every single one of us is a complete and utter failure. But God proves his love for us in that while we still were sinners, Christ died for us (Romans 5:8).

This is what it says in Romans, and this good news is the power of God for the salvation of the world.

I don't know if you have ever personally found your way into these verses. Maybe for you, as it was in my case, you did not find the verses as much as the verses found you. However it happens, I know from my own experience that when these words sink in, they can set you free.

There I was, a freshman in college, a certified Sunday school graduate, a retired president of my church youth group. We were having a student Bible study on the letter to the Romans. I knew all the Jesus stories, the Genesis stories, a few memory verses here and there. But I had never read Romans.

We were flipping through the chapters for some reason, and I found that verse in the third chapter where it says, "All have sinned and fall short of the glory of God" (Romans 3:23). That verse struck me between the eyes, in all of its honesty. "All have sinned. All have fallen short."

Suddenly a strange sense of relief came over me. *All* of us *have* sinned, and no one is any better than anybody else. *All* of us *have* fallen short — that's the truth! So we can stop punishing ourselves for not measuring up. The truth is, no matter how good we are, we will never be good enough. In an ultimate sense, that's okay, because life is not about us ever being able to measure up. Life is about God, who moves toward us in Jesus Christ to bridge the distance.

If you do nothing else this morning, just let that sink in for a minute.

There is something very comforting about this. If we came to church this morning thinking we were "good enough," Paul says, "Get real." Nobody has the capacity to be good enough, and the good news is that God is not bound by *our* limitations. God loves us because of who we are, in spite of who we are, before we even know who we are.

"There is no distinction," says the Apostle Paul, "since all have sinned and fall short of the glory of God." Then in the very next breath he says, "And they are justified by his grace as a gift, through the redemption that is in Christ Jesus ... (made) effective through faith" (Romans 3:22-25).

That is the point of why we are here, after all. Before the church got to be big business, this is what all the excitement was about. God loves us, and for that reason alone, God has sent Jesus Christ into the world. Sometimes a preacher needs to stand up and say it.

Essentially, that is the claim Paul is making in this section of the letter. It is so large, so heavy, that it is tough to let it sink in.

We find some help at this point from an Episcopalian priest named Robert Capon. He writes theology books and cookbooks. One of his books is called *The Supper of the Lamb,* and a reader is never really sure if he is talking about eschatology or mint jelly. Capon is a highly imaginative theologian, which is probably why I like him, and he had been known to overdose on the letter to the Romans.

In one of his books he raises the question of how we are to make it through this world. One way is the high school yearbook way, and another is by way of the ticket window.

Remember the high school yearbook? It is full of good things that happened in the past. We see the pictures; we remember the accomplishments. In particular, we fondly recall all those special events that happened years and years ago. Capon observes that, for a lot of people, faith is a memory of past events, like the crossing of the Red Sea, or the death of Jesus, or the high school prom. If some of us hang on to those events from long ago, we think we can get through life. But Capon says that is a dead end. Remembering the past does not always get us through troubles here and now.

By contrast, consider the ticket window. You go up to the box office, make a purchase, and then you are allowed in. We can think of God in Christ as the official ticket agent who lets us into the stadium, and that is true enough. The problem with a ticket window, however, is that you must have some earning power to get your ticket. You need to work hard and long to accumulate enough money, and then you will be allowed through the gate and shown to your seat. The problem, however, is that the ticket costs too much for anybody to buy. Nobody else can afford it, either. The only available tickets are the tickets that somebody gives you.

So how do we make our way through the world? Not by remembering memorable achievements in the yearbook. Not by buying our own admission. We make our way through the world by responding to the free gift of God.

Imagine, says Robert Capon, a sign over a stadium that announces, "Open to all for free." You draw near and discover *somebody* has already stuck a free ticket in your pocket, given you a fine seat, and brought you a hot dog and a drink. You did not ask for any of it. It is given to you, and you have to decide if you can accept it. There is nothing else to remember or forget. There is nothing you need to do to earn your way inside. You are already there, as a gift — unless, of course, you refuse the offer which has been offered to everybody.

Capon says the work of Jesus on our behalf is like this.

> *It says not only that we don't need to have the wherewithal (good works) for a ticket, but that even to think we could buy a ticket is to misunderstand the whole setup ... The only appropriate thing to do about such a fantastic arrangement is just shut up, believe it, and enjoy it — because we've already got it.*[1]

In the church, the ten-cent word which we use for all this is "justification." It's the idea that God-in-Christ justifies us; that Christ makes us right in God's sight; that in our unacceptable state, God accepts us, because Jesus has done all the necessary work on our behalf.

Can you believe it? That's the question upon which all of this pivots. Can we believe it?

I know people who work their entire lives to make themselves acceptable. They put in long hours, they keep at it all the time, they bring work home with them. If you get them in a chair long enough and say, "Why are you working so hard?" they might admit, "I work so hard because I always wanted my father to accept me; I always wanted my mother to approve of me."

Listen, there's a news flash: our Parent in heaven already accepts you and approves of you. So stop working so hard. If you wanted to earn your way into the pearly gates, you would never be able to make enough money. You would be so busy trying to prove yourself that you would overlook that free ticket that Jesus has already slipped into your pocket — before you even knew he had done it.

That, my friends, is something of what it means to be justified before God. The point is, life is not about us and our long list of checkered achievements. Life is about God, and what God has accomplished in the death and resurrection of Jesus.

For our part, all we need to do is trust the ticket has already been slipped into our pocket.

It's like old Abraham. Remember him? According to the book of Genesis, he was an amazing man. When Abraham was 75 years old, God said, "Go!" Abraham didn't ask where; he just went. You might think that God loved him *because* he was obedient to God.

The truth is, for some reason, God said, "Abraham, I'm going to make you somebody special," before Abraham could even respond.

When Abraham was 99 years old, God sneaked up on him and said, "Abraham, I'm going to make you the father of a huge multitude. I'm going to change your name to mean 'Grand Exalted Father of an Exceedingly Large Family,' or in short, I'm going to call you 'Big Daddy.'" And Abraham laughed, and said, "O God, get serious." And God said, "I am serious; in fact, I'm so serious, I want you to get circumcised at the age of 99, after which you're going to become a father." Abraham did as he was told, even though it felt like his body was as good as dead. Maybe you might think God loved him because he did what God wanted him to do. The truth is, God had already said, "I'm going to make you the father of a huge multitude."

Then came that day, that very dark day, when God sneaked up on him one more time, "Abraham! Take your son, your only son Isaac, the son whom you love, and offer him on the mountain as a burnt offering." Abraham didn't say a word. He saddled the donkey, stacked the wood, and took his son up the mountain. He built the altar, put Isaac upon it, and raised the stone knife. There was a great silence, and God said, "Stop! Now I know that you fear me." You might think, "What a test that was!" Abraham passed the test, and therefore that's why God loved him. But all these events came long after the moment when God had already reckoned him righteous.

That happened late one night, many years before. God said, "Abraham! Go out and count the stars. That's how many children you're going to have." I picture the old man squinting toward the sky, and beginning to count: "One, two, three, four, five, ten, twenty, thirty, one hundred, two hundred, ten thousand and one, ten thousand and two...." As he counted, for some miraculous, inexplicable reason, he believed the promise of the Lord.

That is all it took. Abraham believed that God was going to keep the promise. For the first time in all the Bible, God said, "Here is a child who is made right with me." Abraham believed, and said, "Yes," to God. That's all it took.

That is all it ever takes. All that faith requires is to trust that the one ticket you could never earn has already been slipped into your pocket.

---

1. Robert Farrar Capon, *The Mystery Of Christ ... And Why We Don't Get It* (Grand Rapids: William B. Eerdmans, 1993), p. 84.

Proper 6
Pentecost 4
Ordinary Time 11
Romans 5:1-8

Still Sinners, Still Forgiven

I have an announcement to make. Today's sermon is not for everybody. It was not planned for a general audience. It was not written to whom it may concern. No, today's sermon is intended for people who have a hard time feeling forgiven. The rest of you can listen in.

Once in a while, I run across somebody who has difficulty feeling that the good news of the gospel is for them. They don't have any problem believing all the outrageous things that church takes to be true, like God becoming a human or the resurrection of Jesus. They may generally go along with, even enjoy, the church's commitment to mission in the world. They like church people, and choose to spend time around them. But when it comes to accepting God as a positive and joyful presence in daily life, well, it simply doesn't come as good news.

At the heart, this seems to be a matter of forgiveness. The heart of the gospel is the news that God in Christ forgives us. "While we were yet sinners, Christ died for us." It's one thing to go to church, sing the hymns, say the prayers, stand and affirm this truth. It's another thing to know in your veins that this is good news for me.

Tom Long tells about his first failure in ministry. All his seminary books were unpacked. All the pencils were sharpened at the desk. A church member knocked on his door and asked if he had a few minutes to talk. She started right in: "I know that I shouldn't feel this way, but I just don't think God can ever forgive me."

The few minutes became an hour. Tom asked, "What is the burden that you're carrying?" She was a devoted mother, a loyal spouse, a committed church member. She had never robbed a bank, did not have a secret addiction, had no shameful secrets to bear.

He tried giving her some spiritual sound bytes — God loves you, God forgives your sins — just trying some quick fix to get her through the moment. Her reply: "I know God loves me. I know Jesus died for my sins. I know all that. I just can't overcome the feeling that God stands in judgment of me."[1]

Anybody know how that feels? As Tom quips, it is like living in rural France in 1944 and hearing the news of D-Day over the radio. The word of conquest reaches your ears, but the army of liberation has not yet arrived at your village.

The letter of Romans seems to be sent to folks in that village. It's sent to people like us. It's a gift to people who gather every week to confess their sins and hear the assurance of God's pardon, yet they can't help but sense that nothing really has changed. Maybe that's why Paul keeps hammering away about the power of forgiveness. He insists that the atoning death of Jesus is a foundational issue which calls the very church into existence. We are included in the power and purpose of the gospel because Christ died for us.

The difficulty is in believing that it's true, really true, that we are forgiven.

I recently heard a minister who served a little church in a sleepy little town on the Susquehanna River. "Sometimes the high school has a good wrestling team," he says. "Other than that nothing much happens." A college professor retired and moved back to the town, back to the family homestead. He was well-educated, well-traveled, and the minister found him to be a breath of fresh air. He had a strong speaking voice, and when he wasn't assisting in the worship service or singing in the choir, everybody could still hear him when the congregation would say some words together.

Every Sunday, they would say the Lord's Prayer together. When they got to "Forgive us our debts as we forgive our debtors," the retired professor would say "Forgive us our trespasses." With his strong voice, everybody could hear it. It used to annoy the minister.

"Forgive us our debts ... Forgive us our trespasses."

One day during coffee hour, he moved over to the man and said, "I notice that you say, 'Forgive us our trespasses,' even when the rest of us say, 'Debts.' I know you grew up in this church, and people around here have always said, 'Debts.' I'm curious about that."

The retired professor said, "My father was the town banker. He always taught us that debts must be repaid, not forgiven. Every dime must be repaid. It was irresponsible to let a debtor off the hook. And so, our family has always said, 'Trespasses.'"

I suppose there are a lot of people who believe that, regardless of whatever words they say. Everybody has to repay everything. That old banker and his son might both be shocked to learn that the touchy word in that prayer is not translated "debt" or "trespass." The really touchy word is translated as "forgive." In Greek, the word is translated as "cancel," as in, "cancel our debts, cancel our trespasses, cancel our sins." Everything destructive is cancelled. That's what Jesus accomplished on the cross.

That's why Paul's proclamation is so powerful. We don't have to keep beating ourselves up about the things we have done or the things we ought to have done. All of that is over. God lets go of it. It's done. It is accomplished. In the final words of Jesus, "It is finished."

Perhaps you heard about the woman in a large city who claimed she was having visions of Jesus. She was a Roman Catholic, and the word spread all over the diocese. The reports reached the archbishop, who decided to check her out. "Is it true, ma'am, that you have visions of Jesus?" he asked.

"Yes," she replied.

The archbishop said, "The next time you have a vision, ask Jesus to tell you the sins that I confessed on my last confession."

The woman was stunned. "Did I hear you right, bishop? You actually want me to ask Jesus to tell me the sins of your past?"

"Exactly. Please call me if anything happens."

Ten days later, she called his office and requested him to come. He arrived within the hour. He said, "You told me on the telephone that you actually had a vision of the Lord. Did you do what I asked?"

"Yes, bishop," she replied. "I asked Jesus to tell me the sins that you confessed in your last confession."

He leaned forward with anticipation. His eyes narrowed. "What did Jesus say?"

She took his hand and looked into his eyes. "Bishop," she said, "these are his exact words: *I can't remember.*"[2]

The Christian faith happens when people accept with complete trust that their sins have been forgiven and forgotten. Somebody else may carry a grudge against you, but it isn't God. Jesus Christ has already gone to bat for you. His sacrificial death has already released you. What he accomplished on the cross continues to set us free. There is nothing that you or I could ever do to erase the power of Christ's one sacrifice.

The problem, then, is not with God. It's with us. We keep hanging on to things. Our memories of sins are longer than God's memory. Either we keep holding those things over somebody else's head, as if we exert power over them, or we are afraid to believe that God loves us so much that God put away our deficiencies and sins when Jesus died on the cross.

I suppose all of us fall into bad habits now and then. For a while, I got into the habit of apologizing for everything. Everything. Somebody would say, "It's raining today," and I'd say, "I'm sorry." I'd be sitting with some people in a restaurant and one of them would get a lousy dinner. And I'd say, "Gee, I'm sorry," as if it was my fault.

Of course, if I actually did something wrong, like cut somebody off mid-sentence in a conversation, they might bring it to my attention. I would apologize once, and then twice, and three or four more times. A week later, I would still be apologizing.

In fact, a few different times during that stretch of time, I was considering committing a few robberies and a murder or two, maybe even jaywalking, and I couldn't stop apologizing for it. What was all of that about?

I went out for breakfast with some friends. One of my friends got a runny omelet, and I said, "I'm sorry that we came here for breakfast."

He said, "Why do you keep saying that?"

"Saying what?"

"You keep apologizing. Don't you believe in the atonement?"

I said, "What?"

He said, "Jesus died once to take away the sins of the world. You keep hanging on to most of your little sins, and amplifying the rest." His words were a well-needed slap. Not a slap across the face, so much as a slap to start a baby breathing. As Paul Tillich once said somewhere, "The greatest burden and joy of the gospel is accepting God's acceptance of you."

You are forgiven, of sins committed and not committed. You are free from the burdens of your natural inclinations. God is done with giving you a report card for everything. Do you know why? Because on the day that God was grading our papers, his Son spilled gallons and gallons of Wite-Out® over everything. It happened once and for all. That's the favorite phrase of a lot of New Testament writers, including the preacher of Hebrews. In Hebrews, for instance, it means two things. First, the cross is the singular, conclusive, and final display of God's forgiveness: once and for all! And second, the cross is the single far-reaching event with universal effect — it happened once ... for all. For everybody and everything. For all.

In one of his theology books, Robert Capon tells about a married woman who made a bargain with God. After her daughter got in a terrible ski accident, the woman promised God that she would end an extramarital affair if her daughter pulled through. Her daughter began to recover, and she began to have second thoughts about the promise. To be blunt about it, the accident sent her back into her boyfriend's arms. So she goes to see Father Capon. She confesses how guilty she feels.

He listens for a while. Then she says, "I feel like I should keep my promise to God, even though I don't want to."

Robert smiled and said, "Do you really think it's going to do any good?" She is shocked, as he goes on to remind her of other people (like the Old Testament character Jephthah) who make rash promises to God.

"The problem," he goes on to explain, "is that the God of the Bible isn't interested in making any more deals with us. He has dealt with us decisively in Jesus. 'While we were still sinners, Christ died for the ungodly.' A broken promise is one more trespass nailed to the cross. We are forgiven and accepted by God. It has nothing to do with how good we are, or how bad we are, or how good we say we're going to be."

She said, "But I'm still stuck in this awful situation with this other guy. What am I going to do?"

He said, "That's your decision. But I need to tell you this: If we believe the gospel, sin can't condemn us — and just as important, not committing sin can't save us. What saves us is the free forgiveness of Jesus, not our works — not even our good works."

She stammered, "Yes, but ... I thought my religion says that ..."

"Helen, excuse my French," he replied, "but Christianity is not a religion. It's a living faith in Jesus, and you've got to trust that he takes away the sins of the world ... Religion can't do the job. The blood of goats and bulls can't take away sins; your performances on your vows have no value when it comes to getting your act together so that you can con God into being on your side. Only Jesus can take away sins; and he's done it all in one shot, for everybody."

"Yes, but ..."[3]

"Yes, but ..." How long are we going to hang on to our objections?

The way I figure it, somebody took Jesus down from the cross a long time ago. There is no reason for any of us to keep him up there.

---

1. Thomas G. Long, "Bold in the Presence of God: Atonement in Hebrews," *Interpretation*, Vol. 52, No. 1 (January 1998), p. 53.

2. This version is retold by Brennan Manning, *The Ragamuffin Gospel* (Multnomah, Oregon: Multnomah Publishers, 2000), pp. 115-116.

3. Robert Farrar Capon, *The Mystery of Christ ... And Why We Don't Get It* (Grand Rapids: William B. Eerdmanns, 1993).

**Proper 7
Pentecost 5
Ordinary Time 12
Romans 6:1b-11**

Thank God, We're Already Dead

If you ever find yourself on the corner of 56th Street and Lexington Avenue in New York City, stop in to see the baptismal font at St. Peter's Lutheran Church. Not long ago, a small group of tourists went for a visit. We were astonished by what we saw.

The font is off to the left, by the main entrance into the sanctuary. That in itself is appropriate, for baptism is the entry into the Christian life. We are brought into the church when we are baptized, so the people in St. Peter's put the font right by the door.

But this particular baptismal font is unlike anything we had ever seen. It is a large deep pool. It's elevated, about chest high as I remember. A casual visitor might confuse it for a hot tub, large enough for three or four people. But there are no spa jets inside, and the water, as I touched it, was quite chilly.

I asked the pastor of that church, "How do baptisms get done at St. Peter's Lutheran?"

"Just like anywhere else," he replied.

"Do people get dunked in the Lutheran church?"

He answered, "Some do. Others stand outside the font, and water is sprinkled on their heads."

"The most important thing," he added, "is that, however we do the baptism, sprinkling or dunking, we have to use enough water to kill people."

Like a lot of ministers, I have been accused of using a lot of water when I baptize people. Sometimes the benediction is barely over, the baptismal family reassembles for pictures, and the sexton is standing close at hand with a mop. In fact, in my first church after seminary, I tried to be generous with the water whenever it was time to baptize. Once I took a pitcher of water and dumped it on the head of some unsuspecting child. The mother was shocked, and thought I was trying to drown her son.

Theologically speaking, I was.

Paul says, "We die when we are baptized." Whether you remember your baptism or not, you died at the baptismal font. That is one of the keys to what it means to be a Christian.

Most of the time in this church, we baptize little children. We don't often know what to expect. The baby could start screaming (and we've had a couple of those), or the baby could coo and smile. Either way, the cuteness factor is pretty high. We also have the tradition of walking the infant down the aisle and introducing her or him into the household of God. Nobody has ever frowned when that happens. Usually most of us are melting into a brief moment of proxy parenthood.

But Paul reminds us that something deeper is going on. At the moment of baptism, we are so deeply united with Christ that we are "buried" with him. Our entire life up to that point has been finished off, and now something new begins. Christian baptism is not a ceremony on anybody's social calendar. It is not a predictable little ritual at a certain time in a person's life. At its deepest meaning, baptism is the event when we are marked as clearly as a Jewish child being circumcised. Life is going to be different from that day forward.

In one of her short stories, Flannery O'Connor tells about a four-year-old boy named Harry Ashfield. He lives in an apartment with parents who neglect him. Their lives are more concerned with drinking, partying, and recovering from hangovers. A cleaning lady takes young Harry to hear a preacher down by the river. Harry has never heard anything like that preacher. As the preacher stands hip deep in the river, he speaks about Jesus and a kingdom of God where every child is safe. Little Harry starts paying attention.

"Hey, preacher," cries out Mrs. Connin, the cleaning lady. "I'm keeping a boy from town today. I don't think he has ever been baptized."

The preacher says, "Bring him over to me." Turning to Harry, he adds, "Have you ever been baptized?"

Harry asks what that means. The preacher says, "If I baptize you, you'll be able to go to the kingdom of Christ. You'll be washed in the river of suffering, son, and you'll go by the deep river of life. Do you want that?"

That sounded pretty good to Harry. He wouldn't have to return to the neglect of his parent's apartment.

"You won't be the same again," the preacher said. "You'll count." And he takes the boy, swings him upside down, and plunges him into the water. The child comes up, gasping for air. Then the preacher says, "You count now."

At the end of the day, Mrs. Connin takes Harry home. Everything is different for him now. He wants no part of his parents' parties. He is no longer comfortable being cooped up in their apartment while they ignore him. All he wants is to go back down to the river, where he can jump in and go looking for the kingdom of Christ.[1]

Paul says, "The old life dies when we get baptized." All our sins are killed off through Christ's death. All our destructiveness is destroyed. Everything that kept us from the joy and freedom of the gospel is now loosed, and we are free to live in the love of Jesus Christ. Provided, of course, that we let the old life die.

In a book on leadership, Garry Wills writes about Harriet Tubman, the remarkable slave woman who led African slaves to freedom by way of the Underground Railroad. That invisible railroad came through these parts, and some of the whistle stops were in eastern Pennsylvania.

Here is a remarkable detail about her. When Harriet Tubman was a teenager, she tried to stop the beating of a fellow worker. Her master hit her on the head, and the blow broke her skull. Harriet lingered near death for weeks. For the rest of her life she suffered from occasional catatonic spells due to the injury. But the injury also set her free.

As Wills notes, "The blow that cracked Tubman's skull struck off her psychic chains. She had already died once; she had nothing to lose."[2]

Ever notice? Sometimes people can have an experience when they were as good as dead. When they emerge, everything is fresh and new. They are not bound and held captive as they once were. In a very real sense, life begins after something has died.

Paul says that this experience lies at the heart of the Christian life. For a couple of chapters, he has been arguing on behalf of grace. As he continues to remind us, God saves us through the death and resurrection of Jesus Christ. We are made righteous, not by our own righteous deeds, but by the righteous work of Christ's sacrificial love. In the cross of Jesus, God has forgiven us even before we knew we needed to be forgiven. The grace of God surrounds us. We can't earn it; we can only trust it and welcome its power in our lives.

Not a bad deal, says the critic. We sin and God forgives. If that's true, we can keep sinning and God will keep forgiving. In fact, we can do something really, really bad, and God will let us off the hook.

But Paul says, "No!" Baptized people must not keep sinning, because they have passed out of a life of sin. Look at what happened: The *old you* was drowned in the baptismal font. Now you are a *new creation*, raised to live a new life. All the powers that hurt and destroy don't have any dominion over you.

A man was talking to me about his gambling problem. It started small: the football pool, a few lottery tickets. Before he knew it, he was taking grocery money and losing it in the slot machines in Atlantic City. Then it got worse. He confessed, "I lost my job, I lost my house. I lost everything and everybody dear to me. I sank so low that I wanted to lose my life. Then I realized I already had lost that life. Everything was gone, and I couldn't pretend otherwise. That was the day when my life began to turn around."

That may sound harsh. Some of us would like to coast along and get by on our own steam. Sure, we get into a little trouble now and then. Everybody does. Most of the time we merely recalibrate the carburetor, without ever getting a whole new engine. We don't allow any interruptions to affect our schedule, our pocketbook, or what we do after dark. Paul sounds rather blunt when he claims that we cannot live unless the old life has died.

But then again, some people are lifted right out of the dust, because they were willing to let go of the wreckage they once suffered.

I was talking with a woman in the hospital. She was there because she lost her gall bladder. But what she wanted to talk about was losing her life. "I married a man when I was twenty," she said, "and my son was born six months later. Shortly after that, my husband drove off and never came back. I didn't know if I would ever make it." But she did. Forty years later, she says that ending became her beginning. A whole new life began when it looked like she reached the end of the road.

From time to time, we lose jobs. We give up routines. We watch our children grow up and move away. We change addresses. We lose marriages. We mourn loved ones. All of these losses are real, and hurtful — and all of them are also reminders that we cannot completely become Christian until we say, "Good-bye" to the old ways.

Remember that poem by T. S. Eliot? It's an Epiphany poem called "The Gift of the Magi." One of the three Wise Men reflects on seeing the newborn Christ child, and he says, "Were we led all that way for birth or death? There was a birth, certainly ... I shall be glad of another death."³

It is a curious line. In Christ, death looks like birth. When Jesus is born, the whole world is silently, secretly, changed. Because of the child in that manger, because of the things he has said and done, everything is different. So Eliot puts those words on a Magi's lips, confessing that he is "no longer at ease in the old dispensation."

Paul says, "Don't you know that all of us who have been baptized into Christ Jesus were baptized into his death? We have been buried with him by baptism into death, so that, just as Christ was raised from the dead by the glory of the Father, so we too might walk in newness of life."

Now, look. According to our church calendar, we are scheduled to baptize a little girl in two weeks. She is a precious little child of God. I am sure she is going to smile at you and win you over. She is a precious gift of God who is being raised by her loving parents. Two Sundays from today, a lot of people are going to be thrilled and delighted when she is baptized.

I have only one request to make. After we baptize her, would somebody please tell her what she has gotten herself into?

---

1. Flannery O'Connor; "The River," *A Good Man is Hard to Find and Other Stories* (New York: Harcourt Brace Jovanovich, 1983), p. 44.

2. Garry Wills, *Certain Trumpets: The Call of Leaders* (New York: Simon and Schuster, 1994), p. 41.

3. T. S. Eliot, "The Gift of the Magi," *Selected Poems* (New York: Harcourt Brace Jovanovich, 1964), p. 98.

**Proper 8
Pentecost 6
Ordinary Time 13
Romans 6:12-23**

Slaves Of A Different Master

Earlier this week somebody asked what the sermon was about. I said, "I'm preaching about slavery." That was a good way to stop a conversation.

Slavery. In Romans 6, Paul talks about slavery. It was an established institution of his time. There is no evidence that he tried to reform it. One of his letters was written to a slave owner named Philemon. During one of his vacations in jail, Paul met a runaway slave named Onesimus. They got to talking, and Onesimus became a Christian. When his sentence was up, Paul put a letter in his hand, and sent him back to his owner, who was also a Christian. And Paul says, "Now you get him back, as more than a slave — he's a brother." It was a nice thing to say, but the young man was still a slave.

You might remember that Paul likes to give advice in his letters. Sometimes he gives advice to all the key figures of a household. "Husbands, give your lives for your wives. Wives, give your selves to your husbands. Children, obey your parents. And slaves, obey your earthly masters with fear and trembling" (Ephesians 5 and 6).

Paul was a preacher. Even if he was so inclined, there was no way he could reform an institution like slavery, which was the economic backbone of the Roman empire. Slavery sounds strange and repulsive to us, but it was a part of his life and his culture. So much so, that he could see slavery as an image — or a picture — of some of the fundamental relationships in life.

He signs this letter to the Romans with the words, "Paul, a slave of Jesus Christ." The word in Greek is *doulos*. That can be translated "slave." It can be translated as "servant."

I was speaking somewhere, and was about to read the opening words from this letter. Right before I read the text, I realized there were a number of African-Americans in the congregation. I didn't know how they would feel about slavery, so I changed it on my feet. I made it, "Paul, a servant of Jesus Christ." You know, it can be translated both ways.

Afterward, one of the men that I noticed came up to me and said, "I was following along in my Bible. I noticed you changed that word. Why did you change it?" I began to explain how you can translate the word both ways, and all of that. He listened with a smile on his face.

Then he said, "You know, Paul calls himself a slave. And if you're going to belong to anybody, you ought to belong to Jesus. He is a tough master, but he is more than fair. And if you belong to Jesus, nobody else can have a piece of you."

He's right. Paul believes that he has a master. In fact, if you listen to this whole passage from Romans 6, it sounds like Paul believes that everybody has a master. Somebody owns us.

That sounds strange to people like us. We live in a land where freedom is always defined as independence. If you are free, it means you are independent. For over 228 years, we have been independent from British rule. That has become the governing metaphor for American life. I am free. I am my own person. I don't need anybody else. I am an island unto myself.

That's what a lot of people want: to become independent. When I was about fifteen, I sat down to watch the Miss America pageant with my sister. We were watching the pageant for different reasons; you know, I was watching to hear all those meaningful speeches, right?

Debbie pointed to one of the candidates. "Watch that one," she said. "She is going to win."

Why? "Because she gave a really good speech about being her own person." Sure enough, she won.

Our culture would like us to believe that stuff: You are free to do whatever you want, go wherever you wish, buy whatever you desire. Meanwhile, there are a lot of people telling us what to do, where to go, what to buy. We think we're free; what we're doing is merely accepting somebody else's story.

I saw a group of teenagers at the local ice cream store on a summer night. It was a good night for ice cream. It was a typical scene: clusters of teenagers orbiting around one another, trying to think for themselves and trying to fit in. If you asked them, every one would value independence and freedom. But look at them: all the girls were wearing the same jeans. All the boys were driving their dad's expensive cars and looking cool. "Be your own person" means, "Don't be a geek. Buy your clothes at the Gap, and borrow your dad's Lexus when you go for ice cream."

Paul is right. Even in a land of freedom and liberty, somebody has shackled us in chains, whether we know it or not. The question is: *Who is yanking your chain?*

Some people are slaves to shopping. They cannot pass up a sale, even if they have a house full of things they don't need.

Some people are slaves to cholesterol. They have never met a donut or a piece of bacon they didn't like.

Some people are slaves to their jobs. They do not like their jobs, but the company is paying them too much for them to quit, so they go to work in golden handcuffs.

Some corporations are slaves to greed. Everybody answers to the bottom line. If the bottom line is not high enough, somebody has to go. In the last few years, we have had all kinds of revelations about that, but it's not news to anyone.

I have a friend who is a slave to Budweiser. If he doesn't have a drink in his system, his body drives him crazy. He's admitted that he is embarrassed about it, and he ought to be. Two weeks ago, he wrecked another truck. His friends hope it's a wake-up call.

The question is: *Who — or what — is yanking your chain?*

C. S. Lewis has a great little book about heaven and hell. It is not so much a story about the next life as it is an allegory for understanding this life. In the book, some people have been reduced to shadow creatures. Others are solid people. These divisions happen because of the choices and commitments that people make, or refuse to make, right here and now.

In one scene, a woman who is a solid person, encounters her husband, who is a shadow creature. Actually he is not one phantom, but two. The first is a great tall ghost, horribly thin and shaky, who seemed to be leading on a chain another ghost no bigger than an organ-grinder's monkey. Her husband is the little guy, and he's holding the chain, which is attached to the collar of the tall ghost.

Every time the wife asks a question, the short man yanks on the chain, and the tall ghost speaks for him. He always speaks in large, self-important tones, as if he has a reputation to maintain. She tells him that she loves him, and he yanks the chain, so that the tall actor can respond with a theatrical flourish. She tries to have a real conversation with him, for the first time in years, and he pulls the chain, so that the tall dummy will speak for him.

Pretty soon, you know why he is the ghost.

Finally she says, "Frank! Frank! Look at me. Look at me. What are you doing with that great, ugly doll? Let go of the chain. Send it away. It is you I want. Don't you see what nonsense it's talking?" Lewis says, "Merriment danced in her eyes ... her laughter was past her defenses. He was struggling hard to keep it out, but already with imperfect success." The short man was struggling against joy.[1]

Who pulls your chains? Whom do you serve?

About twenty years ago, singer Bob Dylan went through a brief spiritual phase. A lifelong Jew, he got serious about God, even thinking about becoming a Christian. He wrote some new songs, hired a back-up group of gospel singers, and went on tour. One of the songs said, "You gotta serve somebody. You gotta serve somebody. It may be the devil, or it may be the Lord, but you gotta serve somebody."

One night on tour he sang that song and the crowd began to boo. The more he sang, the more they booed. He stopped playing and left the stage. Afterward, one concert-goer said, "I didn't come to hear that kind of bologna. I'm free. I don't serve anybody but myself."

Believe me, friends, there is no greater slavery than serving only yourself.

Paul says he is a slave of Jesus. He struggles with his own urges, just like anybody else. But he knows in his gut that no good can come from listening only to his own desires. He is bound to a greater purpose than following his nose or listening to his stomach. He belongs to Jesus Christ. That is his identity. That gives him a purpose.

He says this because he knows if the only thing he does is what he wants to do, if the only opinion he listens to is his opinion or his friends' opinions, if the only purpose for his life is to cover his tail or save his skin, then he is in a whole lot of trouble.

The power of sin is so pervasive that it can take and twist our best impulses into something foul. There are so many kinds of sin that work on us and bind us. It's hard to be free for all of it.

But it's possible.

In a few minutes, we baptize a little child. We're not doing this because it's the fashionable thing to do. It's not a rite of passage. It's not a culturally sanctioned event. We are not announcing, "Here is a little child who from this day forth will be her own person." No, we're saying, "God has one more child. Before she even knows it, she belongs to God through Jesus Christ." From this day forward, we will do everything we can to nurture her into that new identity.

Just like any other child, we're going to give her something important to think about. We are going to tell her how much she is loved. We are going to teach her the story of Jesus, which is now her story and ours.

The day may come when she'll say, "Mom, do I have to go to church?" We can laugh about that; most of us have said that, some time or another. There are a lot of things in church that seem like forms of imprisonment. Like one parishioner once said to me, "Reverend, how long am I supposed to serve on this committee? It's been 42 years."

There are a lot of things in church that seem like slavery. We come here, and pray for forgiveness, and somebody tells us we're forgiven. Then across the aisle we see somebody we'd rather not ever spend any time with. And we pray, "Forgive us our debts as we forgive our debtors," and we think, "Oh, I don't want to forgive him. I'm not going to forgive him." But we've said those prayers, and we are bound to those words.

There are some things we learn through the church that feel like burdens. We get to know somebody, and discover that they are hurting, and we don't know what to do. We don't know how to help. It would be a lot easier to slip away and ignore them. But we can't do that because we are bound together through Christ, even when we'd rather go our own way.

There are some occasions when the church decides it has to do something. A widow with seven kids comes to our neighborhood. She speaks with an accent. We don't know where we're going to put them. We are wondering how much money this is going to cost, and what else this is going to put off the plate. But we know it's the right thing to do, and we are bound to the work of justice and new beginnings.

There are a lot of times when it would be easier to do our own thing. To play it safe. To back away. To retreat in comfort. Then we come to church and remember that we are bound to Jesus Christ. Not only that, he has bound himself to us. We are never free from him.

The good news, of course, is that in this kind of bondage, there is great freedom.

---

1. C. S. Lewis, *The Great Divorce* (New York: Macmillan Publishing Co., 1946), pp. 113-114.

**Proper 9
Pentecost 7
Ordinary Time 14
Romans 7:15-25a**

At War With Myself

In a certain church, a woman was leading the congregation in the prayer of confession. She called the people to confess, reminding them of the sin within their hearts, and then all joined in reading the prayer of confession. She paused for the silent confession, and she kept pausing for a good long while. So long, in fact, that the people began to rustle as they waited for the next part of the service.

It was awkward, and more than a few worshipers thought she had lost her place or mislaid the piece of paper with the proper words written on it. Finally someone was overheard to murmur, "Just hurry up and forgive us, so we can shake hands and sit down."

I wonder sometimes, if that is how we feel when we come to the prayer when we confess our sins. For some people, it seems rather perfunctory. Read a short prayer that mentions some things that you may or may not have done or felt. Pause for a moment to appear properly penitential. Then move on to more cheerful and uplifting aspects of the service.

We don't talk much about sin any more. It's not a topic of public discourse, and if it is, it's usually reduced to some obvious misdeed of some prominent public figure. And since we would rather joke about our public figures on late night television than forgive them, we often regard sin as some extravagant mistake that any intelligent person would laugh about.

We hear about a congressman accused of taking bribes and making a fool of himself. We pretend to be shocked, and poke fun at his rough language. It is our way of saying it couldn't happen to us. Either we are not that stupid, or we are not that extravagant.

In other words, "Just hurry up and forgive us, so we can shake hands and sit down."

We don't like looking too closely at the dark side of human existence, unless, of course, we can turn it into some form of entertainment. But all of us know it's there. All of us are acutely aware of the dangerous power of sin.

Years ago, there was a *Peanuts* cartoon where Lucy was explaining to her brother Linus about the division in the human heart. She drew a picture of a heart, put a line down the middle, and said, "One side is filled with hate and the other side is filled with love. These are the two forces which are constantly at war with each other." Linus says, "I think I know just what you mean. I can feel them fighting."[1]

So Lucy has him tip to one side, so the good part can drain into the evil part. If only it were that easy!

The Apostle Paul describes a constant war going on within himself. "I do not do what I want, but I do the very thing I hate ... I can will what is right, but I cannot do it. For I do not do the good I want, but the evil I do not want is what I do ... I find it a rule that when I want to do what is good, evil lies close at hand. I delight in the law of God in my inmost self, but I see in my body another law at war with the law of my mind. Wretched man that I am!"

A lot of people don't like the Apostle Paul. They think he ought to act more like a twenty-first century person. But the truth is, he understands us better that we understand ourselves. He knows that to be human is to find yourself in one tangled mess after another. Sometimes the mess is of our own making. Sometimes it comes from our own rebellion. Sometimes our best efforts are corrupted by the power of sin. Today he simply holds up a mirror and invites us to look at ourselves.

Paul speaks about his own spiritual struggles in the seventh chapter of Romans. He holds up himself as a sermon illustration. A lot of scholars think he is talking about the old life before he became a Christian. He says, "I am a slave of sin, a captive to the law of sin," even though one chapter before he said we are no longer under sin's dominion. Now we are slaves to the righteousness of God. Our lives are directed toward serving God.

That is true, as far as it goes. But most of chapter 7 is in the present tense. He speaks about a war continuing within himself. He tries to do the right thing, but it doesn't always work out that way. He knows he has been claimed by Jesus Christ, called to live as God's apostle, and filled with the gifts of the Holy Spirit. He knows this; yet it is one thing to know it, it is another to live it day to day. He says, "I detect another force at work in my life." Even his best efforts can be corrupted. Such is the power of sin.

Walker Percy once asked:

> *Why is it that the self — though it professes to be loving, caring, to prefer peace to war, concord to discord, life to death; to wish other selves well, not ill — in fact secretly relishes wars and rumors of war, news of plane crashes, assassinations, mass murders, obituaries, to say nothing of local news about acquaintances dropping dead in the streets, gossip about neighbors getting in fights or being detected in sexual scandals, embezzlements, and other disgraces?*[2]

Paul says we are at war with ourselves. Why do we do some of the things we do?

I went to see a man in the hospital. He smoked cigarettes his whole life. The doctor told him he had to stop, so he changed doctors. He kept smoking. He got emphysema. He got really sick. He went to the hospital. They told him he had to stop. He kept smoking. He got lung cancer. He went back into the hospital. They removed a lung. The day he got out, he started smoking again. They wheeled him into the hospital again. This time he had burned out his trachea. They had to remove his voice box. They put a little tube in his throat. I heard about it. I went to see him. He wasn't in his room. I looked all over the place. Finally one of the nurses said, "I'll show you where he is." She took me downstairs, out the back door. There he was, out in the courtyard, taking a long drag from the Marlboro that he put in the hole in his throat.

Why does he do that? Doesn't he know better?

There's a woman who likes being a good friend. She has a pleasant personality, a gentle demeanor, a pretty smile. She loves to listen to people when she meets them for coffee. She's very friendly when she stands next to people at a soccer game. People tell her all kinds of things. She listens sympathetically, intuitively nods her head. Then she excuses herself, pulls out her cell phone, dials a number, and says, "You'll never believe what I just heard."

One friend got damaged by her gossip and confronted her. "Why did you treat me like that?" There were a lot of tears, an apology, "I'll never do it again." The accuser slips away, still wounded. The woman watches her go.

Then she pulls out the cell phone, dials the number, and says, "Can you believe the nerve of her?"

Why does she do it? Doesn't she know better?

Paul says, "I don't understand my own actions." We can take him at his word. All of us do stupid things, destructive things, things that don't make any sense. I remember when I was ten years old, I threw a snowball at the windshield of a moving police car, and hit it. What was I thinking? Surely I knew better, but I couldn't help myself.

A few years ago, some of us went to Haiti. We lived among the poor in an effort to understand how two-thirds of the world's people live. Rice and beans were our daily diet, except for the day we received fried goat and fresh Spam. The experience opened my eyes to see just something of what it must be like. Then we hopped on a plane and flew back to New York. As soon as we hit the ground, I begged our group to stop at a Burger King so I could gobble down two double Whoppers with cheese. What was I thinking? When it dawned on me what I had done, it made me sick. Of course, the Whoppers didn't help.

Sometimes, we like to rebel against some standard. Some authority says this is the way things are, and we say, "No, it's not." Somebody says, "Short hair," and we grow it long. Dad says, "Turn down the music," and we turn it up. Most of us have been there.

I had a philosophy professor in college. It was a class on consciousness, if you can imagine that — for college students. This guy would walk over by the window, then put his foot up on the desk. He would stand in front of a "No Smoking" sign and light up a hand-rolled cigarette. What was that all about? I think you know.

Earlier in this chapter, Paul says, "I wouldn't have known what it is to covet, except the law said, 'Thou shalt not covet.' As soon as I heard that law, I started wanting what other people have."

It's like the mother who says, "Now, kids, don't get dirty. Stay out of the mud." The kids look at one another. There's mud? Where's the mud? Next thing you know, they are up to their ears in it.

She yells at them, "I told you to stay out of the mud!" But, Mother, they didn't know it existed until you told them to stay out of it.

Paul says this is the dark power of sin. Sin takes something good, like the Law of God, and twists it all around. The Law says don't covet. Paul says, "Sin, seizing an opportunity, produced in me all kinds of covetousness. I was deceived, and it killed me."

Now pay attention here: He was trying to do the right thing, and he got all messed up. Do you think it's possible for people to comb their hair, go to church, sing the hymns, pray the prayers, make the offering — and then turn on one another? Attack one another? Yes, it can happen. Even at the point of our best efforts — personally, nationally, ecclesially — sin seizes whatever it can.

In one of her books, Kathleen Norris writes about "good old sin." That's how some of the ancient Christians called it, sin as a persistent and troublesome force in our lives. She writes:

> *These days, when someone commits an atrocity, we tend to sigh and say, "That's human nature." But our attitude would seem wrong-headed to the desert monks, who understood human beings to be part of the creation that God called good, special in that they are made in the image of God. Sin is an aberration, not natural for us at all. This is why Gregory of Nyssa speaks so often of "returning to the grace of that image what was established in you from the beginning." Gregory saw it as our lifelong task to find out what part of the divine image God has chosen to reveal in us ... We can best do this by realistically determining how God has made us — what our primary faults and temptations are, as well*

> *as our gifts — not that we might better "know our-
> selves," or in modern parlance, "feel good about our-
> selves," but in order that we might become instruments
> of divine grace for other people, and eventually return
> to God.*[3]

The early Christian mystics understood both the perils and possibilities of the human heart. The great danger is rooted in the ever-present power of sin, that frequently fatal tendency to turn in on ourselves and turn away from God. But the great possibilities come in the power of God through Jesus Christ. In Christ, God has come right into our tangled messes to rescue and restore. Jesus came to us, and our sin was so pervasive that we killed him. But God raised him up. And Jesus Christ keeps after us, keeps rescuing, keeps restoring — until the day comes when he turns his kingdom over to the Father — washed, renewed, redeemed.

That is our Christian hope. We trust that the work of Christ is greater than the work we can do. On the cross, he takes away the sin of the world, and serves notice that God's forgiveness can cancel every debt and trespass. In the power of his resurrection, he remains with those whom he has claimed, offering guidance and help in time of need.

That is one reason why we don't rush through our prayers on Sunday morning. We take the time to name before God the places where we have fallen short and fallen down. We try to be as honest with ourselves as Christ our judge.

Then we take his hand and let him lift us out of the mud, always trusting that we have a second chance and a new beginning.

---

1. As discussed by Robert L. Short, *The Gospel According to Peanuts* (Louisville: Westminster John Knox Press, 1965), pp. 35-39.

2. Walker Percy, *Signposts in a Strange Land* (New York: Farrar, Straus, and Giroux, 1991), p. 153.

3. Kathleen Norris, *The Cloister Walk* (New York: Riverhead Books, 1996), p. 127.

**Proper 10
Pentecost 8
Ordinary Time 15
Romans 8:1-11**

No Longer Damned

The text for today is Romans, chapter 8, verse 1: "Therefore, there is no condemnation for those who are in Christ Jesus."

I'm not sure all of you were paying attention, so I'm going to say it again. The text for today is Romans, chapter 8, verse 1: "Therefore, there is no condemnation for those who are in Christ Jesus."

You know, this is really important, so I'm going to say it one more time. Romans, chapter 8, verse 1: "Therefore, there is no condemnation for those who are in Christ Jesus."

You know what the problem is in the church today? I don't know a lot of people who believe that verse.

They look at all those other verses that talk about the way you need to live, and what you need to do, and how you need to keep busy doing the Lord's work. I hear people talk about how hard they are trying, how fast they are moving, how tired they are trying to do the right thing. I also hear them speaking about how they don't measure up: "I don't have enough time for my children." "I don't like the way my house looks." "I wish I had more hours in the day." "This dress makes my legs look fat." Nobody believes that verse from Romans 8, verse 1: "Therefore, there is no condemnation for those who are in Christ Jesus."

You listen to some people, and it sounds like the Christian life is all about being condemned. Somewhere in our past, we had some finger-wagging preacher trying to scare us out of hell.

I recall such a minister, now in his seventies, who used to stand up and scold people for things they hadn't even done yet. He would tell them, "Don't drink, dance, or chew, or date the girls that do."

He used to stop by the youth group meeting, listen to what they were planning to do, and start giving them speeches.

"So you want to go bowling?" he said. "A lot of good people have gotten stuck in the alley. Don't let it happen to you."

One time, they were talking about going to see a Disney film. The minister heard about it and stopped by. He said, "Don't even think about it — it's a waste of time. The Lord is coming back at any moment. When he comes, do you want him to find you in a movie theater?"

He ruined a lot of fun evenings with speeches like that. More than that, he tried to influence an entire generation by giving the distinct impression that the Christian life is a matter of duty and obligation. The duty is so demanding, the obligation is so heavy, that nobody can live up to such requirements.

Paul says, in Romans 8, verse 1, "Therefore, there is no condemnation for those who are in Christ Jesus." I wish I knew somebody who believed that verse. I wish I knew a church that lived as if that verse is true.

I received a call from a family to do the funeral of their mother. Two of the family members don't go to church. Another is a Presbyterian in the Midwest. She told the funeral director, "Get a Presbyterian minister." So I got the phone call.

The three of them told me about their mother. She had good domestic skills. She could cook and sew. She was a devoted wife. There was a lull in the conversation.

Just then, the youngest daughter said, "Reverend, we should probably be honest with you. Our mom never went to church. She got thrown out of her church."

I said, "That sounds interesting."

The story began to emerge. She was born into an Irish family on the west side of town. There were lots of children, all of them were baptized in an Irish church. Then she fell in love with a Baptist and her family turned on her. Her neighbors tried to talk her out of it, but she married him anyway. She loved him.

One day, the priest knocked at the door and called for her. He didn't come in. She came to the door. He said, "Mary Catherine, you cannot come back to the church. You are no longer welcome."

He turned and walked away, and the young bride never went into a church ever again."

I said, "I'm sorry about that."

The other daughter said, "Mom always believed in the Lord. She read her Bible every day. She prayed all the time. She never lost her faith. It's just that they threw her out of the church for marrying a Baptist."

"After that," another grown child said, "none of our aunts and uncles had nothing to do with us, even at Christmas. We were like the black sheep. But Mom told us Bible stories, and we talked about them."

"Once," another said, "Mom had a newspaper clipping. I think it was back in the 1960s. The Vatican decreed Catholics couldn't be excommunicated for marrying Protestants. Mom showed us that article, and we said, 'You can go back to church.'

"She said, 'No, I can't. I can't go back.' And she never did."

Then they told me one more story. When their mother was near death, at one point she reached out her hand, as if she were reaching for something or someone. It was as if she was remembering her favorite hymn, "Precious Lord, Take My Hand." She reached, and then she was gone.

We sat in silence for a minute, and then concluded: The church let her down, but Jesus did not.

That story reminds me of Romans 8, verse 1. Do you remember the text? "Therefore, there is no condemnation for those who are in Christ Jesus."

At this point in its history, the Christian church has a lot of brand names. It doesn't matter if we are Presbyterian, Baptist, Mennonite, Orthodox, or Catholic. What matters is that we belong to Jesus. That's what it means to be "in Christ Jesus." We belong to him. Nobody can take that relationship away. One of the things that most brands of Christians do is to declare who belongs and who doesn't, who fits in and who stands outside, who speaks with the right vocabulary and who does not, who believes fervently enough and who has an inadequate faith, who votes the right way and who votes the wrong way. We want to declare all these things, as if we are the real authorities. As if we are God's gatekeepers. How shortsighted!

It reminds me of what Kathleen Norris says about predestination. The South Dakota writer says:

> *The most intriguing thing about the doctrine of predestination (which John Calvin inherited from Saint Augustine) is not his belief that some are gratituously predestined by God to eternal salvation and some to damnation but that no one but God knows who is who. There, among the heroin addicts, is one destined for eternal joy. There, among the faithful of an ordinary church, is one destined for damnation ... It strikes me that only a French lawyer could have come up with so complex, if not bizarre, a justification for treating all people as if they could be among the elect, the chosen of God. If the history of Christianity has taught me nothing else, it reminds me that it takes all kinds.*
>
> *Evil acts daily oppress this world we call home, but we do not know enough to say that another (person) is irredeemable, condemned, destined for damnation. That judgment is reserved for God.*[1]

How can we limit God's judgment and God's grace to our own understanding?

There is a family where one cousin did time in prison for armed robbery. He couldn't feed his family, so he put a gun in his pocket and robbed a gas station. There is another cousin who served in the first Gulf War as a demolitions expert with the Marines. He blew up things for a living. Mostly he blew up things that belonged to other people. Can you help me sort out which one belongs to God, and which one does not? It's a mystery to me. I think only God can sort it out.

All I can say is Romans, chapter 8, verse 1: "Therefore, there is no condemnation for those who are in Christ Jesus."

Tony Campolo tells the story somewhere about getting a phone call at home. A voice said, "We need a minister. Our friend died, and we need a minister to do the funeral."

"When's the funeral?" Tony asked.

"Tomorrow."

Tony said, "I will be there." So the next day, he put on his preacher suit and went over to the cemetery.

He was walking up to the graveside to do the service as people were gathering. Not knowing the man who died, he was putting together some thoughts as he walked. Just when he resolved to do this, he looked up to smile at the people who were gathered. There were about a dozen men. No women, all men. Something began to dawn on him, so he asked, "How did your friend Jerry die?"

One of them said, "He died of AIDS."

Tony said, "Did Jerry have any family?"

"They haven't talked to one another in years. We looked in on him when he got sick. I guess we were the closest thing to family he had."

Tony said, "Did Jerry have a church background?"

"Sure, Preacher, all of us grew up in a church. That's why we wanted a Christian minister."

Tony said, "Well, it's my privilege to be here. I thought I would read some passages from the Bible."

One man said, "Could you read that passage from John 3:16?"

Tony said, "Sure." He started, "God so loved the word that he gave his only begotten Son," and suddenly the rest of them chimed "so that whosoever believes in him would not perish but have eternal life."

Somebody else spoke up, "How about that passage about many rooms in the Father's house?"

Tony said, "Sure," so he read from John 14: "In my Father's house there are many rooms...." By the time he said the first half of the Bible verse, all the guys were joining in, "and I go to prepare a place for you, so that where I am, you may be also."

Someone else said, "I remember where Paul says, 'Nothing shall separate us from the love of God,' " and most of them started completing the verse.

Tony said, "Here I was, a straight guy, with a dozen gay men, doing a funeral for their dead friend. Every single one of them knows the scriptures. They grew up memorizing those words. We stood there trading verses for about half an hour. It was incredible!"

Finally he said, "All of you know your Bible. Where do you guys go to church?" And they got very quiet. They didn't say a thing.

Tony said, "Friends, I'm going to give you one more verse, and then we're going to have a prayer. The verse is Romans, chapter 8, verse 1: 'Therefore, there is no condemnation for those who are in Christ Jesus.' "

That verse was still hanging in the air, when one of the men said, "I wish I knew a church that believed so strongly in Jesus that it would take me in."[2]

"No condemnation." I believe it says, "No condemnation for those who are in Christ Jesus."

Is there anybody here who believes that verse?

---

1. Kathleen Norris, *Amazing Grace: A Vocabulary of Faith* (New York: Riverhead, 1998), p. 168.

2. From a personal conversation, August, 2002.

**Proper 11
Pentecost 9
Ordinary Time 16
Romans 8:12-25**

Speaking Of The Spirit

There's something you might not know about the Apostle Paul. The Apostle Paul never tells any stories about Jesus. But he does talk about the meaning of those stories. For instance, Paul never tells the story of Christmas, but he does say, "When the fullness of time had come, God sent his Son, born of a woman, born under the law, in order to redeem those who were under the law" (Galatians 4:4). He doesn't speak of shepherds, angels, or Magi, but he talks about the meaning of Jesus' birth.

Paul never tells about the crucifixion — never a word about the nails in the flesh, the cry of dereliction, the ripping of the Temple curtain — but he has a lot to say about the cross: "We proclaim Christ crucified, a stumbling block to Jews and foolishness to Gentiles, but to those who are the called, both Jews and Greeks, Christ the power of God and the wisdom of God" (1 Corinthians 1:23-24).

In fact, Paul doesn't have much to say about the story of Easter — he never mentions an empty tomb or angels in white. He does, however, affirm Jesus Christ is risen. "Death has been swallowed up in victory ... Thanks be to God, who gives us the victory through our Lord Jesus Christ" (1 Corinthians 15:54, 57)

Given this pattern, what do you think Paul has to say about the Day Of Pentecost? Absolutely nothing. There is no word of the rushing wind, Peter's sermon, or the testimony in various languages. But Paul does have a few things to say about the Holy Spirit. Listen:

> *For all who are led by the Spirit of God are children of God. For you did not receive a spirit of slavery to fall back into fear, but you have received a spirit of adoption. When we cry, "Abba! Father!" it is that very Spirit bearing witness with our spirit that we are children of God, and if children, then heirs, heirs of God and joint heirs with Christ — if, in fact, we suffer with him so that we may also be glorified with him.*
> — Romans 8:14-17

The Holy Spirit is the most mysterious person of the Trinity. Presbyterians, for the most part, get stuck when it comes to ghost stories. We focus a lot of energy on God, who holds both Old and New Covenants together. We have a lot to say about Jesus, who lived, and died, and lives again. But we don't always know what to tell our children about the Holy Spirit. As people of order and reason, the topic has often been elusive, as fleeting as a ghost in the night.

This isn't the case among churches that emphasize experience, excitement, and enthusiasm. Most of them have much more to say about the Spirit. For example, I remember a memorable line by a Pentecostal preacher. He stood up one day and said, "The Spirit is the electrical current in this congregation. Whenever God sends the Spirit, we always get charged up." That's what he said. A few months after he said it, the congregation had problems with its fuse box, and needed to have the whole building rewired. Perhaps the amperage was too high.

As we heard in the short section from his letter to the Romans, the Apostle Paul took a quieter approach. He struggles to define what he means by the Holy Spirit. A few verses before our text, he said the Holy Spirit is God dwelling in us (8:9). Then he claims the Holy Spirit is "Christ in (all of) you" (8:10). He goes on to affirm that the very power of God that raised Jesus from the dead is the power that raises us — first, raises us out of bed; and finally raises us out of the grave. Either way, the Holy Spirit is God himself giving us life and power and peace. If we are looking for a definition of the Holy Spirit, phrases like these are the best Paul can do.

But we still struggle to find something to say. In the four verses we heard today, Paul doesn't talk so much about the person as the work of the Holy Spirit. What does the Spirit do? There are three answers in the text.
1. The Spirit leads us.
2. The Spirit frees us.
3. The Spirit witnesses through us.

Behind them is the affirmation that, through the Spirit of God, we belong to God. Thanks to the Spirit, we are God's children.

Sometimes people know who they are by who they look like. Others may say to us, "You're the spitting image of your mother," or "You talk like your dad." One of the frightening things that happens when children grow up and become parents themselves is when they suddenly hear their parent's words coming out of their own mouths. They may have vowed it never would happen, but it happens anyway.

Sometimes we are known by whom we resemble. In the Gospels, some people ask of Jesus in Nazareth, "Isn't this Joseph's son?" (Luke 4:22). Others weren't so sure. They discerned that Jesus was led by a deeper purpose and motivation. Not merely appearance, but action. What does God do? That is what we should do.

In our text, Paul reminds us that we are known by how we act. "If you are led by the Spirit of God, you show that you are God's very own children." All of us are made in the image of God, but when we act like God acts, we show that we belong to God. Not only are we God's spitting image, we are called upon to do his work. We are invited to act as God acts toward us.

Needless to say, that is something of a challenge. A lot of times we follow our own spirits. We act our own ways. We behave as if God is no force in our lives whatsoever. We do what comes naturally. The fact of the matter is, some of that can look pretty ugly. Here we are: prone to jealousy and superstition, always bending in our own direction, always wanting to know, "What's in it for me?" If we do anything that reflects the justice and mercy of God — if it coincides with what we naturally want to do — that's one thing. If it doesn't coincide with our desires, we say, "We're going to be ourselves."

Believe me when I say that "being yourself" is not all it's cracked up to be. The gift of God is the Spirit of God. Christians believe that Someone Else's Spirit comes to claim us and direct us. When we reduce our daily behavior simply to saying, "I was being myself," that means we follow the will of the "flesh," and not the will of God. God gives us a spirit of freedom, not a spirit of license, not a spirit of "I can do whatever I want." There is no passage in the Bible that says, "Be yourself." No, we are told to become who we were baptized to be. The only way to grow into our Christian identity is to follow the lead of the Holy Spirit, who offers us the direction of holiness, truth, and mercy.

The greatest human need is to justify ourselves. Do whatever we want, and say, "I deserve this, because...." But the news of the gospel is that God has already justified us in Jesus Christ. We don't have to strive to measure up or prove ourselves. God has already shored up the difference. For our part, we only have to trust that it's true, live as people who have been freed by the death and resurrection of Jesus, and trust that nothing can ever separate us from the love of God through Christ Jesus our Lord.

It really comes down to this: Do you belong to God, yes or no? "All who are led by the Spirit of God are children of God." That's what Paul has to say to us.

I usually pick my sermon titles by Monday or Tuesday. Sometimes picking a title is a trap, because you think you know what you're going to say before you finish preparing to say it. By the time Sunday arrives, God leads me down a different path to say something else. When I thought about the Romans passage earlier in the week, I was taken by the word "adoption." It's a rare word in the New Testament, and I started thinking about the church. Thanks to the Holy Spirit, we are adopted in a blended family, with our Single Parent who art in heaven. But the more I think about it, and now that the bulletin deadline is past, I think I might retitle this sermon, "Why 'Being Yourself' is a Bad Idea."

Today, I am not speaking against being authentic, or being real, or taking stock of the gifts and abilities which God has given us. No, the gifts of God are to be used by God. If you are a baker or a painter, you need to bake or paint because God gave you that gift and intended it to be used.

Rather, my concern is getting out from under the burden of being an individual, getting free of the burden of being "your own person" while the rest of the world is ignored and left to rot. The gospel of Jesus Christ lifts the burden of thinking the world is mine to conquer, mine to plunder, and mine to do with whatever I feel like doing.

There is nothing in the gospel to justify that kind of thinking. What we hear instead is the news that we belong to God, and through God, we belong to one another. Coming to terms with that central truth is what it means, I think, to be led by the Holy Spirit.

I saw it happen. We took the confirmation class down to Philadelphia for an overnight. It seemed like a good idea to see what the church looks like in a different place. There we were: four adults with ten adolescents, on a sunny weekend. You could feel the energy surging in our ten young people. Developmentally they are at a time in their life when they are spreading their wings ... and testing the adults all around them. I know some adults who might think that taking a trip like that, with kids so full of energy, would be more trouble than it was worth. But that was not the case.

At lunch on that Saturday, we went to St. Vincent's Catholic Church in Germantown. That parish runs a soup kitchen in their fellowship hall. The kids in our class dished up canned ravioli and vegetables for about 200 people who came through the food line. They themselves didn't get to eat lunch until almost 2:00, and not one of our kids complained about it. I think I know why. For the moment, they knew it was more important to feed some hungry people, to do a beautiful deed for God, than to demand a fat meal for themselves. Even if they didn't have the words to explain it, they knew what it means to be led by the Spirit.

It is no coincidence that we have been working on some catechism questions with those confirmation students. The first question asks, "Who are you?" The answer is not, "I am my own person" or "I am so and so," or "The child of so and so." No, among the baptized, the first and most appropriate answer is, "I am a child of God."

We do not belong to ourselves. We belong to God. We are adopted into God's family. God willing, we will be continually haunted by the Holy Ghost, so that we might be who we were baptized to become. If our only pursuit is doing what comes naturally, then what separates us from the animals? If the only thing we do is our own thing, then we are suffocated by our own limits. As Christians we are called to be led by the Spirit, to follow the lead of the Somebody who is far more loving and wise than we are. God is greater than our own conscience, broader than our own imagination, more generous than we would normally choose to be. To live into all of that is to live into the full inheritance of all God chooses to give us.

The poet Wendell Berry sums this up when he prays these words:

> *O Thou, far off and here, whole and broken,*
> *Who in necessity and in bounty wait,*
> *Whose truth is light and dark, mute though spoken,*
> *By Thy wide grace show me Thy narrow gate.*[1]

---

1. Wendell Berry, "To the Holy Spirit," *Collected Poems* (San Francisco: North Point Press, 1984), p. 209.

Sermons On The Second Readings

For Sundays After Pentecost (Middle Third)

Complete Joy

Jeff Wedge

*To the memory of
the Rev. Dr. Richard Carl Hoeffler*

Introduction

My homiletics professor in seminary used to caution his students that sermons were an oral form. Because of this, the form of writing he advocated for sermons was a specialized form which he termed "oral writing."[1] He also insisted that the written form of a sermon was never fully a sermon. In many ways he was almost certainly correct. A written sermon is something different from a sermon delivered to a congregation as an oral presentation.

The history of great preachers is a lengthy one, and it is filled with many examples of the power and ability of some masters of this form. John Chrysostom, for example, took his very name from his ability as a preacher. Chrysostom means *golden-mouthed*. In the late fourth and early fifth centuries, Chrysostom not only was a powerful preacher, but the influence of his skill is reflected in the structure of church buildings to the present day. He had special platforms built from which to preach. From the platform he was able to be heard by more listeners, and the platforms reflected his desire to proclaim the word to more people at a time. Chrysostom's platforms are still found, in various forms, in many churches, often under pulpits or as ambos in more traditional configurations.

Few modern preachers will ever face the challenge once faced by Laurence Chaderton, the Master of Emmanuel College in Cambridge in 1584, when he had preached for a mere two hours and proposed to end his sermon. The congregation was very disappointed and some members shouted out sentiments such as, "Go on, sir! For God's sake, go on!"

In fact, the art of listening is something which is not as common as it perhaps should be today. Today, print is omnipresent and often illustrated with color pictures, and even, on the Internet, with video clips and background music. Simply listening to a sermon is something many people find difficult to do.

If the oral sermon is facing problems, the written form comes with a different set of issues to confront. The written form of sermons also has a long and venerable history. Generally a collection of sermons, particularly when arranged according to the lessons appointed for consecutive Sundays of the church year, is known as a *postil*. Originally a word to describe a commentary attached to a biblical text (from the Latin phrase, *post illa verba textus*), by the time of Luther the word meant an annual cycle of homilies.

Martin Luther wrote a number of postils during his life, and often wrote as he did to George Spalatin in August, 1521, when he sent the last portion of a manuscript of a postil to the printer. In that letter Luther included instructions about typefaces, binding, and prices for the final volume, but realized that his preferences were not likely to be followed. While Luther's often stormy relationship with printers is well beyond the scope of this volume, it is an interesting note on the history of volumes such as this.

Luther also expressed his recollection of a postil which had influenced him early in his life, and a hope that a postil could help preachers improve their sermons if they were studied before entering the pulpit. On occasion, postils were even meant to be read during worship, particularly in parishes without a pastor, for whatever reason.

In more modern times, Bishop Lajos Ordass was oppressed and imprisoned by the Communist government of Hungary, deposed from his office, and placed under house arrest for much of his life under the Communist regime. The issue was his refusal to submit to the demands of the government for the church to abdicate its prophetic position. On the few occasions after his initial imprisonment when he was allowed to preach, his words were recorded by a group of church stenographers. His sermons, as well as his public testimony at his trials, were later typed, printed, and sold to defray the costs of upkeep for the church buildings throughout the country.

These texts are more a record of actual preached sermons than those usually found in traditional postils, but they also represent another aspect of printed sermons. In a transcript of a preached sermon, there is more likely to be a clearer relation between the preacher and the congregation than in a sermon written entirely for a postil, not a congregation.

The written form of a sermon that was not originally preached is actually more of an essay based on a text than a sermon. It is certainly less oral than a transcript of an actually preached sermon. It is also more formal, and often less specifically directed at a particular situation.

The present collection is intended to help a preacher formulate thoughts about a particular lesson, not provide an easy way to avoid the hard labor of preparing to preach. I hope these sermons will present one perspective on a lesson which can be used as a basis for the actual proclamation of the Word.

The most serious problem with these sermons is that they are not particularly topical. The famous comment of Karl Barth that a Christian should read with the Bible in one hand and the daily newspaper in the other is particularly apt when considering the preparation of a sermon. As these sermons were written, the first openly gay Episcopal bishop was the subject of a national convention of that communion, a pedophile priest was killed in prison, California considered the recall of its governor, and Mel Gibson's movie about the Passion were all prominent in the nightly news. None of these news stories is mentioned in these sermons.

If these sermons had been prepared for preaching in a parish, any of these stories, in some form or another, would likely have been included, at least in passing. If they had been included here, by the time this volume was published, the topical mentions would have been historical, and could easily have forced many potential listeners to wonder when that event might have taken place. It seems likely that sermons should include appropriate references to current events, that is, events current at the time the sermons are preached.

Not that the topical references to current events necessarily need to be judgmental comments on the events. Condemnation or praise is not necessarily required, but illumination of the present situation with the light of the gospel is something basic to the preacher's task.

Thus, in some ways, the preacher's task can be understood to take the ideas in these sermons, add current events and personal reactions, and then formulate the message for a given Sunday.

In many instances there are themes which connect two or more of these lessons. This should not be a surprise, especially when the lessons are taken sequentially from a particular letter (in this case from Romans and then Philippians) of Paul. It can be worthwhile to determine these themes and follow them through a number of weeks. While these sermons generally stand independently of each other, connecting the themes is also a potentially illuminating approach.

It can also be a daunting task, but it does allow for an in-depth study of various aspects of Paul's view of a Christian life, a subject which can be very meaningful. Some of the aspects of the Christian life which Paul deals with specifically include love (in various forms), prayer, death (from a theological and philosophical basis, not from a pastoral, comforting perspective), and congregational conflict.

These sermons are somewhat diverse, but generally attempt to explicate the text assigned for each Sunday.

---

1. Richard Carl Hoefler, *Creative Preaching And Oral Writing* (Lima, Ohio: CSS Publishing Company, 1978).

**Proper 12
Pentecost 10
Ordinary Time 17
Romans 8:26-39**

Effective Suffering

Many people have heard a part of this lesson before. Most particularly, the last two verses, the part about "neither death, nor life, nor angels, nor rulers, nor things present, nor things to come, nor powers, nor height, nor depth, nor anything else in all creation, will be able to separate us from the love of God in Christ Jesus our Lord."

These verses are often a part of funeral services. In the context of a funeral service, these verses are a source of comfort for those in attendance, a consolation for the bereaved, and a strong reminder of the reward which awaits us all at the conclusion of this life. In the context of this lesson from the letter to the Romans, these verses are the summary of a very important passage, one which is about much more than simple consolation at a funeral.

Back at the beginning of the lesson, we start with our weakness. That can seem a rather inauspicious place to start — our weakness. We likely would prefer to begin with our strengths, the things which are to our credit; not with our weakness, the things which are likely to embarrass us.

Many parents seem to take a special delight in humiliating their adult children by bringing up embarrassing stories about growing up. Stories about odd manners of dress, especially when backed up with pictures; stories about difficulties with toilet training or bed wetting; stories about the things a child once did when growing up, but has long since ceased to do. No matter how cute the story might seem, particularly to the parents, the result for the child is often utter embarrassment, diminished self-esteem, and humiliation.

And here we are, at the beginning of this lesson, speaking of our weakness. And a very specific weakness at that, our inability to pray. To pray. Such a basic activity for a Christian, praying. Hans Kung, the Roman Catholic theologian, once wrote a book titled *On Being a Christian*. In over 600 pages of text, he never devoted a chapter to the subject of prayer. When asked about this curious lapse, he responded that prayer was so basic a part of a Christian life it could safely be assumed to be a part of every page. And we have trouble with prayer.

Everyone has heard the definition of prayer — a conversation with God. But most people have trouble with the dialogue. Instead, our prayers often sound more like a monologue or an inventory of our troubles and desires or even a listing of our failures.

While the controversy goes on about prayer in the classroom, many people have pointed out that as long as there are tests, there will always be prayers in the classroom. While that might be true, many of those prayers are mostly acknowledgments of a student's failure to prepare properly, and a demand, or at least a certain amount of begging, for divine intervention to take the place of the lapses in studying — listing of a failure and an inventory of troubles and a desire for help.

And many, if not most, of our prayers are like that. Not the sorts of prayers we should be making, but the ones we can manage, often under pressure, even though we know our prayers are less than perfect, even less than they ought to be. And, before it seems we are getting too personal here, consider a comment of Martin Luther's on the subject.

A man who devoted hours every day to prayer and devotions, Luther was once sitting at his dinner table when a roast was brought out. He noticed Topol, his dog, staring at the meat, and he said, "Oh, if only I could pray the way my dog watches this meat! All his thoughts are concentrated on this piece of meat. Otherwise he has no thought, wish, or hope."

"If only." Two little words which can serve as a summary of our weakness — our weaknesses in general, and our weaknesses regarding prayer in particular. But things do not end in "if only," with our weakness. Our weakness is only the beginning, not the end, no matter how often we are tempted to end the discussion as quickly as possible when we start with our weakness.

In our weakness, the Spirit helps us. We are not alone in weakness, but helped, mentored, and coached by the Spirit. And even if we really do not know everything we should about prayer, the Spirit helps us, and more. More than merely standing on the sidelines and yelling encouragement, more than simply providing the words for us, more than instructing us in the proper ways of prayer, the Spirit actually intercedes for us. To express that in another way, when we pray in our weakness, the Spirit takes our place, and prays with and for us.

And when God searches hearts to discover the content of prayer, it is not our hearts that are searched, but the mind of the Spirit. This is likely a good thing, as our hearts can be a significant problem. Our hearts can be filled with the details of our weaknesses, with all the things that distract us from our prayers. But, even if we are unable to concentrate our thoughts on our prayer as we should, the Spirit focuses properly on prayer, on our on-going discussion with God.

And so, we begin in our weakness, and we find that we are not alone there. The Spirit is with us, even to the point of standing in our place and interceding for us with God. In the midst of our weakness, we find that our strength is with us, the Spirit saves us from our failure and weakness.

And then, as we read this lesson, we come to a sudden shift of thought. Rather than a further discussion of the role of the Spirit, or prayer, the thought of the lesson shifts rather abruptly to a sentence we can easily find ourselves rejecting. The sentence is: "We know that all things work together for good for those who love God, who are called according to his purpose."

"All things work together for good"? Are you kidding me? How can we really say something like that? That statement is almost as bad as the old cliché, "God's in his heaven, all's right with the world." And for that cliché, there is some good news and some bad news. The bad news, in case you haven't watched the evening news recently, is that all is, most emphatically, not right with the world. The good news, on the other hand, is God's not in his heaven either. God's right here, with us.

But that idea of all things working for good? There's plenty of bad news about that, too. There are certainly things happening to people which do not seem to be working for good. The difficult events can be explained in a variety of ways.

We could talk about the need for bad things to enable us to appreciate the good things that happen to us. While this might sound quite rational and comforting, it is a terrible, gruesome interpretation of this verse when it is applied to things such as sudden, accidental deaths, incurable illnesses, debilitating diseases, and the long list of things which abruptly change people's lives.

It is also not a correct view of a loving God who listens to the Spirit rather than us to imagine that God sends or allows the bad things to happen so we can appreciate the good. Rather than a God who is with us, this is a picture of a remote God who is cold-hearted enough to allow the destruction of people and families and lives simply for the sake of encouraging a sense of appreciation in the survivors.

Alternatively, we could talk about how everything that happens is really a part of God's greater plan. Even though this is an excuse which has been offered frequently, the same objections apply.

This excuse requires a God who is somewhat cruel in the details required for the sake of a greater plan. Our human plans often impose suffering on individuals for the sake of a larger plan, which is intended to provide good things for a larger number of people. This is because of our human failure to grasp the full implications of the plan.

For example, consider the idea of providing high-quality, low-cost housing for people. While the idea sounds very good, and as if it could be an example of "working for good," when the current residents have to be moved out to allow for the building of the new structures, substantial difficulties and dislocations usually occur.

But if our best intentions and efforts often lead to problems, we might expect that God's efforts should avoid these problems. We believe in an all-powerful, all-knowing, loving God. To suggest that some people have to suffer in the course of God's greater plan is really a misunderstanding of what it means to have an all-powerful, all-knowing, loving God. There is no good reason that explains why such a God would punish his people.

There is plenty of bad news about that verse, "All things work together for good." But there is also good news. The bad things that happen to people are really a result of our own sinfulness. But the good news in the midst of our suffering, in the midst of all the things that result from our sinfulness, as we go through the bad stuff that is such a part of our lives, is: God is not in heaven; God is here with us.

Those who study such things say there are few things which are worse for an individual than to have one's child die. And we should remember that this is precisely what happened to God, when Jesus died on the cross.

Suffering is aggravated for most people when it is done in isolation. Quite often the response to people who try to help is, "You wouldn't understand." Or even more, "You don't understand." But the good news is, God understands. The terrible isolation that means people are forced to suffer alone, with no one to share their problems, need not be a problem for us. Our suffering, our sorrows, our problems are all understood by God. Because Jesus came and lived among people, as a person, and suffered all the things that happen to people. And, most especially, because God has suffered the death of his Son.

And the good news is even more than simply a companion in our difficulties. Some people are able to understand that their suffering is a path to help them grow in their faith and their connection to God.

Today's lesson concludes with those sentences often read at funerals. Once, at a funeral, a comment was made in the sermon, "Some people suffer more effectively than others." It sounds strange to speak of "effective suffering," but the phrase is worth our attention. We can be fairly certain that at some points in our lives we will suffer. It might take different forms for different people, but the fact of suffering is a part of our lives.

And since we will suffer, it makes sense to learn about the idea of effective suffering. If nothing else, perhaps we can learn how we can manage effective suffering.

First, we should be clear that this does not mean that we should go looking for more ways to suffer, just for the practice. It should be clear that we face plenty of suffering without looking for more.

But in our suffering, we need to be clear that God is with us. We are not abandoned, not alone in our suffering. We are always accompanied by God and by Jesus. In part, this is the answer to our problems with prayer. Even when we might doubt it, even when it seems as if we are absolutely alone, God is with us in our suffering. More than just a presence, God has a complete and total understanding of what we are going through, and complete comfort for all our sorrow.

Effective suffering is the way we learn that these things are true and we learn to take strength from them. Effective suffering is a growing of our faith and a developing closeness with the God who is with us at all times.

And it is effective suffering which allows us to understand what Paul means when he asks, "What then are we to say about these things? If God is for us, who is against us?"

"Who is against us?" Would you like a list? Most of us can provide a long list in response to that question. We can start with the way things seem to work against us. The refrigerator that stops working just after you put all that expensive food in it. The computer that swallows your file just as you finish making it perfect. The car that won't start when you are late for a critical meeting. And on and on.

"Who is against us?" There are people who seem to take delight in making us look and sound foolish. Not that we need a lot of help, most of the time. But even when things are going well, there always seems to be someone who particularly enjoys calling attention to our shortcomings.

"Who is against us?" If the truth is to be told, entirely too often we are against us. Even when we know what we should be doing, we don't do it. Even when we know what we should say, we keep quiet. We can make quite a list of people who are against us, and the place for the foremost person who is against us is reserved for — us.

That is where the really good news begins in this lesson. Even though we begin in our weakness, and progress to our suffering, and then come to the point of learning that our biggest problem is ourselves, through each of these stages, through each of these points, there is one thing which is constant.

In our weakness, our failures, and our problems with prayer, the Spirit is with us and beside us, praying for us, interceding with God.

In our suffering, as we learn about effective suffering, we also learn that God is with us comforting us, and supporting us in our suffering.

Finally, as we realize that the answer to "Who is against us?" is us, we also realize that Jesus intercedes for us.

There is a pattern here. Father, Son, and Holy Spirit are all involved in interceding for us, helping us, supporting us, comforting us as we go about our lives. And the best part of the promise comes in the last few verses.

In our lives there are people who come and go. Today, with the Internet and various listings of people and addresses and phone numbers, it is not uncommon to get letters saying things like: My name is ... I once knew someone with your name ... We were in school, the military, college, or some other place ... Are you that person?

Are you that person? Are you the person who once knew the person writing the letter, but over the years drifted apart? Eventually you were separated by distance, time, other interests, and any number of other things.

That separation happens quite easily today, and it is possible that similar separations have happened for much of human history. Certainly, Paul's comments at the end of this lesson sound as if he was familiar with such things. And he knew about the Good News. We face separations, but there is one separation we will never face.

"For I am convinced that neither death, nor life, nor angels, nor rulers, nor things present, nor things to come, nor powers, nor height, nor depth, nor anything else in all creation, will be able to separate us from the love of God in Christ Jesus our Lord."

That's the good news. Amen.

Proper 13
Pentecost 11
Ordinary Time 18
Romans 9:1-5

Families In Christ

Aren't families fun, at times? Paul reminds us in the lesson for today that families can be a source of many things in our lives.

Consider the husband who had promised his wife to replace the kitchen cabinets, but kept putting off the home improvement. The wife had to leave to care for her sick mother for two weeks and returned to find the new cabinets installed in the kitchen.

She was very pleased with the surprise, at least until a few days after her return, when a neighbor stopped by for coffee. After the wife praised her husband for finally installing the cabinets, the neighbor commented, "Yes, we were all very happy the fire damaged only the old cabinets."

Joy, anger, frustration, disappointment, care, concern, and many other emotions are all tied up in that incident. It often seems as if that is how it works with families: a blending of many, often contradictory, emotions and multiple responses to our families and the members of our families.

In many ways, what is involved is more than merely the people we happen to be related to in any of the ways we usually understand that term. Many years ago, a Hungarian was asked if he thought of the Russians, who had recently invaded his country to put down a bid for independence, as friends or brothers. His immediate response was that the Russians were his brothers. The response was so startling, the Hungarian was asked to explain further. He pointed out that relatives are simply a fact of life, but people choose their friends.

It is so very true. Our relatives and our family are most often not something we choose. It is something that happens to us as a part of our living. Family is a fact of our lives.

Paul certainly understood that point. Listen again to what Paul said. "I have great sorrow and anguish in my heart. For I could wish that I myself were accursed and cut off from Christ for the sake of my own people, my kindred according to the flesh."

Families can work that way. Parents, particularly parents of grown children, are quick to point out that just because their children have grown up doesn't mean that they stop thinking about the kids and worrying about what happens to them. Sometimes, it seems that parents with adult children are more concerned because they don't always hear about what is happening with the kids as frequently as they would like.

Most parents sound very much like Paul when it comes to the problems confronting their children. Most parents would gladly substitute themselves to endure the adversities that face their children. Even though we realize such substitutions aren't possible, we often find ourselves wishing, like Paul, that we could take the problems on ourselves, in the place of our family members. We wish those things happened to us "for the sake of my own people."

And who might be included in that term, "my own people"? Most individuals have a rough and ready definition in mind when asked about what constitutes a family member. Often this definition is expressed in terms of a "blood relative," a term that sounds very much like Paul's term, "my kindred according to the flesh."

Most people aren't aware that the term "blood relative" is often defined in the law. For example, in the state of Florida, a blood relative seems to be defined rather broadly. It includes people who might not normally be thought of, such as nieces and nephews and in-laws. Of course, the purpose of the law is not to provide an academic definition of the official limits of a family, but to define precisely who is considered a "blood relative" for specific legal purposes.

Most families seem to have some idea of who is really part of the family, and who is a member of the family only for some other reason. The boorish spouse, the cousin who is chronically broke, or perhaps the rather distant relative who showers only once a month and insists on long hugs whenever the family gets together are only a few examples of the folks who are often thought of as only vaguely part of the family.

Then there is the difficulty of the "black sheep" many families have as a part of their membership. The source of the designation varies greatly from family to family, but the result is often similar. Relations with the black sheep are usually strained, sometimes severed, on occasion to the point that the rest of the family changes its name to avoid any association with a black sheep who has become especially well-known or even infamous.

Sometimes the situation is based on our own misunderstanding of who is to do what in a family. This was certainly the case with two young girls walking home from Sunday school. One of the girls asked, "Do you think there is a devil?"

The other girl responded, "No, of course not. It's just like Santa Claus. He's really your father."

That is almost certainly a misunderstanding, not an accurate view, of a black sheep in the family.

The church has often been referred to as the family of Christ. And the church seems to come with the same problems and difficulties we find in our biological families. Joy, anger, frustration, disappointment, care, concern, and many other emotions are all part of our experience with families, and they are also part of our experience with the church family.

As much as we would like to believe that only the best parts of families are present in church, when we approach the point honestly, it is clear that some of the less savory aspects of families are also present on a regular basis. There are, unfortunately, gossips, boors, and other less desirable types in many congregations. There are, in the church family, some disagreements and arguments and even a black sheep or two. It is simply a fact of being part of the family of Christ.

There is a hint of such difficulties in the first verse of this lesson. Paul begins by insisting he is "speaking the truth in Christ — I am not lying; my conscience confirms it by the Holy Spirit." Not only does this opening suggest there might be rumors about Paul circulating in Rome and other places, but also that there is a strong possibility that Paul is seen as deserting his own people by his actions. Paul's defense, that he is speaking the truth, is bolstered by the witnesses he produces for the truth of what he is saying. As required by the Jewish law, Paul provides the names of two witnesses — the Holy Spirit and Christ. Even at the beginning, it would seem that life in the family of Christ was not quite as perfect as we might expect.

The situation is worse than that, for the difficulties are not limited to simply our congregation. They extend past our local boundaries to include the national church. More than that, we are related to all Christians, all around the world. We are all members of the family of Christ.

The story is even more inclusive than that. We stand in the line of all those who have borne the name of Christian. All those folks, who, for the last twenty centuries, have claimed to be followers of Christ, are part of the family.

Many people know some details about the history of their family. The grandparent who took part in World War II, the ancestor who was part of the Civil War, the first member of the family to come to North America can all be important people to remember and honor. Less important is the ancestor who abandoned the family, the bigamist, or the person sentenced to be transported for his crimes. Even if the less desirable ancestors are often the more interesting folks we find hanging off the family tree, they are only rarely the people we would want to hang out with for very long. Most families, if we only knew all the details, have both heroes and knaves among their members, both among the current generations and the ancestors.

Paul recognizes this issue in the conclusion of this lesson. In two brief verses he recounts the highlights the history of Judaism, "the adoption, the glory, the covenants, the giving of the law, the worship, and the promises." And then he points out the event that should be the high point of that history, the coming of the long-awaited Messiah, who is born a Jew and comes first to the Jews.

This is a point made by both Jesus and Paul. Jesus came first to the Jews as the Messiah and proclaimed the kingdom to the chosen people. Of course, Jesus was not exactly what the Jews expected as a Messiah, so his coming was not recognized as clearly as it might have been.

His coming presents the Jews with a choice. They might either believe in the Messiah and follow his instructions, or they might turn their backs on him. By the time of Paul, the decision had largely been made. The majority of Judaism had turned away from Christ — thrown him out of their family, so to speak.

This rejection is the source of Paul's sorrow and anguish. The people who should have recognized Christ have turned their backs on him and his offer of salvation. Paul is greatly distressed by this decision. He makes it quite clear that he would do almost anything to make things different, but there is very little he can do.

In many ways, these last verses of the lesson sound rather foreign to us today. We are not Jews or former Jews, as many of the people of the church in Rome were. The highlights of Jewish history are only vaguely a part of our background. Rather, we usually focus on Christ as the center of our lives.

Before we dismiss this part of the verse as unimportant and unrelated to our situation, we should consider it in a little more detail. Rather than being literally applicable to our situation, consider it as a model which leads us to examine our heritage as Christians.

They are Israelites, those who have the name of the favored people of God.

We are Christians, those who bear the name of the Son of God.

To them belongs the adoption, those who were selected to be the chosen people.

To us belongs the adoption, which makes us part of the family of God.

To them belongs the glory of the *shekina*, the continuing presence of God among the chosen people.

To us belongs the glory of the promise of Christ, that he will be with us, always, to the end of the age.

To them belong the covenants of Noah, of Abraham, and of Moses.

To us belongs the new covenant of Jesus.

To them belongs the giving of the law.

To us belongs freedom from the law.
To them belongs the worship of God in the Temple.
To us belongs the worship of the Father, Son, and Holy Spirit.
To them belong the promises — when God speaks and says, "I will be your God, and you will be my people."
To us belong the promise of Christ — to be equally with Christ children of God and participants in the kingdom.
To them belong the patriarchs.
To us belongs the apostles, the disciples, and the Son of God.
And to all of us, both the Jews and we Christians, belong the confrontation, the choice we face. Will we accept what God has promised us? Will we accept our adoption as children of God? Will we be a part of the family of Christ? Amen.

**Proper 14
Pentecost 12
Ordinary Time 19
Romans 10:5-15**

Beautiful Feet

There are some things which are not often associated with the word "beautiful." Our lesson today ends with an image associating such an item with "beautiful," and then bringing up another topic which seems completely unrelated.

This odd sentence is: "How beautiful are the feet of those who bring good news."

It is strange enough to call feet beautiful. Most often we think of feet in a much more utilitarian context, as something we stand on and walk on, our basic support for standing upright. People who spend substantial amounts of time focusing on the beauty of feet are generally known as "fetishists."

More often we are about as familiar with our feet as the peasant in a story told by the nineteenth-century theologian Soren Kierkegaard. The man normally went barefooted, but once, when he had some money in his pocket, he went to the city and purchased a pair of shoes and stockings. After his purchase, he had some money left over, so he proceeded to get drunk. He was still in that condition when he tried to get home, but managed only to stagger out of town where he lay down in the middle of the road.

A wagon came along and the driver yelled at the peasant to move or he would drive over his legs. In his condition the peasant looked at the unfamiliar shoes and stockings and replied, "Drive on; they are not my legs."

Feet are simply not something commonly regarded as particular points of beauty in modern society. Usually, they are thought of more like the comment of a fashion-conscious woman. When asked about purchasing shoes, she replied with her rule for shoes: "If the shoe fits, it's ugly."

So this image from our lesson sounds rather strange or, more frankly, weird. Is it possible that Paul is simply using an image which he understood, something he liked? Is this simply Paul's own, weird image? Actually, the image did not start with Paul.

The image comes from Isaiah 52:7. At that place the prophet says: "How beautiful upon the mountains are the feet of the messenger who announces peace, who brings good news, who announces salvation, who says to Zion, 'Your God reigns.'" A little more specific detail, but not really much help in understanding the image.

Isaiah is speaking, in general terms, of the restoration of Israel to what he and other members of Israel regarded as its rightful place, of the return of her people to their homes, where they will live in peace. More than that, he is speaking specifically of the return of those people who are still pure, clean, and ready to live as God's people and worship God as they should.

Paul certainly knew of this background, especially considering the context in which he used this quote from Isaiah. He uses it as the answer to a series of rhetorical questions about the way in which people will hear about God and the good news of Christ. For Paul this reference to the words of Isaiah is both an answer and a call to those who hear his words.

Even though this helps us understand the way the statement is used, it still leaves us with that odd image of "beautiful feet." While feet are not usually seen as beautiful today, and in fact are often the subject of jokes, and derogatory comments and frequently regarded as a subject unfit for polite conversation, they filled a different place in the ancient world.

Hospitality in the time of Paul and Jesus involved a ritual we no longer employ. Guests at a dinner were greeted by having their feet washed. People were expected to wash themselves before they left their homes for the dinner, but walking from one home to another, especially when wearing sandals, resulted in feet that were, at the least, dusty. Both to keep the home and its furnishings clean, and to welcome the guests and restore them to a feeling of freshly scrubbed cleanliness, greetings involved the washing of the guests' feet.

In the Gospel of John, Jesus follows this ritual when he washes the disciples' feet as a part of their last meal together. When Peter objects that it is not seemly for Jesus to wash his feet, Jesus tells him if his feet are not washed, he has no part in the kingdom. And then, in a command which is still a bit bothersome to many people, Jesus commands the disciples to follow his example: "You also ought to wash one another's feet" (John 13:14).

An image that reminds us of the value of humility, of the need to humble ourselves, and to remember that it is not our efforts which should lead us to pride, but the efforts of God working through us. Paul reminds us of all this in his series of questions leading up to this comment about feet.

"But how are they to call on one in whom they have not believed?" Paul begins with a basic question: How can people call on the name of the Lord, if they have not believed in Jesus before they call on him? It seems like a basic question, but Paul builds on it with a second question.

"And how are they to believe in one of whom they have never heard?" Paul is building a series of questions, a series that sounds very familiar. He selects a key word from the first question and builds the second question on that word, and again with the third, and again with the final question. And the series reminds us of the many times something like that has cropped up in other contexts. There is a classic folk song about an old lady who swallowed a fly, and then swallowed a spider, a bird, a cat, and an increasingly diverse series of animals to get rid of the fly and each other. This is only one example of the same sort of thing Paul is doing with his questions.

And how are we to expect that people could come to believe in someone they have never heard of? Obviously the situation is an absurdity, but Paul goes on to ask the next question.

"And how are they to hear without someone to proclaim him?" In order to call on Jesus, people must believe in him. In order to believe, people must hear the good news. In order to hear the good news, someone must proclaim that good news. Everything is quite logical, and it all builds clearly to the conclusion in the form of the final question.

"And how are they to proclaim him unless they are sent?" How can anyone proclaim unless they are sent? To proclaim the Good News, to tell the story of Jesus and God's love for the world, people need to be selected, called out, commissioned, and sent. If that sounds like a description of what happens to missionaries, it quite likely is.

But things don't stop with missionaries, with people sent to far-away lands to proclaim the good news. Those who lead in our congregations are also called and sent to proclaim. As are we all, each week, called together here for worship and sent forth from our worship, back into the world, called and sent to tell others about the good news of Jesus and God's love, called and sent to proclaim him where we already are.

So, in the final analysis, it is really our feet Paul is talking about. Our feet are beautiful because we bring good news. Our feet are beautiful when we announce peace, as Isaiah puts it. And our feet are beautiful, as Paul reminds us, when we proclaim the good news of Jesus.

Beautiful feet is still a strange image, but when we think about it, how beautiful are the feet, and everything else, about the people who announce peace. In our modern world there are not all that many people who actually get to announce peace. There are some who try hard, announcing peace in louder and louder tones, even as those around them blow themselves up, shoot others, and generally behave in very unpeaceful ways.

In our modern world, some people who announce peace and actually seem to accomplish it are given awards such as the Nobel Peace Prize. More often, however, the people who spend much of their time working toward peace are faced with violent reactions from those around them. Rather than getting praise from most people, they are accused of things such as being unpatriotic, seditious, cowardly, and worse.

It has often been said that Dr. Martin Luther King, Jr., who proclaimed passive resistance and non-violence, was regularly surrounded by very violent behavior. In fact, the same thing can also be said about the example who inspired Dr. King's plan of action, Mahatma Gandhi. There are some peacemakers who seem to have very unpeaceful activities swirl around them.

Often, it is only in retrospect that peacemakers are recognized for their labors. And there have been times when even after the peace is accomplished, those who were most important in bringing it about are still not recognized. Of course, recognition is not what peacemakers are really seeking. The obvious reward they seek is peace.

And peace, true peace, is certainly something to be sought. Not merely the absence of war, but a positive force, an opportunity for growth together, a situation where people are able to work together so all can accomplish a better life is certainly something everyone would recognize as a thing to be sought, at least in an ideal sense.

But Isaiah doesn't stop with peace, as desirable as it is. Isaiah goes on to say beautiful feet also belong to those who bring good news, the part of the verse that Paul seizes upon. Isaiah continues with other thoughts, but Paul is content to quote the part about those who bring good news.

We often think that the only people who can bring the Good News are those who are ordained, who preach on Sunday mornings, those specially called to be pastors. There is a story that reminds us of the true situation.

A minister found himself in the line waiting for Saint Peter's attention at the Pearly Gates. He was behind a guy dressed in a Hawaiian shirt, jeans, and a leather jacket, and wearing sunglasses. Finally Saint Peter addressed the man in the outlandish costume, "Who are you, so I might know what to do with you?"

"I'm Joe Green, a New York taxi driver."

After a moment consulting his list, Saint Peter broke into a big smile and gave the taxi driver a silken robe and a golden staff along with a hearty welcome.

The minister announced, "I'm Harold Snow, head pastor at St. Mary's for the last 43 years."

Saint Peter consulted his list, provided a thin cotton robe, a wooden staff, and jerked his thumb, indicating the minister should enter. Not too clear about this treatment, the minister asked the reason.

"We work by results here," Saint Peter replied. "When you preached, people slept; when he drove, people prayed."

The people specially called to bring the good news are not only those who preach on Sunday, but also those who are witnesses on every day of the week. The matter of beautiful feet is not limited to those who get up on Sunday morning and preach; it includes all who show how the good news works itself out in their lives. In truth, beautiful feet are even more common among the people of the congregation than among the people in the pulpit.

This is because it is in our lives that the good news is working itself out. Even when it might not seem that the good news is particularly active, nor particularly present, it manages to work itself out in our lives. Even under the most trying of circumstances, we find the good news not merely present, but often showing itself forth in our lives.

Consider Sir Alexander Fleming, the discoverer of penicillin. He made his discovery in a dust-filled, poorly-equipped laboratory. There were few conveniences, and a culture he was about to examine happened to be the precise spot where a mold spore, carried by a breeze, had previously landed.

Several years later, when he was a world-famous scientist, he was taken on a tour of a modern lab, a facility which glistened in its air-conditioned, dust-free, super-sterile purity.

"What a pity you didn't have a place like this to work in," commented Fleming's guide. "Just think of the wonders you could have discovered in surroundings like this."

Fleming responded, "Not penicillin."

We act like that sometimes. We think the only way to be witnesses to the good news is to find ourselves in some special place, to act in a way unlike the way we act every day, to say and do things that impress other people with how Christian we are.

In reality, we act as witnesses to the good news in our lives every day, where we find ourselves, acting the way we act. Not in some spectacular fashion, but in the normal actions which make up our daily lives.

We witness in that way, in the places where we are. We witness with our actions, with our lives, and with our beautiful feet. Amen.

**Proper 15
Pentecost 13
Ordinary Time 20
Romans 11:1-2a, 29-32**

Irrevocable Gifts

People have had a wide variety of reactions to the idea of politically-correct language. One of the more interesting is a series of books by James Finn Garner. A look at the contents of the volumes gives an insight into the way things are handled. The stories include such titles as the politically-correct bedtime story of "The Three Codependent Goats Gruff," and the holiday story of "Rudolph, the Nasally-Empowered Reindeer."

Under the humorous approach there lurks a problem that can cause us real difficulties. Today there are some terms which are not generally allowed in polite conversation: terms which are thought to be potentially offensive, even if there are no new terms to replace them. This leads to some concepts which are now, suddenly, more difficult to explain concisely. Like "Rudolph, the Nasally-Empowered Reindeer."

Consider a phrase commonly used before it became an issue to use only politically-correct language — "Indian giver." The concept behind the phrase was someone who gave a gift, and then asked for it to be returned, or even took the gift back. Today, of course, there are still people who do this, but we no longer have a convenient term describing such behavior available for our use.

But the idea of an Indian giver, if not the term itself, can serve to remind us of what Paul is speaking of in this lesson. He writes, "For the gifts and the calling of God are irrevocable." Simply stated, God is not an "Indian giver." Once given, the gifts of God are permanent, not able to be taken back.

People often receive gifts, at Christmas, on birthdays, and on other special occasions. Sometimes these gifts are less than thrilling, at least to some who receive them, like a big box of socks and underwear for Christmas when you are only eight years old. At other times the presents are much more lavish, leading to images of a child surrounded by a sea of gifts and discarded wrapping paper.

And there are times, amid the plenty, when frustrated, frazzled people turn to threats in their efforts to maintain some order. "You behave, or I'll take away your presents." Considering the way people behave, it wouldn't be much of a surprise to find that God does the same thing. "Behave, or I'll take back my gifts to you."

It certainly seems that the stories we find in the Bible about the ways people behave could easily earn us threats like that. And the Bible contains a variety of accounts of the way God punishes the people who disobey, the people who do not follow the command to be the people of God.

Paul, of course, is very aware of this history. He knows exactly how the people of God have fallen short, have failed in their efforts, have often not even made any discernable effort to live up to their promises to God. Almost like someone who is trying to lose 25 pounds to fit into a particular article of clothing, and finds oneself promising to follow one's diet faithfully — tomorrow, or as soon as the cheesecake is gone, or right after the holidays, or whenever. Somehow, those 25 pounds never seem to go away, and the clothing never gets worn.

Paul understands, and he begins with "I ask, then, has God rejected his people?" And Paul's answer is, in the original Greek, much more emphatic than the way it gets translated in most Bibles, including in our lesson. "By no means!" Or, "Certainly not!" Or, "Of course not!" All these are rather pale representations of the words in the original Greek.

In a printed document, Paul's answer should at the least be in bold type and entirely in capitals.

When the lesson is read, the answer should be spoken loudly, perhaps even shouted, "No! No! No!"

Because the gifts of God are irrevocable. So irrevocable, that even the threat of taking them back doesn't happen. It is sometimes hard to accept, but the gifts of God are given forever.

There is a need to be careful here, however. We have to understand these gifts quite well, and quite properly. They are given forever, but that does not mean the gifts are always available for our use. The gifts are irrevocable, but that does not mean that we always use them properly, or even use them at all.

Many of the gifts of God are talents and skills which must be developed. An athlete, for example, can be blessed with exceptionally quick reflexes and extremely acute eyesight. These gifts, however, do not mean that this person is ready to join a major league team without learning the rules of the game, practicing the game, and playing innumerable games in preparation for that major league debut. In a similar way, most talents and skills must be used in order to develop them fully. Our gifts are the basic talent and skills, and an ability to refine the basic talent which is also our gift from God.

We begin with potential, but that means only that we must work on that potential to bring it to its full flowering. This was exactly the case with a young lady named Mary Alice. Everyone said she had potential. And she did. But she was deeply concerned that she might misuse her potential, or that it might somehow be taken from her, or that if she used it, it would somehow be diminished and go away. So she hoarded the potential very carefully.

Mary Alice never actually used any of her potential, but she knew that no matter what else might be said of her, people would always say, "She has potential."

The story of Mary Alice is, all too often, only an extreme example of the ways we avoid our own potential, the ways we avoid using the gifts God has given us. Everyone can think of examples of people who are like Mary Alice, people who have gifts, people who have potential, but who allow their gifts to languish.

Or, perhaps, we can think of people who seem to have no gifts. President Andrew Johnson was once described by a congressman as a "self-made man." One of the president's most vocal political opponents, Thaddeus Stevens, commented that he was quite glad to hear the president was a self-made man, as that relieved the Almighty of a tremendous responsibility.

It seems obvious that any gifts we have are gifts from God. Without God and the gifts all people have been given, we have no claim to be or do anything. Even so, it can be uncomfortable to make the effort to utilize our gifts. Most often, the gifts do not merely happen, but require us to exert ourselves. Most often it is not a matter of simply applying our gifts with no further effort. In reality, we often find ourselves confronted with situations which require intense personal involvement and no promise of complete success. Instead, we face situations which require us to become personally involved, which require us to risk opening ourselves to other people and to risk getting hurt, with only a hope of success, not even a promise.

In the face of this situation, it is not surprising that some people choose not to utilize their gifts. It would seem, however, that our problems with gifts don't end with a failure to use them at all. An even more serious problem is the way it is possible to misuse our gifts.

At least in theory, the gifts we receive from God should be used to the glory of God. It seems so obvious, and yet, in practice, it is so difficult actually to do that.

We sometimes suspect that the only way to use our gifts is to work for or in the church. And there are certainly a large number of things that need to be done around the church, and a number of ways gifts can be utilized within the church. There are often opportunities for using our gifts that are not filled because people are reluctant to use their gifts, or because they don't want to use their gifts in the church, or because they are acting like Mary Alice and hoarding their potential so it won't be thrown away.

But the story of how we are to use our gifts does not end with the church. It does not end with the ways we use our gifts in furthering the mission of the church. There is a world outside the walls of the church, and everyone who is a part of the church also finds themselves in the world on a regular basis. We are also expected to use our gifts in the world.

Using our gifts to make a living, to earn an income for ourselves and our families, to find fulfillment for ourselves in our work are also ways that we should be using our gifts. We have been provided with a variety of gifts that we can use in the world for a variety of things.

Work is one thing, and we are often reminded that our work in the world provides us with more than mere sustenance. It also provides us with an opportunity to display our gifts, especially our gift for behaving ethically and responsibly. By setting an example for those around us, by acting appropriately, we also act as witnesses to the God who gave us these gifts.

In many ways this is the way it works with all our gifts. We have been given these gifts, and we are expected to use them responsibly and ethically, as a form of witness to the God who gave them to us as our irrevocable gifts. This is the responsibility that comes attached to the gifts: that we use them as we witness to the love of God in our lives.

That responsibility can be troubling. It can lead people to look at the gifts of God in the same way we sometimes look at the gifts we receive from other people. There is always the relative who thinks no one ever ages past the age of seven, and somehow manages to give gifts which are quite inappropriate. Or the clothing that is at least two sizes off, either too large or too small. Or the third or fourth copy of the same gift. Or almost anything that is not completely appropriate.

To handle these problems, many stores set up special "gift return counters" on the day after Christmas to accommodate the long lines of customers who have gifts to return. Some people even give gifts with receipts enclosed in envelopes so the gifts can be returned more easily. If the gift isn't what we want, we often return it.

It isn't quite that easy with God's irrevocable gifts. Sometimes the gifts are difficult for us to cope with. The gifts present us with duties and responsibilities that appear to be beyond our capacity. Giving the gift back begins to look like an option with promise, if only promise of relief from the demands of the gifts.

Our biggest problem is that when we begin to turn our backs on God's gifts, we very quickly, even without meaning to, turn our backs on the ultimate gift of God's mercy, as it was shown to us on a cross.

We try to cope with the gifts, we try to use them responsibly and ethically, and we fall short, we fail in our efforts, we sin. When we are honest, we know we are not what we should be. We don't live up to the gifts we have been given.

There is a way to arrange one's possessions known as an irrevocable trust. This is often used as a way to arrange the final disposition of a person's belongings and resources, both for the remaining years of life and after death. While the idea is attractive, and often quite beneficial, there is one important aspect to the arrangement that must be taken into account. As an irrevocable trust, if your ideas about what should be done with your belongings and resources change, the instrument is extremely difficult to change.

The concept of an irrevocable trust is what God has given us in his Son. We have been given an irrevocable gift, something that is never taken back, something that never can be taken back. We have been given God's mercy, God's love, as an irrevocable gift. What we do with the gift is our witness to God, our reflection of God to the world. Amen.

**Proper 16
Pentecost 14
Ordinary Time 21
Romans 12:1-8**

Body Parts And Pride

It sometimes happens that small parts of the Bible seem to become dated, especially when they echo particular periods of time. When these small portions are brought up later, they seem out of touch with the modern world. The lesson today might serve as an example of this phenomenon.

When we read the lesson it sounds almost as if it should be a part of the '60s. Early on, there is a comment about not conforming, then something about transforming by renewing your minds, and finally, the ending about everybody working together. It all sounds as if it would fit right in if we were watching a nostalgic television special about the good old days of the 1960s. While it is uncanny that something written almost 1,900 years before the time the words seem to suit can evoke memories of a period only forty years ago, it is an unfortunate mistake to consign these words, along with other faded sayings of those days, to the collection of discarded remnants from that time.

These words are quite pertinent for our situation today, and they should carry a lot of meaning for us. It is worth our while to make the effort to listen carefully to what is being said in our lesson this morning. After all, it isn't as if the issues Paul speaks about have ceased to afflict humanity.

Consider, for example, a man who was promoted to a position that had the title of vice-president. The man was exceedingly proud of the new position and developed the annoying habit of speaking of himself in the third person. Many of his sentences began like this: "Your vice-president would appreciate ..." or "Your vice-president says...."

Finally, the man's wife was so tired of this behavior that she told the man, "Vice-presidents are a dime a dozen. Why, down at the supermarket they have a vice-president in charge of prunes."

Furious, the husband demanded that his wife prove her statement. She called the supermarket and asked for the vice-president in charge of prunes.

"Which kind," came the reply, "fresh or dried?"

It sounds like that husband needed to listen to Paul's advice in our lesson today: "I say to everyone among you not to think of yourself more highly than you ought to think." In fact, it sounds like advice that could at one time or another apply to all of us.

This isn't the only part of the lesson that is not dated, but is still applicable to our situation today. The last portion of the lesson is a listing of various roles in the church that Paul suggests as important in the life of a congregation. This is not meant to be an exhaustive list of all the roles that will ever be needed in every congregation. For example, many congregations have found individuals knowledgeable in the operation of electronic equipment to be quite useful in spreading the good news, but Paul doesn't mention specifics, such as webmasters in establishing and maintaining websites. This does not mean such individuals are not important and quite helpful. Nor does it mean that Paul was less than we might think because he didn't mention specific roles useful in the church 1,900 years after he wrote these words.

It does mean that the list here is not meant to include every specific role the church might ever need. Rather, this is a generalized list of some of the more important roles necessary in the life of the church. This list of roles is mentioned to support an idea that is even more important. In the life of the church, the concept Paul expresses here is more important. That concept of the roles is mentioned to support and to serve as an example for others.

The concept is something that has become known as the Body of Christ. Paul's insight here is that the Body of Christ can be compared to a human body, especially in the fact that a human body has a multitude of parts and all of the parts need to work together for the good of the whole body. If the commercials are correct, the human body consists of at least 2,000 parts. And they need to work together for a person to live in a healthy way.

It sometimes happens that a human body has difficulties with a particular part. Some newborns need an immediate blood transfusion to ensure their survival. The blood they are born with is unable to work with the rest of the body, and it must be replaced.

This example must be taken carefully. It is an extreme example of the importance of the various parts of the body, both the human body and the Body of Christ, working together. It is not an endorsement of any efforts to replace parts of the church that don't seem to be working together.

A better understanding might be that of the effort many people make to attain a well-proportioned body. Exercise, diet, and other activities all have a part to play. Further, as most people are aware, doing some unfamiliar activity often leads to the comment, "I'm using muscles I didn't know I had." If this is the case, you will likely be aware of them in the next few days, when the newly-discovered muscles are quite sore.

Perhaps what the Body of Christ needs more than replacement of the parts that aren't working is an exercise that puts all the parts of the Body to work, particularly the parts that aren't working very hard.

Rather than trying to drive out the more difficult parts, it is important to remember that we are all parts of the Body of Christ, and we all have different functions. Paul puts it this way: "For as in one body we have many members, and not all the members have the same function, so we, who are many, are one body in Christ, and individually we are members one of another."

In one body we have many members, in one church we have many members, in one group we have many parts. It is this fundamental truth that underlies the list of the parts Paul offers. There are times when we seem to expect people in the church to be good at everything. It can be humbling to realize that not everyone is good at everything that needs to be done around the church.

This is even more difficult when we realize that in many congregations the people who are likely to volunteer for an activity in the church are the same people time after time. This issue is so significant that one rather frustrated leader in the church once commented that most churches would be stronger if they were significantly smaller. He theorized that the first third of a church's membership was committed, the second third was the outer fringes, and the last third was already out of the church. The loss of the last third would likely result in a more active congregation.

While this perspective might sound rather harsh, it does have some truth in it. But we must be very careful not to push this idea too far. Consider the story of a young man who desperately wanted a part in his third-grade play. He confided his desire to his mother, and she considered her son briefly. She realized that, in all honesty, he was not particularly likely to be awarded a part. So, on the day when the parts were announced, she made sure to be at school to cheer up her son after what she strongly suspected was going to be a sad experience. To her surprise, the young man came out of the doors of the school with a big smile and bursting with pride. Before she could say a word, he announced, "I made it. I've been chosen to clap and cheer."

Not all members in the church have the same function, and we must be very careful to value the functions of all members. One of the most important functions, perhaps, is the function of attending worship weekly, the people who clap and cheer in the church, as it were, the ones who form the congregation, who fill the pews, who are present to worship. It seems so simple, so basic, that sometimes we don't realize how important a function it is.

A youth once commented that he always knew who he would see in church on Sunday morning. And he then gave a list of ten families and individuals he could count on seeing each time he was in church. Even without realizing they were doing it, these people were ministering to the youth simply by being present for worship. A ministry of presence. Nothing particularly flashy, perhaps nothing to brag about; simply, merely coming to worship. Not only a basic function, but also a function of great importance.

It is important to note, this is not a ministry that must be based on what a person gets out of being present for worship, but a ministry of providing a witness to others in the congregation. By being consistently in worship, people are establishing a witness that worship is an important part of life. This is a ministry and a witness that is essential in a congregation, but it is easy to overlook.

The same is quite true of all the functions Paul lists. They share a tendency to be important even when they appear innocuous and common. This aspect of these gifts should remind us that Paul does not list these gifts in any particular order, certainly not in any order of importance. Rather, Paul lists gifts that are the bedrock of a healthy congregation, those things that will certainly be found wherever the church is found.

Think about the list. Prophecy ... Ministry ... Teacher ... Exhorter ... Giver ... Leader ... Compassionate.

There are all important functions, all important gifts, that will be found in a healthy congregation. Some of these things happen more publicly than others. Leaders are usually known by many other gifts when they fill that role. Exhorters, which we might also know as speakers, are often noted as they are those speaking to others. Teachers, of course, have students. Ministers, both ordained and lay, are well-known by those to whom they minister.

But many of these functions are also quite unobtrusive for some people. Givers, of course, are often anonymous. Teachers, ministers, and the compassionate are also often found working in obscurity, unknown to many others. These are important functions, important work, and often they are done quietly.

But, as we are all part of the Body of Christ, all the functions work together for the health of the body. That can be a difficult concept — the Body of Christ. Paul says, "We, who are many, are one body in Christ, and individually we are members one of another." It sounds so simple, such a natural image, something we should grasp with very little interpretation. Perhaps it should be like that, but all too often it isn't.

Consider, for example, an old ostrich James Thurber once told a story about. This old ostrich was instructing a class of young ostriches in the excellence of the ostrich species, when a young skeptic named Oliver said, "Man can fly sitting down, and we can't fly at all. How can we be so excellent?"

The old ostrich replied, witheringly, "Man is flying too fast for a world that is round. Soon he will catch up with himself and there will be a great rear-end collision. And Man will never know that what hit Man was Man."

Not only are the ostriches rather unclear about their own place, but the old ostrich also has an interesting understanding of the eventual fate of humanity. As humorous as the image is, and as physically impractical as it sounds, it is philosophically and metaphorically quite a challenge to avoid exactly such a fate.

Whenever we lose sight of Paul's image of the Body of Christ, which we are all part of, which we all share and work to strengthen, then we run into the danger of catching up with ourselves and being part of a great rear-end collision. And Man will never know that what hit Man was Man.

Keeping our focus on being a part of the Body of Christ is really a result of Paul's advice in the beginning of this lesson. The part that sounds the most like the rhetoric of the '60s. "Do not be conformed to this world, but be transformed by the renewing of your minds, so that you may discern what is the will of God — what is good and acceptable and perfect."

Do not be conformed, because we are only accidentally in this world. We are really part of the Body of Christ. We are part of the people who are transformed by the renewing of our minds. The ways of the world, the ways the world judges and evaluates things are not the way things really are. And that is precisely Paul's point.

As we study the word of God, as we participate in worship and find ourselves renewed, as we minister in a variety of ways, most of them not flashy but all of them as part of the Body of Christ, we find that our minds are renewed by the promises of God. Because of that renewal, we are enabled to see what is the will of God.

This is often an idea used in a judgmental manner, particularly in an effort to eliminate the Body parts we dislike. Paul points out the real purpose. As our minds are renewed, we are able to grow in our ability to see what is good, what is acceptable to God, and what is perfect. And as we begin to see these things more clearly, we are also inspired to seek them more closely in our own lives.

We are better able to work for the growth and betterment of the whole Body of Christ.

When we continue as part of the Body of Christ, we are able to be transformed, we are able to live more fully as members of the Body, and we are better able to fulfill more completely the functions we have been given in the Body. Amen.

**Proper 17
Pentecost 15
Ordinary Time 22
Romans 12:9-21**

Heaping Coals And Virtues

A French writer and historian once wrote, "We owe to the Middle Ages the two worst inventions of humanity — romantic love and gunpowder." While many people might be tempted to agree that gunpowder has been an invention which has caused many problems for humanity, it is the other item which is surprising to find on a list of the worst inventions of humanity, particularly on the very short list.

Even though this isn't the time of year when people think especially about thoughts of love, this is only a few months past spring, when young people's fancies are thought to turn to thoughts of love, and past June, when many people get married. So it might seem strange to hear about romantic love as one of the two worst inventions of humanity.

But there is certainly some evidence that romantic love is not quite as wonderful as the stories might make it seem. For one thing, there is the terrible rate of divorce in this country, which might be seen as the result of romantic love meeting the real world.

One old pastor used to tell every couple he spoke with during pre-marital counseling that romantic love, the love that is supposed to see a couple through the rough spots, was likely to be quite surprised the morning after the wedding, when both people woke up with bad breath, mussed hair, and all the other unlovely details of waking up and seeing someone for the first time without any effort to prepare for the encounter. No longer a vision of loveliness (or handsomeness) ready for a date, but now another person waking up, perhaps even a little cranky until that first cup of coffee.

Romantic love faces some serious challenges from the real world and all the unlovely details of life there. It is possible that elevating romantic love to a position of being the answer for all problems, as has sometimes been suggested, has contributed to some problems growing out of control. The lesson on this day begins with love, in fact, with two kinds of love. It is likely that taking either of these uses as romantic love would be very misleading.

In fact, this is more than simply two comments on two different types of love. This lesson begins with some rules for Christian behavior. In many ways this list is a sort of "Ten Commandments for Christians."

The list begins with "Let love be genuine." In many ways this injunction is also a summary of the entire list. The word used for love here is *agape*, a word which is difficult to translate fully. It means *love*, but that simple word hardly includes everything the word meant when Paul wrote it here.

Before Christians came along, the word *agape* was hardly used in Greek. It was one of the words used to mean love, and it had little meaning beyond that rather vague use. Christians took the word over and began using it to describe the activity of God, most particularly to describe the loving action of sending his only Son.

Genuine love, which is held up as the first and most important Christian Commandment, is parallel to the divine love, especially because both are best understood by looking at the actions which spring from the love. Paul has written famously about divine love and the nature of the actions that spring from divine love. Those same thoughts lie behind Paul's words here. The call to let the divine love be genuine is a call to us to let our entire lives be ruled by the model of divine love.

As people who live their lives by genuine divine love, we know that this divine love is not merely a matter of things to be avoided. Rather, genuine divine love is something that reaches out to help and support and manifest God's love to the people we meet. As George Bernard Shaw once stated it: "The worst sin towards our fellow creatures is not to hate them, but to be indifferent to them; that's the essence of inhumanity." Genuine divine love is never indifferent.

The second in this list of Christian Commandments continues this theme: "Hate what is evil, hold fast to what is good." Far from being indifferent, this is an active approach to living. More than mere lip service, Paul uses very strong words. The word translated as *hate* appears only here in the New Testament. It is a very strong word, which means more than merely hate, more on the order of *hate strongly* or *abhor*. Not a matter of saying the words, simply expressing a distaste for, but taking an active stance against what is evil and also uniting with what is good.

The term used here to mean *hold fast* also has a translation which is not used in many texts, but one which is very evocative of what Paul is saying. The word can also be translated as *glue together*. More than hanging on, Paul is reminding Christians of the need to glue yourself to the good, attach yourself to the good, literally become a part of what is good.

The first thing that comes from gluing yourself to the good is to "love one another with mutual affection." This time the word translated as love is one which is familiar to most people — *philadelphia*. While the word is more familiar as the name of a city, it is also a Greek word that describes brotherly love or affection. Rather than the divine love that underlies the entire Christian life, this word embodies the idea of affection for a brother or a sister, and in the New Testament, primarily an affection for a fellow believer.

Many congregations have, at some point in their past, faced issues of conflict. The conflict comes from many sources, and there are usually people who ask something like, "How can this happen in the church?" The answer is clearly that it can happen because the church is full of human beings, and conflict often occurs when people gather together.

Clearly conflict in congregations is not something that has only surfaced in recent years. We might reasonably suspect that Paul's comment, coming as the first result of gluing ourselves to the good, comes from a person experienced with conflict in congregations, from a person who recognizes the danger of such situations and the best way to deal with and prevent such situations. This is not to say all conflict in congregations will be entirely avoided. In fact, some conflict might even be healthy.

North Sea fishermen often face a problem. When they have a large catch of herring, the fish can become sluggish and lethargic and lose most of their value. To resolve this problem, the fishermen put a couple of catfish in the tanks to keep the herring stirred up so they flourish. It is quite likely that congregations can similarly find a few people who challenge the easy assumptions and remind the congregation of some hard facts to be quite important to the on-going life of the congregation. But even a congregational catfish is still bound to try to fulfill this injunction to "love one another with mutual affection."

The remaining items in the list continue to clarify the way that Christians are to live, particularly together. "Outdo one another in showing honor" sounds a little foreign to most people, but it seems that Paul is using a fancy way to remind Christians of the importance of humility. A noted scholar was once approaching the dais when a loud round of applause broke out from the audience. The eminent scholar immediately stepped back to allow the person following him to step up and accept the honor being done to him by the audience. It was simply impossible for the scholar even to consider that the applause might be meant for him.

"Do not lag in zeal, be ardent in spirit." Christianity is, or should be, a passionate adventure. When Paul wrote, being a Christian was likely to cause a series of problems for believers, possibly even ending in death, as it did for Paul himself. Only those passionate about their belief need bother to participate.

While it seems as if this passionate level of participation has diminished greatly today, the fact that Paul includes such a comment in this list indicates that passion was something people in his day could have trouble sustaining, just as some people have problems with passionate Christianity today.

"Serve the Lord." This sounds like the simplest statement on this list to understand. Ironically, it is also one which presents a different problem. When scribes copied the New Testament in ancient times, they regularly used abbreviations to make the work go faster. One system of abbreviation commonly used dropped the vowels from words, much as written Hebrew does. From this system, there are two possible words that could be found here, one meaning *Lord*, the other meaning *time* or *opportune time*, as a footnote in the Bible translates the alternative.

Serve the time. In other words, seize your opportunities. Looking back, it is easy to see the chances and opportunities that have been presented to us, and to rejoice over the ones that were seized and led to great results. It is also possible, if less easy, to recognize the opportunities that were lost because they were ignored. It is likely that either reading of the text can be understood as embodying a central truth about the Christian life.

"Rejoice in hope, be patient in suffering." Two statements that reverse each other. Within the Christian family it is easy to rejoice at the good news of another. It is also fairly simple to join in sympathy with others who are suffering. These reactions are natural and present everyone with opportunities to share with others at times of great joy and sorrow.

While the basic instinct to share with others is present in everyone, as Christians we need to be attentive to nurturing the tendency and helping it to grow into the strong ability to be helpful to others in both times of joy and sorrow.

"Persevere in prayer." It might be a surprise to find prayer listed so far down this catalogue of Christian Commandments. It could be that this lowly placement is a result of Paul's assumption that prayer is such a central part of a Christian's life that it needed only a passing reminder to persevere in it. Archbishop Fulton J. Sheen once said, "I am not going to pray for you. There are certain things a man has to do for himself. He has to blow his own nose, make his own love, and say his own prayers." Paul certainly shared this perspective when he urged his listeners to persevere in prayer. And so should we, as individual Christians who actually do persevere in prayer.

"Contribute to the needs of the saints." Perhaps it should not be much of a surprise to find a comment about our contributions in a list of Commandments for Christians. There are those who think the only purpose of the church is to collect money to ensure that the church continues to exist. But Paul is not particularly concerned with the survival of the church. He is pointing out the need to contribute to support the needs of the saints. In his time, this was largely a matter of collecting funds to support the widows and orphans in Jerusalem who were the responsibility of the Christian congregation there. Not for the congregation itself, but for the people who depended on it for survival. The same thing is true today. Contributions to support and underwrite the projects of the church that provide for people and their needs are critically important. Often, in this world, it is only the church that provides for the poorest around the globe. It is our obligation to provide the contributions required to support those ministries meeting the needs of the saints.

"Extend hospitality to strangers." This is, perhaps, the comment that many people find to be the most difficult of all those in Paul's list. Strangers are a problem. Today, they might be violent, or ill, or something else. Hospitality sounds like it involves inviting people into our midst, either into our homes or into our church building. It all sounds like something we would rather downplay, or perhaps ignore, and not be involved with.

It is unfortunate that the modern world seems to have heightened our concerns about these issues and greatly reduced our willingness to extend hospitality to the strangers we find around us every day. Perhaps such concerns are not completely new or limited to the modern world, however. It is possible to understand the remainder of this lesson as a further comment on how to go about extending this hospitality, especially in the face of the dangers that increase our natural reluctance.

Paul encourages those who hear his words to "live peaceably with all," at least as far as such behavior is possible. No evil for evil, but do what is noble. Let all those provocations go and do good to all. It sounds like a nice idea, but one that will never work in reality.

It is a plan that is not easy to carry out. But consider the youngest child in a family. Older brothers have a tendency to tease and bother the youngest, and the treatment only gets worse when the youngest reacts by screaming, shouting, crying, and running to parents to complain mightily about the treatment. It is a difficult lesson to learn, but when the youngest begins to ignore the teasing, and the reactions stop, much of the teasing also stops. It isn't as much fun when nothing happens as a result.

This works beyond the family as well. Rather than being hard with people, Paul suggests giving others more than they deserve, even feeding your enemies when they are hungry and giving them a drink when they are thirsty. When these basic needs have been met, the generosity should continue.

Paul suggests, in a wonderful burst of insight and humanity, that "by doing this you will heap burning coals on their heads." A desire for revenge is a part of most people, and it seems as if the best way to get revenge is to fight fire with fire. But Paul has a better way, a way that helps Christians to resist evil, to prevent being overwhelmed by evil, and finally to overcome the evil that tempts us, a way to hate evil and hold fast to what is good, as he commanded early on in his list.

Paul suggests that we should overcome evil with good. It is not always the way we are familiar with, and it is certainly not the way most of the world seems to work. It is simply the way that Christians let the divine love of God show through them to the world. It is simply the way we live our lives as Christians. Amen.

**Proper 18
Pentecost 16
Ordinary Time 23
Romans 13:8-14**

Doing Well And Doing Good

There is a cliché thrown around the business world that states that people should do well by doing good. This translates into a rationale for doing works of charity and for being generous to employees, customers, and communities. The reason for these good deeds is to engender good feeling and, in the long run, to make more money, in other words, to do well.

By being good to employees, costs for recruitment and training and replacement will be greatly reduced.

By being good to customers, there will be loyalty and an increased willingness to spend money in your place of business or on your brand of merchandise.

By being good to communities, there is often a reduction in taxes, greater ease in obtaining needed licenses and permits, and a general improvement in the opinion of community toward the business.

Many businesses have discovered that doing good often translates to doing quite well financially. Paul almost sounds as if he is saying similar things for Christians in the lesson for today. Christians should do good to do well forever. Or, if we listen more carefully, Paul is really encouraging Christians to do good, live right, and, as he expresses it, put on the Lord Jesus Christ. Surprisingly, all this is without a single shred of a promise about doing anything, either doing well or doing poorly.

Often, especially when trying to convince people that they should act in a responsible, Christian manner, people promise a variety of things as rewards for such behavior. Behave as we know we should, and you will be given eternal life, God's love, and other things. Sometimes the promises are more specific, as when our good behavior is promised a reward of a good life, increased wealth, or the admiration of others.

All in all, it sounds very much like the sort of thing most parents use with their children on occasion. If you sit quietly, I'll stop and get you some ice cream, or a hamburger, or a special toy, or whatever.

Paul does none of this. Most emphatically, he promises no rewards for our living up to the way we are supposed to live as Christians. Rather than rewards, Paul simply presents a picture of some of the basics of a Christian life.

First Paul talks about love as the one word that describes a Christian life. Of course, this message has been proclaimed among Christians for centuries, but it has clearly been misunderstood for about as long as it has been proclaimed. Take, for example, Paul's example of how the commandments interact with love. Paul points out that all the commandments are summed up in the instruction, "Love your neighbor as yourself."

In spite of this, many people still seem to hold on to various commandments from the Old Testament, particularly the Ten Commandments, as some sort of guideline to how Christians should live. The commandments are held up as the Law of God for Christians. And this ignores Paul's comment that "love is the fulfilling of the law."

Perhaps this preference for the commandments is simple to understand. The commandments seem to provide easy limits to what we should do, and by the ways we interpret the commandments, the limits are even easier. The commandment says we should not murder, but that is fairly simple for most of us. The commandment says we should not commit adultery, which people seem to find more difficult, but it at least sounds attainable. The commandment says we should not covet, which is certainly more difficult, but something we can work on and at least make it seem as if we can manage it.

In the time of Jesus, the commandments were often reduced to very achievable tasks. Honor your father and your mother, for example, was simplified to providing for your parents in their old age. Simply placing enough money in the Temple storehouse to provide for the needs of your parents meant, at that time, that you had fulfilled all the responsibilities of that commandment.

Luther, in the *Small Catechism*, takes another approach. He points out that our responsibilities do not end merely with the two people we recognize as our parents. He enlarges our understanding to include all those in authority, and he points out that we should "honor, serve, obey, love, and respect them." While those in authority, by their actions, sometimes make this difficult, Luther has already made the commandment substantially more comprehensive and difficult to fulfill by his explanation.

If we took the Ten Commandments seriously, and tried actually to fulfill the understandings of the commandments we find in the *Small Catechism*, things would not seem nearly as easy. Suddenly Paul's quoting of Jesus' summary of the law sounds like not such a bad idea after all.

Jesus was asked, in Mark and Matthew, for a summary of the law. He responded with a twofold summary. The first commandment is, "You shall love the Lord your God with all your heart, and with all your soul, and with all your mind, and with all your strength." The second commandment is, "You shall love your neighbor as yourself." These are exactly the same words Paul uses in today's lesson. Even in the Greek New Testament, the words are precisely the same.

The basic idea, as Paul expresses it, sounds quite simple. Love everyone, and your actions will fulfill the law. The Greek word translated as love is *agape*, which means a holy love, the sort of love God showed by sending Jesus, and Jesus showed by giving his life for us, the sort of love that does no wrong to a neighbor. When we show that sort of self-giving love for others, we fulfill the law.

Of course, this summation of the law is similar to Luther's explanations of the commandments in the *Small Catechism*. Exactly as it happened with Luther, rather than making things easier to accomplish, Paul makes things much more difficult.

Problems with this idea of love are not new by any measure. In fact, from Paul's writings in the New Testament we can understand that early Christians were quite likely to stress the outward gifts such as healing, prophesying, or speaking in tongues, and frequently to lose sight of the basic duty of love. Not a simple theory, often nothing that looks impressive, but a bedrock for Christian behavior — You shall love your neighbor as yourself.

No longer are we able to reduce the commandments to simple little actions we can hope actually to do, or a few things we should avoid doing, such as murder and adultery. Instead, everything we do or fail to do must be examined against a higher standard. Is this action an expression of the holy love we are called to be showing the world, or is it not?

There are times when the answer to this question is not completely clear, and times when it is painfully clear that we are on the wrong side of the answer. Even worse, it is quite possible that different people can understand the answer in seriously different ways.

The law, in our lives as Christians, has been replaced by this summary, this command to love our neighbors as ourselves. This simple summary makes things much more difficult for us. Now we have to consider our actions not as actions under the rules of the commandments; now we have to consider the way those actions will show the way God's holy love for us applies to everyone.

As if this wasn't enough, Paul continues with an innocent sounding phrase, "Besides this." After making every action of a Christian a cause for consideration, Paul goes on to address those who hear his words. "You know what time it is, how it is now the moment for you to wake from sleep."

Today we know such a statement as a wake-up call. And, regrettably, such a call is sometimes needed. There are incidents when Christians can seem to be sleeping. There are times when we would rather not be confronted with issues that create problems for us. Issues such as the behavior of other people, while quite suitable for gossip, are often ignored when it comes to our actions.

It is a wake-up call not merely to condemn sinful behavior and move on, as if we have never sinned, but rather to show that holy love for fellow sinners in our lives. It is certainly a given that there are sinful people in this world, and, most certainly there are sinful people sitting in every congregation in the world. And the roll call of sinful people, when we are being honest, begins with a glance in any mirror. When we do that, we see the face of the sinful person we are most familiar with — ourselves.

This is precisely the path Paul takes. Even though we are closer to salvation now than when we became believers, we are still plagued with our tendency to act sinfully. We often know what we should do, but we regularly fail to do it. Paul uses the image of night and day.

We know the night is ending, but in the few waning hours of the night, we are sorely tempted to give in to the easy ways — to follow the ways of the night and not allow ourselves to be bothered by the call to do no wrong to our neighbor.

Paul reminds us of our duty to "lay aside the works of darkness and put on the armor of light." That can be the hardest part of all. If only there was something we could do to earn a share in this salvation, then the whole system would be so much easier. If we could do things, if there was a nice list of the things we needed to do to ensure our place in eternal life, everything would be much easier to understand.

But Paul mentions the things we do, our actions to earn a share in God's salvation, our works as "works of darkness," and he is clearly correct. This is really the root of the problem, and the source of our affection for the Ten Commandments. We would really like to be able to do something to be sure we had earned our way into salvation.

In this world virtually everything people have is the result of somebody doing something to earn it. People who have great resources have often worked hard to gather the resources. At the least, they have parents or grandparents or more remote ancestors who worked hard to gather the resources, and others who worked hard to conserve them. Those who have little are sometimes the object of scorn for a perceived lack of initiative, or creativity, or ambition, or opportunity, or something. What we do has a great part to play in what we have.

It seems as if this should also be true about our relationship with God. A simple list of the things we should do to make that relationship better or stronger, or at least to ensure the relationship exists would be quite helpful. Unfortunately, such a list does not exist. If anything, the very idea of looking for such a list of things for us to do is contrary to the basic message of the New Testament and the church throughout the centuries.

We are already assured of God's love for us, because we do know what time it is. This is the time after Jesus died on the cross for us. This is the time when we are called to live out the holy love of God for us in our lives with our neighbors. We have no list of specific actions to take, but we are given the more difficult thing, to "put on the Lord Jesus Christ"; to let our actions and our lives be guided by the example of the self-sacrificing love of God; to follow the example of Jesus in our relations with all our neighbors, everywhere; to spread the good news of God's love in all the ways we act for our neighbors. Amen.

**Proper 19
Pentecost 17
Ordinary Time 24
Romans 14:1-12**

Life, Death, And Judgment

In 1741, Jonathan Edwards preached a famous sermon with the title, "Sinners in the Hands of an Angry God." In great detail Edwards spoke of the wrath people rightly faced when they confronted the judgment of a God who was angry at the way the people had failed to do what they were called to do. While many people understand only this much about that famous sermon, and hold it up as an example of the worst sort of preaching meant to terrify those who hear what is said, the sermon itself is actually quite pastoral. Once Edwards established the implications of the human behavior of his followers, and the rather gruesome rewards this behavior had earned at the coming judgment before God, he turned his attention to what he described as the door of mercy which Christ opens wide so that all can come through. Rather than merely terrifying the listeners with a vision of the impending doom they faced, Edwards works hard to make the doom real so that he can also proclaim the real mercy that is ready for Christians.

Jonathan Edwards certainly has a notable place in American religious history. And as a result of his most famous sermon, as well as the hundreds of sermons he preached during his life, he is noted as a leading religious figure in early American history, including his central place in the Great Awakening. But his importance on this day is more a matter of his emphasis on the judgment of God. At least in his most famous sermon, Jonathan Edwards was particularly concerned with the judgment of God on sinful people.

Today that is a concept that is not often dealt with seriously. In fact, the concept of judgment and punishment for our sins is more often like a production of the opera *Faustus*. Toward the end of one evening's production of the opera in Dublin, Ireland, Mephistopheles was conducting the title character, Faust, to and through the trap door in the stage that represented the gates of hell. Mephistopheles made the descent quite handily, but Faust, who was rather obese, got stuck halfway through the opening. No amount of pushing or pulling would budge him. Suddenly an Irishman in the balcony shouted, "Thank God! Hell's full!"

The story is humorous, and it deserves at least a smile, but, unfortunately, the story is also a symptom of the problems involved in talking about God's judgment today.

The first problem is that when we speak of God's judgment, it is very easy to get judgmental and tell anyone listening how they are guilty and worthy of being punished for their terrible actions, particularly if we don't happen to like the actions of those other people. Not that such attitudes are anything new. From what he wrote, Paul encountered the same things back in his time. This is clearly the case when Paul writes: "Welcome those who are weak in faith, but not for the purpose of quarreling over opinions. Some believe in eating anything, while the weak eat only vegetables. Those who eat must not despise those who abstain, and those who abstain must not pass judgment on those who eat; for God has welcomed them."

Clearly in what he writes Paul shows echoes of some of the arguments he must have encountered as a pastor over the years. It is easy to be judgmental when we are convinced that the way we do things is right and the way others are doing things is wrong. Of course, there are some things which are clearly wrong, but listen to Paul's example again. Some folks eat anything, others eat only vegetables. Those who eat anything shouldn't despise the vegetarians; and the vegetarians shouldn't despise those who eat anything. In many ways this controversy sounds very modern.

There are many people today who are vegetarians of various degrees, and some of them look at the rest of the world, or at least the non-vegetarian portions of it, as somehow inferior to themselves, or somehow morally deficient for eating meat, with some vegetable eaters somehow despising those who still eat meat. It might be a bit surprising to find a very similar argument dividing the church at the time of Paul. Or, then again, perhaps it shouldn't be much of a surprise at all. After all, people don't seem to have changed their ways all that much since the time of Paul.

In Paul's day the issue revolved around the fact that the meat in a butcher shop was usually the result of an animal that had been sacrificed to a pagan god, and in eating the meat a person was thought to be worshiping the god the animal had been sacrificed to. Christians generally denied the existence of other gods, and many found no obstacle to eating meat. Some Christians had trouble with this theological concept, so they ate only vegetables in order to be sure they were not inadvertently worshiping some pagan god.

The reasons for the selection of a vegetarian diet may have changed, but the basic dietary positions seem to be much the same now as they were twenty centuries ago in the time of Paul.

Another way we get into trouble with the idea of judgment is when we begin to think that God agrees with our ideas, our positions, and our understandings, and God must, therefore, disagree with anyone who has a different idea. This particular idea leads people to cause all sorts of problems, both in the church and in the world. An example of the mischief this attitude can cause is the history of the Crusades, when some Christians claimed that God must want various sites in the Holy Land freed from control by non-Christians. As the struggle to free locations proceeded, various actions, including attacks on Christian cities, massacres of prisoners, both Christians and non-Christians, and the destruction of many of the sites that were supposed to be freed, took place. In fact, there are some experts who say that the problems in the Middle East today are, in some ways, a result of the Crusades.

Another assumption that causes problems is the way we sometimes feel like God's on our side and against the other side. Paul addresses this issue as well. He writes, "Who are you to pass judgment on servants of another? It is before their own lord that they stand or fall. And they will be upheld, for the Lord is able to make them stand." Paul's point here is that no one is able to be the judge of the actions of someone who is following the rightful orders of one's master. The key point is that we are all servants of Christ. Thus, it is very dangerous to question the actions of someone who is the servant of another, not subject to us.

In the military the idea is quite easy to understand. Everyone in the military is somewhere in something called the chain of command. This is the pattern that lawful orders normally follow. The person in charge gives an order, and the people who are under that person carry out the orders. There are some people who are not in this line. Special officers such as doctors and chaplains are normally outside this pattern. Thus, in many circumstances, these officers are not able to give lawful orders concerning things outside their own area of specialization. And, in fact, it is often dangerous for these officers to try to correct the actions of someone who is already following another officer's lawful orders.

In the rest of the world, we are not often in something as strict as a chain of command at all times. And, in fact, we sometimes think that we are in charge of our own lives. But, as Christians, we are each the servants of God, each with a unique relationship to God, and thus, each following our own instructions. It is, as Paul reminds us, not for us to judge the relationship of others to God.

A third problem with judgment is the natural tendency of all people to avoid the consequences of their actions. Consider the story of a college student whose father had high expectations, perhaps too high. When the student found out he had failed all his subjects, he sent his mother a quick e-mail: "Failed everything. Prepare Papa."

Later that day the mother sent an e-mail to her son: "Papa prepared. Prepare yourself."

This ominous message serves to remind us that we often try to avoid the responsibility for our actions. The college student almost certainly had the ability to avoid failure in at least some of the classes that dismal semester. But, when the word came of the results of a semester's inattention and inactivity, the student tried hard to avoid the parental response to the wasted semester.

We often live as if we expect that there will be no judgment, and we will have no responsibility for our actions. We sometimes live very much like a man who was terrified at the prospect of death, particularly a sudden death he had no opportunity to prepare for. Finally, this man made a deal with the Grim Reaper that the man would receive clear, repeated notices before the Reaper would come for him.

One day, unannounced and completely unexpected, the Grim Reaper appeared and demanded the man's life.

"How could you break your pledge?" the man complained bitterly. "I received no warnings from you."

A hideous grin spread across the skeletal features, and then came a response: "What about your failing eyesight, your dimmed sense of hearing, your grey and falling hair, your lost teeth, the wrinkles on your face, your bent body, your dwindling powers, your vanishing memory? Were these things not unmistakable signs and warnings of my impending arrival?"

We want so much to avoid the results of our actions, especially when they look like something we will dislike, some sort of punishment, what we deserve for our sinful lives, that we sometimes ignore even the clear signs that judgment is coming. Sometimes we even try to ignore things like Paul's clear warning at the end of this lesson. "For we will all stand before the judgment seat of God ... So then, each of us will be accountable to God."

And that, when we take it seriously, is a terrifying prospect. Consider the old couple named Si and Rose who prayed together every night. Every night they prayed, "Lord, when you're ready for us, take us. We're ready."

A playful group of boys heard their prayers and decided to have a little fun. They got on top of the house and spoke down the chimney in a deep voice ... "Si ... Si."

Rose asked, "What do you want?"

The voice answered, "I want Si."

"Who are you?"

"I'm from the Lord, and I've come for Si."

"Well, he ain't here; he's gone."

"Then, since Si isn't here, I'll just have to take you, Rose."

Rose spoke sharply, "Get out from under that bed, Si. You know he knows that you are here."

Even without a detailed inventory of our sins, we might all be seriously tempted to crawl under that bed with Si. We are all aware, when we are honest with ourselves, of the many times we have fallen short of what we are expected to do. All of us are saved from what we deserve, what we have earned, by the Christ who died and lived again.

The potential difficulties of judgment raining down on us are the result of the way we live our lives. But the story doesn't end there. As Paul put it, "We do not live to ourselves, and we do not die to ourselves. If we live, we live to the Lord, and if we die, we die to the Lord; so then, whether we live or whether we die, we are the Lord's."

Our failings are not the end. As Jonathan Edwards traced things in his famous sermon, our failings, our sins convict us when we stand before God. But "we are the Lord's," we are saved because Jesus came and took on a human body and died for us. Because of that, we will not be held responsible for what we have done. Because of that, the prospect of God's judgment holds no terror for us, because "we live to the Lord." Amen.

Proper 20
Pentecost 18
Ordinary Time 25
Philippians 1:21-30

Struggles, Death, And Christ

Many people cling very tightly to life. They refuse to let go of it, and hold onto a shred of life beyond all reasonable expectations. And then there are others.

There was an old man, lying in the bed in the back bedroom, surrounded by his wife, daughter, and his four granddaughters. His breath was coming slowly, almost in sighs, and the time between the sighs was stretching to longer and longer periods.

Finally, when the silence had stretched to an unbearable length, the youngest granddaughter threw herself on the bed and cried, "Oh, Grandpa, Grandpa. Don't leave us," and then she began to cry loudly.

Her grandfather slowly moved his hand to pat her arm, then took a deep breath and said, "Let me go. It's peaceful there."

Many people are very much like the youngest granddaughter, clinging to life and expecting everyone else to cling just as strongly as she does. As people get older, some grow to be more like the old man, welcoming death as an end to the struggles and pains of this life. Some few even pray that they will be released into death.

This attitude is sometimes difficult to cope with, even if it is possible to understand the situation of someone who seems to be nearing the end of their life, praying for a quick end to the struggle and pain. What is very difficult is to grasp what Paul is saying in the first sentence of today's lesson. "For to me, living is Christ and dying is gain."

Even though this letter was written while he was in prison, Paul's experience there did not lead him to despair and hope for death. In fact, just a few verses before this lesson, Paul is rejoicing at the opportunity he has been given to speak to his guards, members of the elite imperial guards, and to convert them to following Christ. Clearly he is not wishing for death as a release from a terrible present situation. Paul's attitude is worthy of our attention for at least two reasons.

First, Paul is seriously saying that he views death as something to be sought, something desirable, something he longed for. Not because the current situation was intolerable, but because he viewed death as the way in which he could "be with Christ."

Paul, as a man in middle age, at the height of his abilities, is imprisoned, but not defeated, or despondent, or suicidal. He is engaged in preaching to his guards and writing to the congregations with which he has been involved before this time. And yet, he is able to say, "My desire is to depart and be with Christ, for that is far better."

It is possible that Paul has an understanding of something that we find hard to follow. This life is something most people hold onto very firmly, only reluctantly submitting to the end of it, and often struggling mightily to hold on to it. But Paul writes that he honestly wishes to depart this life and be with Christ.

Should we view this statement as an example of Paul's unwavering faith in Jesus? Certainly. It is a stunning example of the depth of his faith and how that faith informed Paul's actions. He viewed this life as something that was suited only for doing the work of the church, as something that could be sacrificed easily, as the end result of that sacrifice would be to his gain. This life is something that might be nice, or comfortable, or full of opportunities to serve Christ, but it is something that also keeps us away from Jesus.

While Paul finds it necessary to remain in the flesh, to stay alive for the moment, he regards it as far better to be able to live with Christ, in other words, to die. Paul's attitude toward death is something that most Christians find difficult to accept. Our difficulty is sometimes used as an accusation that our faith isn't strong enough, certainly not as strong as Paul's faith was.

The accusation is, in large part, unfair and often untrue as well. It is unfair because we don't often hear much about the Christian attitude toward this life. And Christians, starting with the disciples and Paul, frequently seem to have put up with this life, but consistently looked forward expectantly to life with Christ. The goal is not a long life, or a full life, or a complete life. The Christian goal in this life is to live a faithful life, which is a prelude to our promised life with Christ.

And that faithful life can be understood as the second part of Paul's attitude that is important for us. In his imprisonment, Paul did not complain about his inability to do anything at the moment, and he did not whine about what he could be doing if only he was free. Paul found himself imprisoned. At that time, imprisonment meant that he was chained to two guards at a time in four hour stretches. Rather than complain about the situation, Paul began telling his guards about the good news.

This is like the story about a missionary who spoke to a congregation about the work being accomplished in remote mission fields. After the worship a gentleman approached the missionary and said he was sorry he couldn't go proclaim the gospel in a remote field, but he had a family to support.

The missionary allowed the man to explain his situation, and finally it came out that the man was the engineer of a train. The missionary smiled and asked, "And what about your fireman? Is he a Christian?"

What about your fireman? Tell him the good news of Christ. What about the men chained to you, who hold you in captivity? Paul's answer was to proclaim the good news to them, and he began to convert his guards to Christ.

And what about us? We hear of the rapid growth of the Christian church in Africa, and the slow, but steady growth in Asia, and the great difficulties faced in many other parts of the world, and we sometimes think there is little or nothing we can do where we are. A contribution to a mission appeal, perhaps, but nothing really substantive.

What about the people who work next to us? What about our friends? What about the people around us? It is sadly and deeply ironic that in America, a country which is often described as a Christian country, there are thousands of people who have no church home. But it is even sadder and more ironic that we work with these people every day and make little effort to tell them about the good news of Jesus.

Many people are somewhat embarrassed by hearing that they are expected to proclaim the good news to the people around them. But consider what Paul wrote in this lesson. "Only, live your life in a manner worthy of the gospel of Christ, so that, whether I come and see you or am absent and hear about you, I will know that you are standing firm in one spirit, striving side by side with one mind for the faith of the gospel, and are in no way intimidated by your opponents."

How can we proclaim? How can we tell people? Paul's answer is really quite simple, and hardly involves any words, at least at first. In fact, Paul's answer is so painfully simple, it is almost embarrassing. "Live your life in a manner worthy of Christ." Our proclamation is centered on our very life, our actions that are worthy of Christ. Not, to be sure, that this is an easy thing. But it is the way we are called to proclaim the good news. We are called to proclaim God's love to the world around us by the way we live out that love.

There are many excuses that are offered for why we don't always carry out this idea, but all those things are only excuses, not reasons why we are unable to do what we should be doing. It is easy to be intimidated and it isn't always easy to proclaim the good news. In fact, it is quite difficult and often a struggle. And Paul knew that, too. "For God has graciously granted you the privilege not only of believing in Christ, but of suffering for him as well — since you are having the same struggle that you saw I had and now hear that I still have."

This is not a matter of having someone who has never faced the situation telling us what we should be about, because Paul is no ivory tower theorist. He has spent the few months before writing the words of our lesson, talking daily with his guards in prison, and telling them about the good news of Jesus Christ. Paul has been struggling for many years, and all those who hear his words know of those struggles. Paul reminds them of the way they, and we, have been granted the privilege of suffering for Christ.

This is perhaps the part of this lesson with which it is the most difficult to cope. We rarely even think in these terms. Who ever tries to convince people that suffering is a privilege? Suffering is suffering; something we generally would prefer not to have to face, certainly something we would rather not find very much of in our lives. Suffering, after all, is what we want to relieve. We certainly do not want to go out and seek suffering as a normal daily activity. At the least, people who do seek out suffering on a daily basis are generally regarded as having significant problems. But Paul recognizes that suffering is a natural part of the struggle all Christians share.

In many ways this lesson seems to present us with a rather bleak picture. Paul begins by pointing out that dying is gain. Then he points out, both in the words he uses and in the example of his own life, that we are called to spread the good news where we find ourselves. Our mission is where we are. Finally, he points out that one result of that mission is going to be suffering and struggle.

If Paul stopped there, his efforts would certainly not involve much of a promise for us. But he slips in a reminder of the promise when he says, "For God has graciously granted you the privilege not only of believing in Christ." The privilege ... of believing in Christ. That is certainly not the way the idea is often expressed, but it is a reminder of the promise we have, the promise we share with Paul and with Christians throughout the ages: The promise that we have the privilege of believing in Christ; the promise that because we believe, we share Paul's perspective that dying is gain, for then we will be with Christ, and that is far better, for Paul and for us, than what we face in this life; the promise that we are saved and assured a place with Christ for all eternity. Amen.

**Proper 21
Pentecost 19
Ordinary Time 26
Philippians 2:1-13**

Complete Joy

There was once a man who decided he was dead. He was actually quite alive, but the man insisted he was really dead. The man's friends were quite concerned over this attitude, and tried hard to persuade the man he was actually alive, but nothing seemed to work.

Finally, one friend with a scientific turn of mind tried to convince the man of the error of his insistence. The friend pointed out that dead men don't bleed. After some time to consider the possibilities, the man who said he was dead agreed. At that point his friend took a pin and stuck the man's finger. Blood began to flow slowly from the wound, and the man stared at the drops of blood forming on his finger. Then, quietly, he said, "Well, what do you know? Dead men do bleed."

In this letter Paul speaks of death as something he regards favorably. Not in some strange way like that man who was convinced he was really dead, but in a healthy way, as the only way he could begin to live with Christ. In the greater scheme of this letter, the desire of Paul for death is only a little thing, something that can be ignored quite easily. It is easy to overlook the little things.

The lesson today begins with another little thing, a phrase it is easy to drop or skip past when we read the text, a phrase that can be forgotten quickly by the time we get to the end of Paul's sentence. "If then.... " Or, perhaps more precisely, "If...."

It is a simple little word, but one which makes everything that comes after it different than it might otherwise be. Instead of a statement of fact or even a command, the sentence that begins this lesson is more of a question and a hope.

Paul does write in long sentences, and this is not only a long one, but also a complicated one to understand. "If," Paul begins, "there is any encouragement in Christ, any consolation from love, any sharing in the Spirit, any compassion and sympathy." The Greek begins each clause with the word "if," which heightens the effect. If there is any encouragement in Christ, if there is any consolation from love, if there is any sharing in the Spirit, if there is any compassion and sympathy. If, in other words, those who receive this letter, if those who hear these words have any of these things, then Paul wants them to do something for him.

If people feel any encouragement in Christ, any strengthening from the body of Christ in the church, any appeal to that part of us which is good and true, any calling of us by Christ to be a part of his work here, then Paul has a claim on them to do what he wishes.

If there is any consolation from love, any encouragement for us from our fellow believers, any comfort in our times of sorrow and loss from the body of Christ, then Paul has a claim on us to do what he wishes.

If there is any sharing in the Spirit, any fellowship with others, any generosity in our time of need, any participation in our grief, then Paul has a claim on us to do what he wishes.

If there is any compassion and sympathy, if there is any affection, love, deep feeling, pity, or mercy, then Paul has a claim on us to do what he wishes.

And that is the critical point — what Paul wishes us to do. He states it simply: He wants the people who heard his words to make his joy complete. In the Greek, the word translated as *complete* can also mean *fill up, be well supplied, fill completely to the brim,* or even *give true meaning to*. In some ways this might sound difficult to do, especially to something like joy.

Our joy is not often thought of as something concrete, something to be filled up, and even the idea of being well supplied with joy is a little jarring. Most often we think of joy as something that is fleeting, something we have briefly, and then the real world intrudes and our joy begins to fade. All too often joy is not something we find in our lives every day, all the time. The idea of complete joy is something we have trouble grasping.

Paul speaks of our actions as something that will make his joy complete. At least, that is one way to paraphrase what he writes in this lesson, allowing for some issues of centuries and distance. It is with our actions that we will make his joy complete. It is fair to ask what actions Paul had in mind.

The answer is to be found in the four items that complete the first sentence. Paul tells his hearers to "be of the same mind, having the same love, being in full accord and of one mind." These actions sound almost like the directions a church official might give to a congregation that is split by various problems and issues. But that, at least as we understand the situation in Philippi, is not what was happening in the congregation.

In fact, later in this letter Paul instructs two women by name, Euodia and Syntyche, "to be of the same mind in the Lord." Then he reminds the rest of the congregation of their obligation to help these women. This rather brief reference, in the beginning of chapter 4, is the only indication we have of the situation that existed in the congregation. It seems that there was a disagreement of some sort, most likely a fairly small matter, with two important members of the congregation choosing sides and attacking each other in some ways.

This is a situation that is entirely too common in too many congregations today. It is also one way to understand the proliferation of congregations in a single locale. One congregation grew until there was a disagreement over something, then one group, one side of the argument, left and organized another congregation.

Consider the small congregation that was exploring options for the floor in the parish hall. Everyone agreed that the old floor needed to be replaced, but the argument came when the subject of covering the floor was raised. The lowest cost covering was the carpet on sale at the warehouse outlet nearby, but one member of the council objected strenuously. While the objections were heard, the council eventually voted to purchase and install the carpet.

The person who objected commented, "Well, you'll install a carpet over my dead body."

Another member of the council was heard to mutter, "That's gonna make one heck of a lump."

Paul was well aware of the potential for this sort of disagreement in a congregation. It is quite likely that he had personally witnessed such flare ups both in the congregations with which he had been associated and, quite likely, in the synagogues he had known as he was growing up. It is easy for people who care deeply about the church to become quite passionate about what happens in the church and about things the church does.

This should probably not surprise us. In every other part of our lives, wherever there are people working with each other, there are some frictions and small disagreements and mild arguments about how things are being done. The church is full of the same sort of people as we find in the rest of the world, and in the church they have the same sorts of frictions and small disagreements and mild arguments about how things are being done.

Knowing this, Paul wants those who hear his words, those who are presently involved in some of those frictions and small disagreements and mild arguments about how things are being done, to work on doing three things.

First, he wants them to be of the same mind. That sounds vaguely uncomfortable, as if everyone should think the same way, never express any ideas other than what a leader says, or else suffer the consequences. In point of fact, Paul was certainly not suggesting that everyone had to have only the same thoughts. However, he was encouraging everyone to have the same attitude and approach to possible dissension.

Paul wants us to have an attitude that is willing to hear both sides of an issue and to listen with an open mind, actually and honestly searching for a resolution of the problem that is appropriate. This, of course, is what many people insist they are doing, even when what they are really doing is insisting on their opinion and trying to force everyone else to accept what they have to say.

Paul was involved in many controversies during his life, including some that led to councils of the early church to settle the issues, near riots in the Temple, and, finally, his arrest and transportation to Rome for a final trial. With this record, it is no surprise that Paul recognizes the dangers of conflict in the church and in a congregation. It should be no surprise that Paul has figured out a way to reduce the danger of conflict in a congregation.

The first step is for the members of the congregation to work to be of the same mind. The second step is similar: The members are expected to have the same love. The same love is an interesting concept. Not that everyone should love exactly the same things and people, but that everyone is equally beloved of Christ, and because of the love of Christ, everyone recognizes the others in the congregation as fellow members of the Body of Christ. In many ways, the idea of sharing the same love is the foundation that makes it possible for us to share the same mind.

The final thing we are to do is to be in full accord and of one mind. Once again, not every person in the congregation is to be identical, as if there were no way that people could differ. Rather, the members of the congregation should work together to attain consensus within the congregation.

Not that differences of opinion are never going to happen, because they will. Not that members will never disagree over what needs to be done, because people do disagree. Not that there will never be doubts and concerns, because people often have doubts and concerns.

To be of full accord and one mind is Paul's way of reminding those who hear his words that with all the problems and disputes and difficulties we encounter within the church, we do come together with the other members and work with each other completely because we are all a part of the Body of Christ.

This sounds very difficult, and it can be quite a challenge. But Paul does not leave things there. He does not simply present some hopelessly optimistic statements of how things should be, and then move on. He goes on to offer some very practical ways to do what will make his joy complete.

First, Paul suggests, "In humility regard others as better than yourselves." It is such simple advice, and such a difficult thing to accomplish. But, if we think about it, regarding others as better than ourselves is quite a practical way to ensure that conflicts rarely get out of hand. In fact, following this advice usually means that what conflict exists is truly centered on questions that matter, never on questions of one person's ego, another person's position, and someone else's pride. If we consistently regard others as better than ourselves, and each person regards others as better than themselves, then it is much easier to do those things that will make Paul's joy complete.

If that advice isn't enough, Paul goes on to say, "Let each of you look not to your own interests, but to the interests of others." Of course each person has one's own interests, but the interests of others are not only important, their interests should be of primary concern to us. Consider, as an example, the manner in which one of the most potent military formations of the ancient world was organized. The Greek phalanx presented a wall of spears and shields and swords to the enemy, with virtually no room for the enemy to penetrate and attack the men who made up the wall of shields. However, the structure of the formation required that each man hold up his shield to protect the next man in the wall. No one protected himself.

An extreme example, certainly. But every soldier who ever served in a phalanx understood perfectly what this advice meant. "Look not to your own interests, but to the interests of others." Once again, Paul's advice works itself out precisely within the church, because when we each look out for others, then the interests of all are taken care of. Just like the shields of the ancient phalanx, each person protects and cares for another, and thus each person's interests are taken care of.

Finally, Paul offers the last part of his advice, "Let the same mind be in you that was in Christ Jesus." This is probably the most difficult piece of advice to follow. Paul expands this advice by quoting an early hymn, and the words of the hymn point out the difficulties we face in trying to follow the example of Christ. The verse of the hymn ends with the reminder that Jesus "became obedient to the point of death — even death on a cross."

That can be the difficult part, that obedience. So long as Paul is giving advice, the situation is only uncomfortable. If we don't manage to follow everything, then we can be uncomfortable, but it isn't really something that could be helped. After all, lots of advice is never acted on. But when we start talking about obedience, things get much more serious.

Let the same mind, an obedient mind, be obedient even to the point of death.

Things are really quite serious with this instruction. Suddenly we are speaking of obedience, even to the point of death, obedience to that advice to "do nothing from selfish ambition or conceit, but in humility regard others as better than yourselves. Let each of you look not to your own interests, but to the interests of others. Let the same mind be in you that was in Christ Jesus."

Paul closes this lesson by re-emphasizing the idea of our obedience. "Therefore, my beloved, just as you have always obeyed me, not only in my presence, but much more now in my absence, work out your own salvation with fear and trembling; for it is God who is at work in you, enabling you both to will and to work for his good pleasure."

And so, we work to obey what Paul wrote, to have the same mind that was in Christ Jesus, to be obedient, even to the point of death. As we struggle with God's call on us to be obedient, we also know that God is at work in us and among us helping us to obey his commands. Amen.

**Proper 22
Pentecost 20
Ordinary Time 27
Philippians 3:4b-14**

Bragging Rights

A mouse was once riding on the back of an elephant, and the pair went across a rickety bridge. As might be expected, the bridge shook and rattled. When the duo had successfully navigated the bridge, the mouse exclaimed, "My, oh my, we certainly made that bridge shake, didn't we?"

It is all too common an experience to meet people who sound as if they are somehow related to that mouse. People who brag loudly about their successes, their skills, the ways they are crucial to the history of the world, or at least to their own little part of it, even when everyone who knows them suspects rather strongly that these people are really much less than they claim to be.

And even though we would like to think that other people are the ones who act that way, if the truth is told, all of us are certainly capable of acting that way at times. In fact, even Paul is capable of bragging this way. Paul begins by reminding his readers that if anyone should ever feel that they are guaranteed salvation, at least according to everything a person can do, the person who should feel most secure is Paul.

As he lists all his qualifications, all his reasons to brag, it sounds as if he had everything possible going for him. "Circumcised on the eighth day, a member of the people of Israel, of the tribe of Benjamin, a Hebrew born of Hebrews; as to the law, a Pharisee; as to zeal, a persecutor of the church; as to righteousness under the law, blameless."

Paul establishes his credentials as a Jew, one of God's chosen people, and then goes even farther. As a Pharisee, Paul was not only aware of the requirements of the law, he was dedicated to carrying out every rule. As a persecutor of the followers of Christ, he was zealous to defend the Jewish faith against the heretical sect of Christians. Finally, as one who would be judged by the requirements of the law, Paul regarded himself as completely and totally blameless under those rules. Sounds pretty good, at least if you're Paul.

But there are two problems with bragging like this. First, no matter how high an opinion we might have of ourselves, it is usually true that there are some areas where we fall short. Even Paul might be convinced that he falls short in some ways, and in other places he does acknowledge that he falls far short in many ways. In fact, here Paul writes this bragging list mostly for effect, not really to brag about how wonderful he is.

But the second problem is more serious than merely our tendency to overlook some of our personal faults and flaws. When we brag in this way, or when Paul brags in this way, or even when that mouse brags in this way, we build ourselves up by comparing ourselves to other people. The other people inevitably end up somehow less than the people doing the bragging.

Bragging always involves elevating ourselves by pushing other people down. Bragging is an exclusive sort of thing, where comparisons are made, invariably to someone else's detriment. Bragging is destructive, poisoning personal relations and threatening peaceful relations in groups of people. For all these reasons bragging is something Paul actually discourages.

Here, Paul brags simply to show how much he seemed to have to brag about. After all, in his situation, he might have appeared to have it made. He had done everything right, so he was assured that he was the most privileged of God's chosen people. And yet, Paul quickly points out what the value of these things he has been bragging about really is. As he puts it, "Yet whatever gains I had, these I have come to regard as loss because of Christ."

All that good stuff he had been so proud of, all the things he had worked so hard to accomplish, the sum total of his life suddenly became a complete loss. The effect of this admission by Paul should be startling. It isn't often that a person who has so much to brag about, someone who is as proud as Paul was, comes to admit that everything he has recently bragged about is meaningless to him. But Paul does acknowledge that all those things are meaningless for him because of Jesus.

Because he knows Christ, Paul realized all the things that people have to brag about are really meaningless. What matters is the simple fact that he now knows Christ. Everything else has lost meaning.

Having established this fact, Paul begins to brag once again. It seems bragging is a habit that is hard to break. But now Paul brags not about his accomplishments for Christ, but about the fact that he has lost everything, and in fact regards everything of this world as rubbish. The only thing that really matters to Paul is his relationship with Christ.

It is this relationship that is the complete opposite of bragging. Bragging shuts people out, diminishes others, and draws exclusive circles in our world. It diminishes others when we try to brag about ourselves and our accomplishments.

The opposite happens in this relationship with Christ that Paul has, and that we share with him, a relationship that opens us up to other people. Rather than diminishing, this relationship with Christ helps us to lift up others, to praise their actions, and to think of others as better than we are. Rather than excluding others, this relationship with Christ invites others to join with us and share in the love of God as we have come to know it through Christ.

Through all of this, we might expect Paul to show a little pride, a little bit of bragging about how he has already established this relationship, and enjoyed the benefits of it such as resurrection and eternal life. We might expect it, but Paul surprises us once again when he confesses that he has not yet obtained the benefits or even reached the goal of a complete relationship with Christ.

Instead, he confesses that he is still working on it. From Christ's side of the relationship, Paul has already been completely accepted and made Christ's own. But, on his side of the relationship, Paul is still working on it, still trying hard to accept the complete relationship. But even Paul finds this to be something he is still working on.

For all our efforts to be perfect, to accomplish things, to be successful, Paul stands as a reminder to us that it isn't quite that simple when we speak of our relationship with Christ. Paul has spent years working on his relationship, trying to get everything in order and to ensure he has done everything possible to perfect the relationship. But he finds, after years dedicated to this project, he is still working on it, still pressing on, still straining forward toward the goal of a full and complete relationship with Christ.

It works that way with us, too. We try hard to get everything right, and then we find that there are always some things that cause us problems.

There was a mother who had a number of children. One day when all the children were home she ran next door to visit with her neighbor for just a few minutes. When she returned home, she found the five youngest children in the living room, excited and huddled in the center of the new carpet with something wiggly and squirmy. At first, everything seemed fine, but then the mother realized that the children were gathered around a family of skunks.

The mother screamed, "Run, children, run!" And the children each grabbed a skunk and ran for the door.

That seems to be the way it works for us, too. The problem is that bragging is so easy for us. It is simple to claim a perfect relationship with Christ; the hard part is actually to have a relationship in the face of all that tempts us to turn away from Christ. And all that tempts us seems to be warm and furry and cute, and we bring it into our lives without realizing just how much of a problem it can be. Our relationship with Christ is threatened by the warm, furry, cute little thing, just as a home is threatened by a family of skunks.

Paul knew the problem all too well, and he told the people who heard his words how he dealt with it. "I want to know Christ and the power of his resurrection," Paul wrote, "and the sharing of his sufferings by becoming like him in his death." There is nothing here about warm and fuzzy, cute and cuddly. Rather, there is talk about sharing the suffering of Jesus, the rejection by family and friends, the poverty, the arrest, beating, trial, and finally, ultimately, his crucifixion and his death.

This is not the sort of thing people brag about. This is the sort of thing people hide and try desperately to ignore. This is like the woman who wanted to be admitted to an upper-crust organization that required a genealogical search and a clean family tree for at least four generations.

The woman hired a genealogist to do the necessary research, and a few days later the genealogist reported to the woman. "There is a problem. It seems your maternal grandfather died in the electric chair in Sing Sing."

"Oh, my," the woman said, "that will never do. Can't you just forget about him?"

"No, I can't."

After some further discussion, the genealogist agreed to put the best possible face on the story in the final report. The final report read, "Subject's maternal grandfather worked in a state institution in upstate New York. Very dedicated to his work, he literally died in harness."

Most people today would prefer to hide the fact of ancestors with unsavory lives. Certainly an ancestor who was executed by the state for a crime such as treason or conspiracy to overthrow the government would be an ancestor who would only rarely be mentioned. Yet, in reality, that is what happened to Jesus.

Here is Paul, an upright man, trying as hard as he can to become like Jesus. Here is Paul, by his words and by his example, urging us to do our best to become like Jesus as well. Our following of Jesus involves more than merely following actions; it involves following attitudes as well. Speaking of both our actions and our attitudes in following Christ, Dietrich Bonhoeffer once said, "Anyone who thinks his time is too valuable to spend keeping quiet will eventually have no time for God or his brother, but only for himself and his own follies."

Paul is urging us to join him in pressing on toward the prize of the heavenly call of God in Christ Jesus; the heavenly call on us of following the example of Christ, of serving others, of working for the betterment of other people, of living for Christ. We know that we will not earn anything by this, but we strive to live this way because Christ has already established a perfect relationship with us. Because that relationship comes from Jesus, we are working hard, straining forward to perfect our relationship with Christ. Amen.

Sermons On The Second Readings

For Sundays After Pentecost (Last Third)

Worthy Of God

Rick Brand

Preface

There is a mixture of blessing and curse in the use of a lectionary. Now after almost forty years of preaching, I have been through these cycles more times than I can compute. It means that I have faced down these texts repeatedly. There is the curse of seeing some of these texts again and again. There was little gold in some of them the first time. Do I just pull out the one used three years ago and let it go, or abandon the lectionary for this week? But there is the blessing possible because one may be tempted to dig deeper. One may accept the discipline and rework the dirt to see if something else is there.

A friend of mine once suggested that "every sermon which was worthy of being preached the first time is worthy to be preached repeatedly. The only trouble is that most sermons were not worthy of the first preaching." I heard Fred Craddock say that congregations enjoy hearing sermons again the way they enjoy watching old movies. I have never been totally convinced of that. These sermons may have been written before their time, but they are not old creations. As preachers, we work together to bring forth our best.

I am grateful to all who have had a part in helping me find a word to say to the glory of God.

Proper 23
Pentecost 21
Ordinary Time 28
Philippians 4:1-9

No Idea

"I entreat Euodia and I entreat Syntyche to agree in the Lord." We have no idea what in the world these two women were quarreling about. Perhaps if we had had *Entertainment Weekly* or the *National Enquirer* or MSNBC or the investigative potential of the Internet we would have more information about the nature of the split. But we have no idea what had set these two women against each other.

Earlier in the letter, Paul had given some advice about trying to have the same mind in them that was in Christ Jesus. He urged them to be less selfish, to look to the interests of others ahead of their own interests. He gave them the example of Jesus Christ not grasping at equality with God but surrendering all that glory to come and to redeem us. Paul tells the church that they need to do all things without grumbling or questioning that they might be blameless and innocent in the midst of an evil and perverse world. So perhaps these two women were somehow caught up in the general selfishness of the church at Philippi.

We know that there were a lot of questions about who Jesus was, about his resurrection, about the Second Coming, about whether the grace of Jesus made it okay for us to do anything we wanted or whether we still had to keep the Jewish laws. What happens to the dead in Christ? Will they get to be in heaven when Jesus comes? There were big and important questions and it is possible that these two women had different ideas about how Christians should be living. Of course, there is never a shortage of controversial questions and tough issues to divide the church. Abortion, homosexuality, praying with your hands up in the air, bringing in a band for jazzy hymns, making a place in the church for handicapped people, war with Iraq: There are always enough reasons for Christian people to get out of sorts with each other.

But it is probably just as true to say that they probably had no idea that they would be remembered down through the history of the Christian Church as the two women who were fussing and feuding. They probably never imagined that their legacy in history would be the fact that they could not get along. They had the potential for being remembered for so much more. As scholars now look back into the scriptures looking for a more balanced approach, looking for women to recognize and hold up as participants in the work of God's people, these two women would have been excellent examples. If we ever needed evidence that Paul lived a better theology than he wrote, all we have to do is listen to his comments about how important and significant he says these two women were in the work of organizing and leading the church. Paul may have said that women should be silent in church, but Euodia and Syntyche labored side by side with Paul in teaching, preaching, organizing, and running the church. These were two exceptional and gifted women who had made significant efforts on behalf of the church at Philippi, and now they were at odds with each other. We have no idea what it was. It might have been theological; it might have been church politics; it might have been personal; it might have been children. But they surely had no idea that this fight that was between them would be the only reason they would ever be remembered. You wonder if the fight would have been as important to them if they had known that the fight was all that would be remembered. Is the fight you are having significant enough to be remembered for 2,000 years?

We really have no idea what these two women were so upset about and why they were so at odds with each other. They had no idea that the quarrel would be the only thing they would be remembered for because they had no idea that Paul would dare mention it in his letter. But it is obvious that it is no small thing. It was a significant issue. There was a deep tear in the Body of Christ and Paul mentions it. This is no inconsequential matter. It is important because it is a quarrel between two leaders, two major people in the church. It is a split that is affecting and harming the life of the whole church. We know it is a significant issue because Paul chose to mention it in the letter to be read publicly before the whole church. Paul mentions it in a very careful way. He is very diplomatic. He "entreats" Euodia and, he uses the exact same word, he "entreats" Syntyche. He mentions the names of the women in alphabetic order so that he does not show preference. He urges them to find a way to come together in Jesus Christ.

They probably had no idea that Paul would dare mention the split and the quarrel in his public letter. But Paul makes it the first thing he says when he comes to the last chapter and begins to give his summary instructions. Paul says it right out loud, in front of everybody, because somehow Paul really believes that it is part of the work of the church, part of the responsibility of the people of God, it is the mission of the people of the way to be the agents of God's reconciliation. Paul mentions the conflict publicly because it is the public work of the people of God to work to make peace. Blessed are the peacemakers. The people who have received the grace of God ought to be the ones who bear witness to the grace of God by acting out the grace of God. It is not that the people of God will never have conflicts or quarrels (why should we think anything so absurd?), but it is that the people of God, the Church, ought to be the place where it acknowledges those quarrels and resolves them. Paul believes that is how the church makes visible the reality of the love and grace of God. People of God show the love and mercy of God to the world by working with these two leaders and bringing them together in grace.

An article in the *Christian Century* suggested that the kind of church that Paul has in mind tends to happen nowadays in the basement of the church and not in the sanctuary. It may never have been able to happen in the sanctuary, but the kind of church that Paul has in mind happens in those groups where people come and confess they are having a problem, and the group then begins the real, difficult, painful work of trying to help that person change. It is in AA groups where the group works to help the person move forward in a life without drinking. It is in "Tough Love" parenting classes where parents and children come and acknowledge that they are in conflict, and the group works to try to help parents establish boundaries and limits and to stick to those boundaries, and to teach children how to negotiate maturity and change the boundaries. It is in "Guardian Ad Litem" programs that meet in the church parlor for training where people know there is a conflict between three or four different sides and they are there to speak up for the child and to work toward some agreement.

The church at Philippi probably had no more idea how to deal with these two women in worship when they heard the letter than we would know what to do if someone stood up now and acknowledged a quarrel with somebody. It is a great compliment to the church at Philippi that Paul mentioned this quarrel and called them to be a part of the ministry of reconciliation. It was an affirmation that they had matured, that he thought they had developed in grace and in understanding of themselves as ministers of grace that he could entrust to them the needs of these two women and to believe that the church in their basement would find a way to help them become reconciled. That is what we have been given, the ministry of reconciliation. In the second letter to the church at Corinth Paul says, "All this is from God, who reconciled us to himself through Christ, and has given us the ministry of reconciliation; that is, in Christ God was reconciling the world to himself, not counting their trespasses against them, and entrusting the message of reconciliation to us. So we are ambassadors for Christ" (2 Corinthians 5:18-20). Paul mentions this quarrel between two of his friends because he believes it is the work of God's people to work with them to bring reconciliation.

Maybe we have no idea what we would do or how we would react to hearing an announcement that so and so were quarreling and we needed to help them become reconciled. But the first prayer request from the cards in the pew rack, when a church put prayer request cards in with the hymnbooks, was from a couple who announced that things are not as solid nor as strong as they believe they ought to be. They want the church to help them become stronger and help them make the marriage survive. They looked to the church to help them agree in the Lord.

The church at Philippi probably had no idea it would hear that assignment when they came to worship. They probably did not expect Paul to mention that embarrassing stuff in the middle of his letter. That kind of announcement expects us to do something. It makes us responsible. Maybe that is why we always want happy stories and pretty music and never want to hear a negative word in our worship. So and so are in the midst of a nasty divorce; we need to help them agree in the Lord. We don't know what to say. We don't want to get involved. So and so are going to court over a contract dispute. We need to entreat them to agree in the Lord. Those words would make us uncomfortable. Mother and daughter are twisted in a nasty fight, we need to help them. Perhaps it asks too much. Perhaps it is more than we can do. Paul seems to think it is part of what we have been called into being to help do. Right there in front of everybody he asks us to help make reconciliation possible.

**Proper 24
Pentecost 22
Ordinary Time 29
1 Thessalonians 1:1-10**

Always?

Now there is a greeting that will knock you back a moment. "We always give thanks to God for all of you." Other translations put it: "We give thanks to God always for all of you." And maybe Paul was pouring it on a little thick, but it is a greeting that will put one on the defensive, because if we are honest, we cannot reply that we have always been praying for Paul. If we are honest, we cannot say that we are always faithful in our prayers at all. Paul tells the church at Thessalonica that he is always praying for them and giving thanks to God for them. But if we are honest we cannot tell each other that we are always praying for each other. In fact, there are days when I never get to my devotional life. So there goes "always" automatically.

Even more typically, the focus of our prayer life changes almost daily. We do not pray for the same thing over and over. We have different issues and concerns each day. We bring to God our prayers to help us deal with our daily issues, and if it takes more than two weeks for God to fix our problems, we are probably praying for something different by then. Always? Paul is praying for the church in Thessalonica always? It certainly holds up for us a standard of devotion that humbles us and embarrasses us. Few of us pray always and seldom does our agenda remain always the same. Paul says he is always giving thanks for the blessings that have been revealed in the saints at Thessalonica, and our prayers seldom touch on giving thanks for the gifts that others have received. If we pray for others, it is because of our desires that they receive a new blessing, that God may help them through a new problem, that God will give to those who are without work new jobs, that God will heal those whom we love from their illnesses.

Paul says he thanks God always for the blessings that are constantly being revealed in the life of the congregation at Thessalonica. Paul says there are three exciting witnesses to the power of God in the life of that congregation: the works of faith, the labors of love, and the endurance inspired by hope in Jesus Christ.

George Barna, president of the Barna Research Group, reported recently that a survey of active believers said their faith is consistently growing, helping them to feel connected to other people, and helping them to feel good about life and to take care of themselves and others.[1] That is part of the work of faith in our lives. When Paul talks about the work of faith, Paul is talking about the effects of faith in the lives of individuals. The work of faith is the change that faith produces in the heart and mind of the believer. Faith is that which links our facts to meaning. Faith is that which leaps into the unknown by trusting the unseen. Emily Dickinson, the gentle recluse of a poet, describes the work of faith: "Faith — is the Pierless Bridge Supporting what we see Unto the scene that we do not — Too slender for the eye." The work of faith is to seek understanding; its job is to take us from the facts and carry us toward meaning.

It is the work of faith to provide us a way to live with all our contradictions into a meaningful and purposeful way. The religious newspaper writer said that "earthly life is full of contradictions and should be savored accordingly. Contradiction, true enough, is unbearable. Nobody wants too much of it. Yet, enormous spiritual work is launched every day on propositions imbedded in paradox, incongruity, contradiction. Four big ones: God is everywhere, yet invisible. Life is lived forward, as Kierkegaard said, but only understood backward. Happiness is best pursued through selflessness. The incarnation is at the center of the Christian story, but just try explaining it to a stranger."[2] It is the work of faith to take our fragile pieces and hold them together in a miracle of purpose and meaning.

But not only is faith supposed to help us find a comprehensive wholeness for our pieces, the work of faith is constantly to be making our picture larger. "Belief makes the mind abundant," said W. B. Yeats. Faith's work is to open up life to larger and larger realities, to open up life on all its sides, at every level to new possibilities and new life.

Beyers Naudé was a 69-year-old white clergyman in South Africa during the struggle against apartheid. He was placed under house arrest for his resistance to the governmental laws. Naudé said it was his faith that changed him. "I should possibly mention that it was in four different areas where I sought light based on the light of Christ. Firstly, the whole question of the unity and diversity of the human race; secondly, on the unity and diversity of the church on earth; thirdly, the responsibility of the church in the different areas of human society; and fourthly, the necessity of the church to play a role of reconciler in situations of serious tensions."[3] The work of faith moved Beyers Naudé from a narrow world of white Christianity to a grander and more exciting kingdom where all people are God's children and deserving of the same love and justice. Faith is not finished with you yet. The Spirit of God is at work in you. Through faith the Spirit is at work to make you into the image of Jesus Christ. It is a work of faith that links us to the meaning that assures us that we are loved, that we matter, that what we do has significance, and that what we do for others has eternal significance.

Thus there are labors of love. There are actions and deeds that we do out of love of God for other people. There are acts of compassion on behalf of other people that grow out of our understanding and vision of life that is given by faith. It is called labor because it is hard. The report from mission trips is that they do a lot of hot, sweaty, and difficult work. There were trucks to unload and food to unpack. There were pots to scrub and dishes to wash. There were hot ovens and stoves to attend. They were labors of love because they were done out of love in response to the love of God in Jesus Christ for us. The mission workers do not know the people they help. They cannot say that they do it because they love them because they were lovable people. Those were labors of love for those people out of response of love for Christ because God has shown his love for the workers. In gratitude for God's love for us, we go and do labors of love for God to those people.

Labors of love are the doing of hard things for others on lots of different levels. There is the glass of cold water to a thirsty person. There is the winter jacket for a school-age child. There are scholarships to camp from individuals. There are deeds of kindness from one person to another. Forgiveness of others is one of the most difficult labors of love we are called to do. Out of the love of God for us while we were yet sinners, we serve that love by forgiving others. The labor of love is to act toward the one who has offended as if they had not offended us. The labor of love is to look at the terrorists as if they were still human beings and to be treated with respect and dignity even while they are punished for the crimes and actions they commit. That is hard labor.

The labors of love are on a personal level. They are carried out on an institutional level as well. There are agencies and groups who are working to provide compassion and justice for all people, like local food pantries and the Red Cross. The labors of love are carried out in the political and international arena as well. There are vast and difficult forces at work in the world that result in hunger, starvation, disease, and unemployment, which can only be changed by political decisions and public will. There are labors of love which must be focused on all levels.

The work of faith and the labors of love can cause us to grow tired and discouraged. There needs to be a patience, an endurance, a steadfastness of hope that sustains faith and love through to the end. It is the conviction that what one is doing is the work and will of God and that God has a purpose and a providence that will sustain and preserve the work we do. The patience of hope, the steadfastness of hope, is joy that brightens all our work. Why are we working and doing these labors? What do we expect and what gives us the reason to believe that what we expect will happen? We can endure almost any kind of how and what when life is sustained by a why. The hope of the Christian faith is grounded in the victory of Christ over death. Our faith and our love is a response to what God has done for us in Jesus Christ, and our hope is rooted in the promise that what we have seen in Christ is God's intention for all life.

Our hope never becomes exhausted because it is not grounded on our own strength or the strength of our economy or the quality of our education. Our hope comes to us from the grace of God we have seen and received in Christ Jesus. On Christ the solid rock we stand and in the wonder of God's resurrection of Jesus, we continue to plant small seeds of goodness and justice in the conviction that they will grow into huge bushes of goodness and justice. We do not become discouraged when resources become low and crowds drift away, because God raised up the one abandoned on the cross. We work in hope and confidence that where we are doing the will and purpose of God, God will not forsake or abandon. We work and live in the steadfastness of hope that the one who has given new life in Christ will be the one to whom we go in the end.

It has stayed with me through the years. The scene from the movie *The Hiding Place* about the ten Boom sisters. Corrie and her sister Betsie were talking with the other women in a concentration camp about the love of God and inviting the other women to share in that love. "You mean that your God of love is sitting up in heaven and cannot smell the burnt flesh of the women who are suffering and being killed down here? Look at these hands, I was first violinist for the Prague Orchestra and now they have been broken and shattered. You mean to say that God intended all this." She waves her gnarled fingers around the barracks. The camera watches as the two ten Boom sisters struggle with the work of faith to include those fingers in their understanding of meaning. But their hope is not built on the prison surroundings, but on the cross and on the Christ who was God enduring our pain, who endured the same hatred and cruelty. The patience of hope is built on the incarnation and so it remains steadfast through all the darkness and the sorrow. Betsie dies with the affirmation on her own lips, "No pit is so deep that God is not deeper." The steadfast hope in Jesus Christ fills us with the confidence that we labor on toward the morning and to the coming of the joy of God's people.

We give thanks wherever and whenever we are blessed by the works of faith, the labors of love, and the patience of hope.

1. Adelle M. Banks "Poll: Active Churchgoers more likely to express life satisfaction," *The News*: Presbyterian Church (USA), Presbyterian News Service, Louisville, Kentucky, July 25, 2003, p. 5.

2. Ray Waddle, "Spell-Checking Spirit," *Image: A Journal of the Arts and Religion*, Number 37, p. 118.

3. Beyers Naudé, *Hope for Faith*: A Conversation (The Risk book series) (Grand Rapids: William B. Eerdmans, 1986).

**Proper 25
Pentecost 23
Ordinary Time 30
1 Thessalonians 2:1-8**

The Cloak

If you can't refute the argument, then you can attack the person, and the best way to attack a person is to question the motives. So Paul is responding to attacks upon the Good News of Jesus Christ by those who have attacked him and questioned his motives for coming to Thessalonica. He rejoices that when he came to preach, people heard the message joyfully. Paul says he preaches because he has to. He preaches to please God. But, of course, there were some who suggested that Paul was really preaching from some other reason. He was preaching in order to enhance his own self-interest.

We have become pretty cynical about public people. Why is that person being so nice to me? Better hold on to my wallet. No sooner does the president get through a speech than somebody on some television talk show begins to tell you the real reasons behind the speech. It is not that the president believes what he is saying. He has more selfish motives. This speech on Medicare in Florida is because he needs the senior-citizen vote in the November election. His visits to North Carolina are self-serving because he wants a Republican majority in the Senate.

The critics were suggesting that Paul had a lot of selfish interests in his preaching at Thessalonica. Behind his efforts to build up the Body of Christ was his own desire to make himself rich by the collections. His preaching of God's grace was a mask behind which he hid his greed. His preaching was a cloak behind which he plotted his economic advances. He was going to ask for a big offering for the church at Jerusalem and keep the purse for himself. He was being kind to the widows so that he could ask them for big gifts. Certainly there have been preachers who have done it that way. Jim and Tammy Bakker seemed to make a pretty good haul with the PTL Club, where they cloaked their greed behind their gospel.

But the larger question now is: Why would anybody bother with trying to hide their greed with a cloak? More and more it seems like there is little embarrassment about greed in the culture. It hardly seems worth the effort to try to hide the motivation of greed. In so many places and in lots of different ways it almost appears as if greed is becoming a virtue.

In the movie *Wall Street*, the leading character gives a speech and he finally declares that greed is good. Greed is motivation for productivity. Greed is the source of great dreams. Greed is the emotion that drives the engines of capitalism. "Individual autonomy is expressed most fully through acquisition and protection of private property. Those who own and consume the most are the most valued human beings." The desire for more, the lust for the new, the artificially created needs make us more aggressive consumers. Human beings have become defined simply as consumers, and that is good because economic growth requires ever-increasing consumption. George Bush blessed greed by declaring an annual "national day of the consumer." Who would want to cloak that? Why try to cover up a national day of celebration for consumers?

Ah, yes, naturally you have a few bad eggs in the equation. Top executives at Tyco, Enron, and AOL let their aggressive consumerism get out of hand, but we try to pretend they are the exception. But the truth is that in the last decade from 1990 to 2000 the average pay for corporation officers rose 463 percent while the profits in those companies only rose 88 percent and the average worker's pay rose only 42 percent in the same length of time. Inflation rose in the decade 36 percent. The current CEO to worker pay ratio of 411 to 1 is nearly ten times as large as the 42 to 1 ratio in place in 1982. If the minimum wage had grown like corporation executive salaries had grown, the minimum wage now would be $21.41 per hour instead of the $5.15 an hour it is now. And nobody tries to cover that up or put a cloak over it and to keep it hidden.[1]

We haven't even begun to talk about how that never-ending desire for more, for bigger, for the highest has affected professional sports and changed the entertainment world, or affected the way we shop and the way we eat, the way we accumulate more and more stuff, to get and to move on to the next thing to get. More and more catalogues for more and more stuff keep coming into our houses, and, afflicted by the same culture that we all live in, we look at them to see if there is "anything I need." There is a new tool. We don't need another tool, but we don't have that tool. We put the catalogue down, but a day or two later we come back to the catalogue. We look at the tool. We can imagine all kinds of projects and pieces of furniture we could make with that tool. We would be so much more efficient. We would be so much better as a craftsman with that tool. We would be so impressed with ourselves as the skilled craftsman we could become with that tool. So we order the tool. The tool comes. We open the box. We plug it in, and the machine makes its wonderful sound. We have all the tools we need for our current projects. So we put the tool back in the box. We put it on the shelf. We come back to the house. We pick up the catalogue and look for the next tool. Why? It is the hunger of greed in us that wants more and more, that encourages us to super-size my meals when we do not need all the calories in the regular serving. But we get more with the super-size.

All of this desire for more, this hunger of the human heart for more, this passion for accumulation never seems to be satisfied. The restless gnawing at the human for that which we do not have is always for more. It is as if we all had hollow legs into which we keep pouring more and more stuff and it is never full. Not long ago one of the state's banks had a series of commercials that would show money in some activity of leisure while it showed the human in some hard-working capacity, and the refrain of these commercials was "I think my money should be working harder." We want more interest. We want more profit. We want more because nothing we ever get satisfies us.

The old preacher in the book of Ecclesiastes went from fame to knowledge to power to wealth, and each time, he concluded that it was emptiness, vanity, vanity, all is vanity, and he was not talking about pride; he was saying it was smoke and mirrors, all mist and clouds; mirage, which offered a promise of satisfaction, but when you grabbed it, it all disappeared. Getting the new tool does not satisfy the hunger that wanted the new tool. Signing the big contract with an NFL team does not answer the insecurity in the heart of the player who signed the contract. Perhaps that is why Walter Brueggeman has written that "consumerism is not simply a market strategy. It has become a demonic spiritual force among us" — the demonic myth that the spiritual hunger in each of us can be satisfied with the things of this world.

Poet Francis Thompson's long poem "Hound of Heaven" traces the journey of Ecclesiastes again as the writer flees from the presence and grace of God because the poet is afraid that in serving God, all the beauties and blessings of earth will be taken from him. In order to serve God, the poet fears that he will have to abstain from all the good things of the earth. But God continues to pursue. God, the Hound Dog of Heaven, keeps stirring up the hunger of the heart. That hunger that is not satisfied with anything the earth offers. "Naught shelters thee," God tells the poet, "Nothing will shelter thee, who will not shelter Me." So that in the end the poet discovers that God is the one for whom he has been looking and hungering all along. God says, "Ah, fondest, blindest, weakest, I am He Who thou seekest, Thou dravest love from thee, who dravest Me." You drive love away from yourself when you drive God away from yourself. As long as we seek to satisfy our itch with more of the stuff around us, the less chance we have to welcome into that space the grace and mercy of God that will begin to quiet that hunger and reduce that drive for acquisition of more and more.

Paul says, "I did not use the gospel as a cloak for greed because I have discovered in the grace of God how to be at peace in the world whether I have lots or have little. I know both how to be abased and I know how to abound every where and in all things I am instructed both to be full and to be hungry, both to abound and to suffer need." The love of God speaks to the insecurity and the need that is at the center of our greed and as we focus on the gift of grace in Jesus Christ, as we rejoice and affirm over and over again that in Jesus Christ we have been given life and life more abundant, there becomes less and less we have to have, less and less we want. We begin to look around and discover that we have too much stuff. We have cluttered our lives with piles and piles and we now begin to wonder what in the world we are going to do with all this stuff.

It is a hunger for God that agitates our souls and is exploited by the world for economic growth. It is the emptiness of the soul for the love of God that sends us to the market place looking for something to fill the hole. It is the love and mercy of God that feeds that hunger with a sense of who we are, with giving us a calling to be faithful people, gives us a work to do in sharing the resources of the world with all people, and brings us into the community of the faithful so that we are a part of a community and not isolated individuals. We need some food. We need some clothing. We need some stuff, but we need the presence and grace of God to touch the deepest hunger in our heart, and in the joy of God's dwelling in us we discover what Paul discovered about contentment. "Everything depends on knowing how much. Good is knowing when to stop."

---

1. Scott Kling and Chris Hartman, "Executive Excess 2002: CEO's Cook the Books, Skewer the Rest of Us," Ninth Annual CEO Compensation Survey (Boston: Institute for Policy Studies, United for a Fair Economy, 2002), p. 15.

**Proper 26
Pentecost 24
Ordinary Time 31
1 Thessalonians 2:9-13**

Worthy Of God

It seems fair to say that the saints of the Lord have always shown us what it is to be worthy of God. It is why we remember them and rejoice for them. They have shown us what a life worthy of God might look like. To talk about the saints, we may talk about Kagawa in Japan, about Mother Teresa, about Bishop Tutu and Nelson Mandela, about D. T. Niles in India, and about Saint Patrick in Ireland. To know the stories of Dorothy Day in New York City and Oscar Romero in Latin America is to have examples of what it means to lead lives worthy of the God who calls you into his own kingdom and glory. But remembering the stories of ordinary, average people, people from the history of any old church, like the people who have died in this church this year, is to remember those who in our own midst showed us lives that were lived worthy of the God who calls us in Jesus Christ. The remembrance of the saints reminds us of the variety of ways people live and also that joy and blessings are to be found as one focuses on the desire to live a life that is worthy of the God who calls us. The saints lived lives that seemed to be made of the same stuff that the gifts of grace were made of. The saints might be said to have lived on the same frequency that the gifts were broadcast on. Saints live at the same level as the gifts. Gifts can be wasted. Gifts are frequently misused. Gifts can be used for the wrong purposes. But there is a great delight and satisfaction when the gifts given are received and used in ways that are fitting and becoming to the gift.

There is an important Tuesday in November; it is Election Day. In 2002, Senator John Edwards may have been the only politician on television telling the truth in his campaign aids. Senator Edwards of North Carolina was urging citizens to vote. The only action which would be appropriate to the gift of liberty we have been given is to vote. We have been given the amazing gift of the right to vote. Long years of sacrifice and struggle have made possible the gift of democracy, the right to choose our own leaders, and the only response appropriate and fitting to that gift, the only obligation demanded by that gift to us, is for us to vote. To lead a life that is worthy of the gift of the ballot is to become an informed citizen and to vote. The great sadness in the land is that so few people will exercise the great gift they have been given and will allow the sacrifices of so many to be in vain.

Or look at the great blessing that this country and this society has given to each and every citizen, the right to a free public education. The gift is being offered every day in each of our schools. The gift is being presented to all children in the community and the only response that is appropriate, the only life that is fitting is the response of participation and cooperation. Our society has decided that it will make available the gift of a public education for all children. To lead a life that is fitting, is congruent, that is seemly, that is relevant, is to study, to behave, to participate, and to attend.

Every gift comes with expectations as to how it will be received and how it will be used. Every gift has a hope that it will be used for a purpose. Every gift brings with it the possibilities of blessings and grace, of responsibilities and obligations. Every gift opens before us a variety of responses and only some of those responses are seemly and becoming to the gift. To hang a Rembrandt painting in the garage is not becoming to the gift. So Jesus looks around him at the way people have responded to the gift of the covenant promise of God to Abraham and David and the prophets. God's promise, "I will be your God and you will be my people," has been converted into a confusing and heavy burden of obligations and rules. Regulations, laws, and traditions now make the gift a heavy burden and diminish the joy of the faithful and living relationship. As Mama Cass wailed, "Look what they've done to my song, Mom." Jesus is distressed at what they have done to the dynamic and joyful covenant of promise. They have killed it with a blanket of rules and regulations.

But when Paul writes to the church at Thessalonica, Paul is worried that the good news of God's grace and forgiveness will lead them to lives that are unworthy of the glorious gift because they will believe that there is nothing that is expected of them by the gift. There were already those who were suggesting that if the Laws of Moses were no longer valid, then it meant that Christians could do anything they wanted: there were no rules. Paul understands that where rules are removed you can end up with a mess. So Paul is eager to remind them that the gift of God's grace is to be received and enjoyed in ways that are fitting for the gift.

Cynthia Gadsen had spent most of her life in the corporate world. Then one day she reached the place where she said, "I would rather be poor than work here anymore." She said it had been a slow process to come to that conclusion. She writes:

> *Over the years I had stitched myself like a tight seam into the fabric of my company. I was loyal, obedient, and enthusiastic. I went where I was told, did what I was asked, and got the job done. My calendar was jammed with appointments, and my time was constantly in demand from colleagues and clients. I became important and busy — marks of success in my mind.*
>
> *Yet as the pace of my life increased, my sense of self-worth diminished. Deep down, I knew something was missing. I consoled myself with money, clothes, and trips, but couldn't shake the subtle ache in the belly....*
>
> *I yearned to step back from this crazy, frenetic dance of doing. Deep down, I was more than ready to move away from the heart-hardening existence of constant demands — more money, more sales, more projects. I wanted out of the harshness that this lifestyle was inflicting on my weary body, mind, and spirit. I longed to dance again in step with the ebb and flow of life and the rhythm of the Creator. I just had to learn to trust that God would meet my needs if I followed my soul's urging. Trusting that I was created for more than a mediocre existence devoted to drive and achievement.*[1]

Wil Willimon, who preaches at Duke University, can add that he knows lots of young adults who can tell you that it is a great, good freedom to strip down, break free, and throw their future away on the kingdom of God rather than harness up for a lifetime of servitude to the kingdoms of this world.

Cynthia Gadsen ends her story by saying, "Each of us is called at some point in our lives — called to be more, to live what we believe, to make visible what we profess. We often are also asked to move from one calling to another. Sometimes burnout is what helps us make the shift. Who will I be? Whose am I? Why am I here?" Cynthia said she found that a willingness to risk, born of an exhaustion and fatigue with the life she was living, helped her decide to try to live by the advice of Saint Paul, helped her to decide to try to live a life that was worthy of the gifts that had been given her.

There is an incredible freedom and excitement, a sense of adventure and risk, a sense of joy and challenge when we begin to guide our lives by the standard, "Is what I am doing worthy of God's gifts to me? Am I using what I have been given in a way that is appropriate for the gifts?" It is terrifying and demanding. To decide to evaluate and to live your life by the standard, "Is this a worthy use of the gifts given to me by God?" is to reject all the other claims upon your gifts. One day when Wil Willimon was feeling low because of the small attendance and poor results he was getting at Chapel at Duke, he complained to Stanley Hauerwas, who was named by *Time* magazine as the nation's most outstanding theologian. Stanley replied to Dr. Willimon, "Cheer up. This university is a bad neighborhood for Jesus. I think you do quite well, Wil, considering that this university is against everything Jesus teaches."[2] To lead a life that is worthy of the God who has called you in Jesus Christ may run you in an entirely different direction than the rest of the world, but as the saints have shown us, it will take us in a direction of contentment and joy, it will take us in a direction where we are at one with ourselves and our gifts. It will give us that sense of being on a level and going in the same direction as the will and purpose of God. To lead a life that is worthy of the God who called us will bring us to end with the saints into the kingdom of our God. To use the gifts that God has given in a way that is worthy of them is to find our Sabbath rest and joy in all we do.

---

1. Cynthia Gadsen, "Dancing in Step," *The Other Side*, November / December, 2002, p. 43.

2. Wil Willimon, "Preaching to Affluent Young Adults, Or Lord, Help Me Shove This Camel," *The Journal For Preaching*, Advent, 2002, Volume XXVI, Number 1, p. 47.

Proper 27
Pentecost 25
Ordinary Time 32
1 Thessalonians 4:13-18

Further On Up The Road

As best I can remember it, the comment came as part of a discussion about the media frenzy immediately following the capture of the two suspected snipers in the Washington, D.C. area. It had troubled some of the participants in the discussion that before these suspects had even gotten charged, before these presumed innocent until proven guilty people had even had a jury trial, there was this zeal on the part of every talk show to get the trial in the place where the death penalty was most severe. Then someone asked this question, "Is America's confidence in the death penalty a result of our moral rectitude or from a disappearance of any belief in an afterlife?" Maybe we would not feel the need to be so quick to impose mortal punishment if we were confident in God's ability to deal with an unrepentant sinner after death. Why are we so eager to kill sinners unless we really do not have much confidence or conviction in a life after death? It certainly makes one stop and think. What do we really believe about life after death? Or if we say we believe in an afterlife, what influence, what impact does that belief have on shaping what we do now? Does there really seem to be a gradual disappearance of any belief in an afterlife in the way we face death?

One minister made these observations, "In my almost sixty years of living, the reaction of society to death certainly seems to have changed. Forty or fifty years ago I don't remember counselors sent to school when children died. Forty or fifty years ago I can't remember seeing public shrines marking the place where a death took place. Out-pouring of grief on the side of the road with flowers, teddy bears, and toys. The kind of public memorial services which took place after the 9/11 attacks or Columbine shootings seem to me to be a new kind of approach to the presence of death. The comments made at those services all seem to talk about what wonderful people those who died were and that we will remember them, and we will live our lives now differently because we want to honor them. But seldom is heard a word about a life or world after death."

There are still radio preachers and pulpit pounders who are preaching the simple message that where we spend eternity, heaven or hell, depends on how we respond to Jesus, so we had better accept Jesus Christ now because we never know when we will die and have to face that judgment. There are some who still talk about life after death, but what kind of influence does it have. Presbyterian Church of Ireland, when it reaffirmed its faith at the beginning of the new millennium with a statement of faith, said that the church "exists to love and honor God through faith in his Son and by the power of his Spirit, and to enable her members to play their part in fulfilling God's mission to our world." The statement calls its members to share life, to worship God, to go forth in mission, and to see itself challenged with "biblical discipleship which is radical in its self-denial, simplicity of lifestyle, stewardship of money, faithful relationships, prayerfulness, concern for the world which God has created, and love for its people whom he loves and for whose salvation he gave his Son." There is not a single mention or reference to a life after death unless you claim it in the word salvation. In the thirty years a minister has been tracking sermons from some of the country's leading journals on preaching, there have only been three sermons published on this text from Thessalonians and one of them is one of his.

Death really is a fearful enemy if this life is all there is. Death is the end. The sniper, the terrorists, anthrax, cancer are all horrendous monsters if this life is all there is. The attack on the Christian faith for its promises of glory and joy in heaven as "pie in the sky by and by" suggests that those who make that claim do not believe in a by and by. Throughout history there have been many who would be willing to trade seventy years of trouble here for an eternity of bliss. But they want their pie now because they do not believe there is something more. Maybe it is there, but it has no influence in how we live. There are even good Christian theologians who have stopped talking about a life after death because they want to point out that heaven can begin here on earth as we live in relationship with God, and hell begins here as we suffer the loneliness and alienation from God. Don't focus on the after death, focus on the kingdom of God in our midst now. There are lots of places where death is exalted as the ultimate. Death and taxes. Grab all the gusto you can grab for you only live once. When death comes, it is over. Finished. Nothing more. We live. We die. That is the way it is. If it happens after you're dead, well, tough, you missed it.

That is what the church at Thessalonica was wrestling with. As the early Christians were celebrating the resurrection of Jesus and anticipating the immediate return of Jesus Christ, they were still convinced that death was the end. When you died, you were finished. They were expecting Jesus' return, but as they waited, some of their faithful members began to die. What a shame. Those devout and beloved members of the fellowship were going to miss it. It seemed like such a pity that they had been so eager and excited about the kingdom of God, and now they had died and would not get to share in that joy. Death had grabbed them. Death had done its work. Death had destroyed them. They had been captured by the power of death and they were gone. When Jesus came to claim his own, he would take those who were living and waiting, and those who had died in the Lord would simply be left behind and taken only in the memory of those who were still alive. Death would keep making the kingdom of God smaller and smaller by taking more and more.

Oh, they knew that God had raised up Jesus Christ from the dead and that the living and reigning Jesus was going to come and bring in his kingdom. They believed in the new heaven and the new earth, but somehow God's power to raise up Jesus did not immediately mean to them that God had the power and would use it to raise up those who had died in faith in Jesus. It is one thing to believe that Jesus died and rose again; it is another step to believe that God will bring with Jesus at his coming all those who have died in faith. What has the resurrection of Jesus Christ to do with the rest of us? Paul had to teach us that the power and promise of the resurrection of Jesus and the coming of the kingdom of God in glory with Jesus Christ is the very reason for our hope in the face of death. It is the reason we do not grieve as those who believe that death is the end. We believe that Jesus died and rose again. We believe that God will fulfill history by the power of Jesus. The resurrection of Jesus is not an isolated, single event, a single solitary rabbit God pulls out of the hat of death to demonstrate that Jesus is the Christ. The resurrection of Jesus is a cosmic event that deflates the power of death and liberates the lives of those who live and love in Christ from the power of death. God established the power of Jesus over the authority of death by the resurrection, and when the kingdom of God comes, God will resurrect from the clutches of death all those who have died in faith and in hope and reunite the living with those who have died before. There is no preference of the living over the dead. The power of God's resurrection will bring forth out of the power of death all those who have lived and loved in the joy of Christ. That is why Paul says we do not grieve as those who have no hope.

This is the great good news that the Christian faith has to speak to a dying world. Without the resurrection of Jesus Christ and the faith that those who live and love in Jesus Christ will be remembered and reclaimed from the power of death when the kingdom of God comes in glory, we have very little that makes much difference. As Saint Paul says, if our hope were limited to this world only, we would of all people be the most to be pitied. Death is our enemy. Death is God's enemy as well.

It is this message that has hope for those who were killed in the snipers' attack, who were killed in the Columbine shooting, who were killed in the World Trade Center buildings. There is not much future in our promise to remember them. But there is a great comfort that by the power of the resurrection of Jesus Christ, in the kingdom of God, there will be a glad reunion with all those who have died in faith. The dead in Christ will rise and those who are still alive when the kingdom comes will meet and rejoice and celebrate a glad reunion. Those who are still alive will not be deprived of the fellowship of those who have already died. Our joy will be complete because it will be shared with all those whose love and blessings have meant so much to us. The kingdom of God becomes more and more important to us as it becomes more and more peopled with the people we love.

Maybe the concern with life after death only becomes important when you have lost somebody you love, for one of the most human desires is to meet again with those we love who have died. "Further on up the road, Where the way is dark and the night is cold, One sunny morning we'll rise I know and I'll meet you further on up the road." That is how Bruce Springsteen sings about it in his album about the 9/11 events, called *The Rising*. "One sunny morning we'll rise I know and I'll meet you further on up the road. I'll meet you further on up the road." It is a rising that the Christian faith awaits as well, resting on the promises of Jesus Christ who died and rose from the dead and in his resurrection has the power to resurrect us into his kingdom further on up the road.

Proper 28
Pentecost 26
Ordinary Time 33
1 Thessalonians 5:1-11

The Day Of The Lord

For a man who claims that he does not know much about the coming day of the Lord, Paul has certainly written us a vivid description of the Second Coming of Jesus Christ. Paul speaks with authority when he says that when the day of the Lord comes, those who are dead and in the grave will be awakened by the trumpets of the angels and they will rise up and meet the Lord first. Those who are still alive when this happens will have to wait until all the dead are welcomed before they get to enter into the joy of the victorious kingdom of God. And that vision of the coming of the day of the Lord, the Second Coming of Jesus Christ, is supposed to comfort us. It is a vision of the coming of the Lord that is supposed to comfort the faithful who have been waiting for the coming of the Lord and yet some of their members have begun to die off and those remaining have been worried that because they died before the coming of the day of the Lord in victory, those who died would not have a chance to celebrate the victory.

Of course, the next question is one that we are always trying to figure out. When is all of this going to happen? After knowing so much about what will happen, Paul suddenly takes a dramatic turn and says, "I really don't need to say anything about the timing of this event, because everybody knows that nobody knows. Everybody knows that it will come when nobody expects it." Notice, Paul says the most likely time for this event will be a time when everything is going well. When the stock market is humming, and there are no wars, and we as human beings are beginning to think that we have mastered this old game of life, then the coming of the

Lord will happen. Paul thinks it is likely to happen when things are going very well. Jesus, who also claimed not to know the day or the hour of this Second Coming, suggests that it is most likely to come when strange events are in the sky. In Luke's Gospel, Jesus says when evil omens and portents are in the sun and moon, when wars and insurrections, earthquakes, epidemics, and famine are happening, when things are shaking and it seems that there is nothing anyone can do and all sorts of hopelessness abound, then look up, for your redemption draws nigh in the coming of the Lord. Jesus suggests that the Second Coming will happen when all hell breaks loose. Paul says when things are going well; Jesus says when things are chaotic. But they agree that it will come suddenly and unexpectedly. The Second Coming of the Lord will involve a cosmic upheaval in which the whole of creation is shaken to its very foundations. The shaking will be a time of judgment when all that is not built on a firm foundation will crumble and that which is built on solid ground, "on Christ the solid rock," will be affirmed.

The Second Coming of Jesus Christ will come suddenly and unexpectedly, but it must not find us unprepared. Jim Moore, who is the Pastor of St. Luke Methodist Church in Houston, Texas, reminds us that in our day-to-day lives we discover *kairos* moments in the midst of our *chronos* time. But when Paul says, "I cannot write to you about the *chronos* (time) or the *kairos* (date) of this event," he is affirming that this Second Coming is an event that is outside categories of time and space. It is God given. This Second Coming of the Lord is an event that takes up and includes and completes both *chronos* and *kairos*.

But Paul says what we have already received is enough light to keep us awake. What we have already been given by God's mercy and by the preaching of the good news is enough to keep us alert and awake, as those who are living and working during the daylight. We are not like those groping in the dark, unable to see, afraid to move, unsure of the next step. We are to be people who are alive, alert, awake, and aware. We need to stay that way. This promise of the Second Coming of the Lord is not an invitation to laziness. It is not an excuse for idleness. The promise of Christ's return is not excuse for indifference. It is the promise of his coming that makes us much more eager to share the good news and to encourage and support each other in faith.

We are the children of the light and people of the wakening hours, and we are to protect and support each other in our work and faith. Robert Farrar Capon likes to suggest as the image of God's providence and mercy an iceberg. For, like the mighty expanse of ice from the polar caps the ice extends out into the ocean in all directions, and the sailors of those areas have to be on guard and alert for the tip of the icebergs where the grace of God makes a brief revelation of its power, light, and love. The iceberg seen is not all there is and someday when the ocean is drained we may see the full extent of the ice, but for the time being all we see, if we are alert, are the iceberg tips. Those who are a part of the people of the light have to keep watch for the icebergs so that they might continue to know and to see the nature and purpose of God. They are to encourage each other with stories and testimonies about the icebergs. We might talk as well about the water table that is underneath the earth. And yet at various places the land dips and the water table becomes a lake or a stream. In the desert those places become oasis and the survival of the journey depends upon the people keeping watch out for the oases so that they may fill the canteens, bathe, and renew themselves. The children of the light, the people of the day, need to be alert for the signs, marks, places of God's revelation, so that they can encourage each other to continue to wait and to hope for the Second Coming of the Lord. "When the earth shall be filled with the glory of God as the water covers the sea."

Paul was convinced that the Second Coming of the Lord would happen before all the people in Thessalonica died. "I can tell you this directly from the Lord: that we who are still living when the Lord returns will not rise to meet him ahead of those who are in their graves." Paul expected it in his lifetime. Others have expected it in their lifetime, and now we are not so sure what we are to do with it. We still have, from time to time, a faith community who thinks that they have figured out the day and the time and the place and they go out to be among the first to be greeted by the Lord.

There are always some faithful people who believe they have outsmarted God and Jesus, or by special gift of the Holy Spirit, they have broken the code and now know the hour and the place. There are others who will tell you that we are all always living in the last days, that this Second Coming of Jesus is always just a moment away from each of us as we go through life with death just a car accident away, just a Heimlich maneuver removed, just an aneurysm erupted. So the day of judgment, the rising to meet the risen Lord, may happen to any of us at any time.

But maybe this passage from Paul is talking to people like us, who aren't interested or worried about when the Second Coming of the Lord will take place. For those who are talking about it, Paul says they should simply continue to be faithful, supportive disciples of the light, to look for the icebergs and the oasis and to continue on the journey of faith. So if we are seeking to be faithful followers of Jesus Christ in what we do and how we live, the date and the time of the Second Coming will not change much of how we live. And the promise of the Second Coming is not a fearful thing for those who now live by faith. Most of the people one hears talking about the Second Coming of Jesus are Christians who are fearful and apprehensive about it, and yet Paul says, "God does not intend to punish us, but to have our Lord Jesus Christ save us." The Second Coming for us is a day of completion and fulfillment. It is a day of judgment and punishment to those who have refused to accept the gift, but for those who have lived and labored in obedience to the light of God's grace, it is the completion of a long journey, not a fearful, destructive moment.

So it seems that the Second Coming of Jesus Christ is an event that for many Christians is far in the background. It is not a high priority item. It is not a doctrine of immediate significance. It will come when it will come, in God's own sweet time, and there is no sense worrying about it. Yet, it is an absolutely essential last chapter to the biblical story. If there was no expectation of the moment when God brings forth his kingdom in fullness, in completion, when God does come to shake and to sort and to judge the powers and principalities of this earth, then we should of all people be the most to be pitied. The Second Coming of Jesus Christ is the symbol doctrine for the completion of the story of God's love. It is the promise which brings together all our journey in faith.

Reinhold Niebuhr once remarked that it makes all of the difference in the world whether the end of history is just the finish of history or is its fulfillment. Does history just fade out when the sun burns up or is it brought to fulfillment when the Son comes again? The promise of the Second Coming of Jesus Christ is the affirmation that history is brought to completion in the will of God. History is moving toward a purpose and a goal, and that history comes to the moment when that purpose is realized. The Second Coming of Jesus links that goal of history to the revelation of God's character and love in Jesus Christ. Jesus is the light by which history will be measured. The acknowledgment that when the Second Coming of Christ takes place there will be a judging and purifying of history affirms what we all believe: that there is a difference between good and evil, that some things are worth doing, and that some things are destructive and evil. It is not all culturally relative. The Second Coming of Jesus declares that the purpose and goal of history is to be found in the conclusion of history given to it by God. We do not know the end of the story until God brings it to an end, and the end is not necessarily included in the story. "There are no achievements or partial realizations in history, no fulfillment of meaning or achievement of virtue by which man can escape the final judgment. The idea of the 'last' judgment expresses the biblical story's repudiation of all conceptions of history by which history believes it can redeem itself, or evolve to the place where it is complete in itself."[1] The fulfillment of history is a gift of God according to the love he has shown in Jesus Christ.

The time, the place, and the possibility of the Second Coming of Jesus Christ does not occupy a prominent place in my daily thinking. It is not the fear of the coming of the Lord on high that motivates my waking hours. But the images, the pictures, the Lord on a cloud, blowing a trumpet to awake the dead, the promise that God will return in Jesus Christ to bring all history to his promised glory is an essential part of the Christian story, for it affirms that history will not come to a conclusion with either a whimper or a bang, nor will it come to a conclusion simply by some human act of destruction. Human history will come to a conclusion by the will and intervention of God. And at that moment when history is fulfilled, the Jesus who was crucified will stand as the one who is Lord and Redeemer.

---

1. Reinhold Neibuhr, *Faith and History: A Comparison of Christian and Modern Views of History* (New York: Charles Scribner's Sons, 1951).

Reformation Sunday
Romans 3:19-28

When is Being Right Wrong?

I finally got a copy of the Rules of Life. We all want them because we think that having a set of rules for life will make life so much easier and less confusing. Just find the twelve rules and follow them and it will take away a lot of worry and agony out of life. So I was excited when I got them. I do not know who made them up, but I got them by e-mail off the Internet, so I know that makes them official. The Twelve Rules of Life:

1. Never give yourself a haircut after three drinks.
2. There are only two tools required: WD-40 and duct tape. If it doesn't move and it is supposed to move, squirt it with WD-40. If it moves and it is not supposed to move, wrap it in duct tape.
3. The five most essential words for a healthy, vital relationship are "I apologize" and "You are right."
4. Everyone seems normal until you get to know them.
5. Never pass up an opportunity to go to the bathroom.
6. If someone says that "you are too good for me" ... believe them.
7. Learn to pick your battles: ask yourself, "Will this matter one year from now?"
8. When you make a mistake, make amends immediately. Crow tastes better when it is still warm.
9. If you woke up breathing, rejoice. You still have a chance.
10. Living well really is the best revenge. Being miserable because of a bad or former relationship just might mean that the other person was right about you.

11. Work is good, but it's not that important. Money is nice, but you can't take it with you. Statistics show most people don't live to spend all they saved; some even die before they retire.
12. Anything we have isn't really ours; it was loaned to us by God. He just let us borrow it while we are here ... even our children.[1]

Of course, these twelve rules give us the same problems Paul had with rules and laws. The more we follow the rules, the further away we go from the happiness we seek from the rules. There is no salvation in the rules. There are some who try to tell us that we can never really keep the rules, but Paul was always claiming that he had fulfilled all the rules. The rich young ruler comes to Jesus and asks Jesus what must be done to inherit eternal life, and Jesus tells him about keeping the law. The rich young ruler claims that he has kept the rules from his youth, and Jesus does not argue with him. We keep looking for the rules so that we can keep them so we can feel contented with our lives. We think that if we can do what is required we can have some peace and satisfaction with ourselves. If we just have the laws and we keep them, then we can have the joy of knowing that we have fulfilled our duty, done our share, proved our worth, contributed our portion, and been good.

Paul talks a lot about the law and about a relationship with God created by obedience. These twelve rules of living do exactly the kind of things that Paul discovered in trying to keep the Jewish Law. First, the law has a way of inspiring us at the beginning to amend our ways, to try to do better, to dedicate ourselves to doing that which the law says. Number 3 urges us to apologize more and to accept the wisdom of others better. We hear that rule and we say to ourselves, "Yes, we are going to do that. We need to do more of that. That would be a good thing," and so we are inspired for a while to try to do different, and to be better.

But the law is a hard master. The law sets the standard and before long the law begins to reveal our failures. There is a book by two professors of theology in New England on the theology of baseball, and one of them says that in baseball, there is no grace. Baseball is all law and rules. We have the rules. We keep all these statistics. We know the score and we know the results we want. It is all law. What will you do this time at bat? The batter comes to the plate with the intention of getting a hit. We celebrate and honor and reward highly anyone who can get a hit four out of ten times. But the law points out that even a 400 hitter has failed six out of ten times. The law may inspire us, but the law exposes our sin, our missing of the mark. The rule about eating crow when it is warm is a clear reminder that you will fail. The law inspires. The law condemns by pointing out the gap between what we should have done and what we did.

Paul knew it so well from his own life. You can hear it in the voice of the rich young ruler as well. The law may inspire us, and the law may embarrass us by showing our failures, but where we are able to keep the rules, Paul says we become arrogant and self-righteous. The better we are at keeping those twelve rules, the more obnoxious we are going to be to live with. The more we can check them off — done that, done that, done that — the higher opinion we are going to have of ourselves; and the more entitled and the more honored we are going to expect to be. If the goal is to be rich, then those who are rich feel entitled and expect things to be given to them. The keeping of the law has a way of making us want what we have earned. We have kept the law the most, we have earned the most, and we want the most. Whatever the rules, we keep them because we want to be known as the best. It is not an attitude that brings us together. You remember the news story of the young girl in a very competitive suburb who did not want to share the honor of valedictorian of her high school class with two other students. There were a couple of small differences in the other students' and her experiences. She had earned it. She wanted it.

A friend of mine said that he had always thought that being elected into the Baseball Hall of Fame was an honor given to players by the public at the end of the career. When Roger Clemens won his 300th game, the news was all about how he was a sure-fire Hall of Famer, because he had earned it. Roger Clemens must have believed that as well, because he began to tell the Hall of Fame which uniform he wanted to wear when he went into the Hall of Fame. He not only felt entitled, but able to dictate terms. The more we keep the rules, the more highly we think about ourselves. The more we keep the rules, the more entitled we think we are to honor, and to recognition, to praise; and the more we create division and separation in the community.

We want a list like the twelve rules of life because as long as we keep trying to find our joy, our rest, our peace, our salvation in the keeping of the rules, the longer we continue to live and act on the conviction that we can control our own destiny. The keeping of the law is a trust in our own ability to determine our own future. It continues to widen the separation between us as creatures and the Creator who has made us for relationships. As long as we say, "Let's see how I measure up to these twelve rules of life," we are the ones who deceive ourselves into thinking that we are the ones who know what justice, mercy, and righteousness are. We make ourselves not only the creatures, but then we are the judge and we check off that we did or did not do that rule. We are the ones who decide who are good and who are not.

No one is declared righteous in God's sight by the keeping of the laws. We can keep the rules. Lots of people day in and day out play by the rules. There are lots of us who say the same thing. We are not bad people. We mow our grass. We pay our taxes. We vote. We have not killed anyone. We have not stolen anything. We love the mates we are with. We have kept the rules. But that kind of being right is wrong if you are hungering for a kind of fellowship with the Creator, if you are seeking a kind of peace of the heart, if you are feeling lost and alone in creation and need companionship and a relationship. If you realize that there is a generosity and bountifulness at the heart of life, to that you owe a debt of gratitude which you can never repay, the righteousness of the law is wrong. You know when you look at the mirror in the morning that most of your waking hours have been focused entirely on your wants, wishes, and whims, and there is forgiveness needed for that selfishness that you can never give yourself. The rightness of the law cannot help you. That kind of righteousness, that kind of being put back into alignment with God, that kind of putting the wheel of your life back on the center of God so that all of it turns and spins smoothly and without wobble or whump, that kind of being put right with God is not a result of the righteousness of the law.

The great good news of the Christian story is that being put right with God in relationship has been offered as a gift by the grace offered in Jesus Christ. That is what makes this message of God acting in Jesus Christ so special, so powerful, so refreshing. The word of the Good News is that God has already offered in his own love for us the possibility of the relationship we have been trying to achieve. For you and me it is not an accomplishment we need to complete. It is a gift that has already been given and we are invited to receive and enjoy. It is a gift of love that opens to us the relationship with God that we know needs to be restored. God has offered that things can be right between us and God by our accepting the gift and rejoicing in invitation to come again into the living relationship of faith, hope, and love.

Making things right by God in Jesus Christ is good news because it frees us from having to keep all of the different rules and laws. The good news is that breath of fresh air, the feeling of a huge burden lifted, a pardon offered for all past failures. God has offered to put right our relationship in love.

The law, the rules, the regulations have a powerful attraction for us, but they cannot bring us to the peace of a restored relationship with God. God comes to us and offers us that restored relationship. The story of Jesus is the story of God coming for us, making another gesture toward us, another invitation, another demonstration of a love that desires to live in communion and fellowship with us.

The life of Jesus is the good story that nothing we have done as human beings is so bad that we do not have a future in God's love. There is no darkness so dark that God cannot find us. There are no deeds we could do that are worse than the cross, and God has not been defeated by that rejection.

The righteousness of God comes through faith in Jesus Christ to all who believe. The grace of God in Jesus restores a relationship that the law can only make more intense.

---

1. These were received as an e-mail from a friend. There was no additional identification as to the author of this list.

All Saints' Sunday
1 John 3:1-3

Say What?

Say what? Saint Paul never thought he got to the place where the power of sin was completely gone in his life. Saint Augustine never preached that once you received the power of Christ into your life all sin was gone. Martin Luther, from whom we get all these Reformation slogans, preached "always sinner; always justified." So what does this mean? "Everyone who commits sin is guilty of lawlessness; sin is lawlessness. You know that he was revealed to take away sins, and in him there is no sin. No one who abides in him sins; no one who sins has either seen him or known him" (1 John 3:5-6).

What does that mean, because there are so many who testify that the deeper Christ comes into one's life the more conscious one is of the power of sin? The more one strives to fulfill the love and will of Christ, the more one becomes aware of the gap between what is desired and what is accomplished. What does John mean that those in Christ do not sin?

What is sin? One gets the impression sin is like modern art. Everybody knows what it is, but don't ask them to define it. When the Old Testament wanted to describe it, the story of Adam and Eve and the fall was told. In the New Testament, rather than give a definition, God sent Jesus and said that is what human life ought to look like and anything else is sin. This passage from 1 John comes as close as any passage to a dictionary-type definition of sin. Sin is the transgression of the Law of God. So it is not surprising that the *Shorter Catechism* uses that as the answer to the question, "What is sin?" Answer: "Sin is any want of conformity unto, or transgression of, the Law of God."

But that just throws us back to the next question: What is the Law of God? And that is why the Old Testament and the Jews are so concerned with the law. You have to know the rules so that you can keep them. And then sin is disobedience. Sin is when you break the rules, and yet all that rule keeping slowly makes you numb. You begin to feel like U2 in their *Zooropa* album: "Don't move, don't talk out of turn, don't think, don't worry everything's just fine. Don't grab, don't clutch, don't hope for too much, don't breathe, don't achieve, don't grieve without leave...." Don't, don't, don't.

Soon, after all those rules, something inside of us begins just to want to break one, just to do something wild and reckless. There are so many rules that we find ourselves longing to rebel, and so sin is often defined as rebellion, as the putting of ourselves in the place of God and deciding for ourselves what is right or wrong. Paul wrestles with this human response to the law. The law is good in that it tells us what is bad, but the law creates a line that always tempts us to step over it, just to assert our own independence. This is the Frank Sinatra theme song sin: "I did it my way." Nobody's going to tell me what to do. There is a sense in which this is quickly becoming our culture's favorite sin. Listen to our ads: "You got to break some rules. Nobody says you have to stay on the roads. Just do it." Yes, there are rules, but rules are made for whimps. Rules are for the other guy. The stop sign on the corner is not intended for us. Others are supposed to stop, but we live here. We know the community; we'll just drive through if it looks clear. For decades the medical community has been telling us the rule that smoking has a negative impact on the quality of life, and people keep saying, "Well, maybe for others but, hey, our mother died at age 87 and she smoked." Here, sin is the rebellion of the heart that refuses to allow something else or another to rule. This is what 1 John is saying. This is the word for sin that is used here. John says when we allow Christ to become Lord of our lives, we no longer fall guilty to the dimension of sin that claims we can be our own boss. With Christ acknowledged as Lord over our lives, we have surrendered that arrogance that claims we don't need any help. Once we have said that Christ is God's Law for life and put that in the center of our lives, we have not become free from all the dimensions of sin, but we are no longer living in the sin of believing we can be our own Lord.

Disobedience, rebellion — two aspects of this thing called sin when sin is seen in relationship to the Law of God. But when we move from the definition of the Law of God as the Law of Moses and the covenant to the life of Christ as the fuller expression of the law, the will, and the intention of God for creation, then sin as the breaking of that law becomes different as well.

The story of the fall of Adam and Eve has always been important scripture to people because it preserves the beginning good and reality of creation. Creation began as God's good work, and creation was created well, is good, and worked properly. The story of the fall provides an explanation for the origin of evil without making the Creator directly responsible for it, and at the same time it gives humanity a place and responsibility of immense consequences. The creature's actions had an amazing impact on the creation of God. When the story becomes the description of the Law and will of God in the goodness of creation at the beginning, then sin becomes different. Or when you look at Jesus Christ and say that there is the full definition of what human life is supposed to be, sin takes on some different definitions.

From the story and the life, our first awareness of sin may come in the feeling that we are missing something. Paul Tillich called it the sense of alienation. Tillich says we are estranged from the Creator. Sin is that universal feeling of having lost something. Homer Rogers writes, "Why is it that you can sit in a rocking chair on the front porch of the house in which you were born and lived all your life and look at the landscape you have seen every day of your life and still feel homesick for somewhere else?" What is it that makes us all feel a little sad when our new clothes get washed and they are not new anymore? When that pretty, clean white sheet of paper has to have an erasure mark on it?

Maybe you saw the movie *Grand Canyon*. Remember the scene where the immigration attorney breaks out of a traffic jam and tries to go around it? He gets off the freeway and since he does not know the town, he begins to enter a more and more run-down area. The realities of urban life become more stark and frightening. Then his car stalls out, and he is stranded there at the corner where a gang of youth gathers. He does use his car phone to call a tow truck, but as he waits, five of the young people surround his car and begin to talk trash and vandalize his car. Then the tow truck arrives and the driver begins to hook up the disabled car. The gang protest. The driver is stealing this plump turkey from them. The tow truck driver takes the gang leader aside and says, "Man, the world ain't supposed to work like this. Maybe you don't know that, but this ain't the way it's supposed to be. I'm supposed to be able to do my job without asking you if I can. And that dude is supposed to be able to wait with his car without you rippin' him off. Everything's supposed to be different than what it is here."

Everything was different, and now sin is felt and experienced as that feeling of deprivation, that feeling of lostness, that awareness of having missed the mark. Sin becomes all those things that we do that we know are not what they should be. Vows should be kept. Marriages should last. Friends don't betray friends. Families ought to be able to talk to each other. Homes should be a place of safety and comfort for children. Sin is whatever causes us to fail to live up to the way it should be. Sin is the missing of the mark. Jesus Christ is the standard and where we fail to live up to that standard of faith and obedience we are participating in sin. This dimension of sin is never left behind completely until we are made perfect in glory.

Sometimes sin *is* manifested by a kind of deceitfulness. Scott Peck, in a book called *The People of a Lie*, suggests that one of the marks of evil is that it will not recognize the truth. We have been told all our lives to honor our fathers and mothers, but in truth we do not like them very much, and yet we refuse to acknowledge that we pretend. We fake it and the deceit poisons us and our other relationships. We acknowledge Jesus is our model and we want so much to be like him, so we deceive ourselves and refuse to see our shortcomings and our failures or to listen when others criticize us. Sin becomes manifested in deceit and pretense, lies and falsehood.

Harvey Cox once suggested that in the story of the fall, the real sin was the refusal to accept responsibility, a kind of lack of ownership for actions, an indifference. Everybody blamed it on somebody else, a dimension of sin which we are not unfamiliar with in our own time.

What John says is that arrogant rebellion and disobedience by breaking the law and will of God is over when we come into the grace of God in Christ Jesus. If we acknowledge that Christ is our Master and that we need his help to obtain life more fully, then that sin which is defined by the wild, reckless lawlessness of life is over for us. We may not always like it. We may not be able to fulfill what we know we should do, but we know we are not God and we know there is a God-intended purpose for life.

When we step back and define sin by the story of the fall and the life of Christ, sin is the smearing of a relationship, a betrayal of a partner to whom we have taken blood-brother bonds. Sin is a culpable and personal affront to a personal God. Sin is the spoiling of the goodness of God. Sin is that which interferes with the will and purpose of God. Sin is what interferes with the way things are supposed to be. When sin is conceived in this larger picture of any and all that is not what God intends for life and creation, then some sins we live in are the results of our own actions and some sins we live in are the results of actions of others, and we live in those sins as conditions with which we must find a way to live in grace. Jesus says marriages are supposed to endure. Some people get divorced because they want the separation, so they live in that less-than-God-intended situation as an action they choose. But some people get divorced who do not want the separation, and so they live in that less-than-God-intended situation as a condition from which they must find a way to continue. Some of us have poor health because of genetic gifts. Some of us have poor health by what we have done to ourselves. God's intended shalom is for all of us to have life and life more abundant. Illness and disease are contrary to God's intentions and will. Sickness and poor health are a result of the power of sin at work in history, but some poor health is a result of our actions and some is a condition with which we must live.

As the people of God who seek to live in the full joy and power and grace of God, we pray that God will infuse in us the power and Holy Spirit of Christ so that we become a place on earth where we get closer and closer to the way God intends life to be. As John suggests, once we enter into that relationship of knowing we are not masters of our own fate and lords of our own destiny, that kind of sin is no longer our demon. Our challenge is to discover how we can live so that life might become more like it ought to be, and how we call to repentance those who sin by the actions they choose, and yet still offer grace to those who are caught in the midst of sin, which is simply the condition into which they have been forced.

For God has intended us all to be called his children. See what love the Father has for us that we should be called the children of God, for so indeed we are.

Christ The King
Ephesians 1:15-23

The Power Of God

The professional observers and media pundits suggest that now Bill Clinton has only his place in history to work toward. He will now be judged against the giants of the past, Lincoln, Truman, Wilson. That is one of the ways that history works. We judge the current events by the standards set in the past. Current NBA stars are now being set against the stars from the last fifty years. Madonna versus Marilyn Monroe. John Updike compared to Nathaniel Hawthorne. And when you compare the preaching and praying of the public church, the church on radio, the church in the public press, with the preaching and praying of Saint Paul, as in this letter to the church at Ephesus, one cannot miss the dramatic change that has taken place in preaching and praying as well. Listen to the preaching and praying of the public church today, and you will hear the message and the prayers addressed to individuals. When you listen to the preaching and praying of Saint Paul, you hear the message and the prayers to God for the church, for the whole fellowship of believers, for the body which is to become the body of Christ. Paul thinks corporately, thinks of the kingdom of God, thinks of the fellowship, prays for the whole church. Today's public praying and preaching are much more centered on individual salvation, praying for God to work in my life, praying for God to help me, and for God to give me the spirit of courage and hope.

Listen to the opening prayer of Paul for the church at Ephesus. Paul begins his letter with the customary greeting and doxology for the spiritual blessings God has brought to history in his work with the covenant people, the Jews, and then in the person and resurrection of Jesus Christ. In the passage before us this morning, Paul moves into telling them what a testimony he has heard about them, about their faith in the Lord Jesus Christ and the way they love all of God's people. So Paul says, "I never stop being grateful for you all in my prayers. Every day, every night, I give thanks to God for the faith of the church of Ephesus and for the love that comes out of that faith."

But that is not all. Then Paul tells them about what he prays for them. He doesn't just pray that they will continue to be strong in the faith and continue to love all of God's people. His great thanksgiving quickly turns into a prayer of intercession for the church. Now what kind of things do you think Paul prays for? Paul says he prays first for them to receive the spirit of wisdom, the spirit of knowledge, and the spirit of revelation which will reveal to them the personality and power of God. Paul prays that the church will receive the spirit of comprehension and understanding so that they will come really to know God, to grasp something of his majesty and greatness, to know the full measure of the scope of the providence and love of God. How many celebrities have you heard say that they really wish the public had a chance to get to know them because they are much more complex than the tabloids have presented them to be? Paul's prayer for the church is that they will receive the spirit of wisdom and revelation that will give them a wider, deeper, broader knowledge of the true personality of God.

Because when they grasp more and more of the personality, purpose, and power of God, they will comprehend more fully the hope that was given to them when they were called by God to his work. The spirit of wisdom and revelation of God would highlight for them the stunning blessings that are planned not just for them, but for all the people of God — no private individual blessings, but awe-inspiring blessings that are vast enough and rich enough to bless all of God's people. Where they become confident of the relationship they have with God, as they get to know God and trust God more fully, they will gain a sense of confidence about the future, about the struggle with good and evil, about the final outcome of history, because they will become more aware of the power of God: the power of God's love, the power of God's goodness to change. The power of God's grace to transform life for the better, the power of God to take that which is broken and make it whole, to take what is dirty and to make it clean, the power of God to take that which is dead and bring it to life.

Paul prays for the spirit of wisdom to come upon the church so that they will know the full quality of the power of God that God has to give to his people. Paul reminds them that it is a power that we have already seen demonstrated. We have seen something of the amazing properties of the power of God as God took Jesus of Nazareth out of the grave and gave him new life. God is not a powerless creator. There is an awesome kind of power in the love of God, and as we come to understand that love and that power we will understand the kind of power that we as the people of God have to turn loose in the world. The power of God's grace and love is an awesome power to transform lives. It is like no other power.

There was a story in the newspaper about the 82-year-old maid in Mississippi who had saved all her life and gave to the University of Mississippi a gift of $150,000, to endow scholarships for black students. The story was about the power of that small act of charity to change things. The woman is now constantly on the go. She is being invited all over the world to be honored for her act of love. She has flown in airplanes for the first time, stayed in the finest homes, eaten whatever her heart might desire, met governors, mayors, and celebrities who have all wanted her autograph. There is a frightening and awesome power in the power of goodness, in the power of compassion, a power which cannot be grabbed or wanted, for the woman did not give the scholarship money in order to become famous. But the act of goodness took an unknown maid and made her a somebody.

Paul says that the power of God took Jesus, who did not count equality with God a thing to be grasped, who did not have the army or the economic power to oppose the political power, who was crucified, and God's power took that Jesus out of the grave and gave him new life. God took that Jesus, who was despised and rejected by humanity, and has now installed him as Lord over all creation. The power of God's love took one who had reached the ultimate bottom and spun the whole wheel of history and established the one who was on the bottom on the top. The spirit of wisdom and understanding will bring into our heart and mind a more complete grasp of the nature and will and purpose of that power of God.

There is a persistent temptation to look at ourselves, to look at our resources, to look at the problems, to look at the needs, and to become discouraged; to look at the evil around us and to despair. We reduce the size and magnitude of the power of God that we have seen made visible in the resurrection of Jesus Christ to the limits of our minds and our understanding. That is why Paul prays for the spirit of wisdom and revelation, so that our minds and hearts might be expanded by the knowledge of God's power, rather than letting us continue with such feeble concepts of God's power. The people of God who constantly renew themselves with a new appreciation and constant reminders of the vastness and greatness of God's power go forward in faith and service knowing that they are the channel through which God has elected to use that power. The church is not a weakling. The church is not a wimp. The church is only powerless when it looks at its own resources. Christ is the head of the church, the church is the body of Christ, and it is through the body of Christ, through the church, that the power of Christ will be fulfilled and expressed into history.

That is why our greatest sin as the people of God against the Holy Spirit is to think negatively or to think realistically, to say that we can't do that now, to think that evil cannot be overcome, to say that nothing can be done about that sickness, to close the doors on options for the future simply because we do not see how we can achieve that. God may not heal our sickness. God may not give us at this moment the resources to give good-paying jobs to everybody. God may know that what we need most is the struggle and not the success, but to say that it is not a possibility, to say that child abuse cannot be stopped, to throw up our hands and to say that we cannot reestablish discipline in our schools, to say that there is nothing we can do to help our young people come to a joyful and affirming understanding of sexuality within commitment, to say we cannot feed, with all the resources and food on this earth, all those in Africa who are hungry, is to deny the power and the potential of the love of God.

Paul prays for the church that it might have a spirit of wisdom and revelation so that it might grow in its knowledge and appreciation of the providence, the personality, the power of God's love, so that we in the church may always be full of more joy and possibility than those who suddenly win the Publisher's Clearing House sweepstakes, for we understand fully that we are the conduit into the world of that same amazing power that resurrected Jesus Christ from the grave, that took that rejected and despised Jesus and made him Lord over all creation and set him as Head of the Church, and who will send that power to his body so that he might continue to fulfill his mission and calling to redeem history.

Paul is praying for the whole body of Christ. Somehow it still seems to me that we have lost something of the greatness of the vision of a redeemed creation and history when all we worry about is the salvation of individual souls. As if all we have to say is that God will just have to deal with individual problems because God is not able to deal with powers, principalities, and kingdoms of this world. Paul says that a prayer for a new spirit of wisdom and revelation of the power of God will send us forth as the body of Christ. What a power! What a God.

Thanksgiving Day
2 Corinthians 9:6-15

Thanks Be To God

It is at this point that so many of us feel the temptation to tune out. "Now concerning the offering for the saints at Jerusalem" is another request for money. That is supposed to be one of the problems with the church. It is always asking for money. If it is not the saints in Jerusalem, it is the hungry in Africa, the earthquake victims in Turkey, or the refugees in Bosnia. Paul is writing asking for money. Jesus talked more about money in his stories than he did about the kingdom of God. The church is always asking for money. If you do not want somebody asking you to give, then it is not wise to be a part of a Christian community.

There is an intimate relationship between who we are and what we do with our resources. Tell us how you spend your money and we can tell you what you believe in. Jesus said that where our treasure is there will our hearts be also. And where our heart is, is where will we put our treasures. We all have our share of blessings, gifts, resources, time, energy, interest, and power. They are who we are and we give them away to the things and causes we love.

Jesus, Paul, and the Christian community all understand the same thing. Until a change of heart has gotten into a person's checkbook, it has not gotten into the person's heart. We direct our resources toward what we love.

Paul asks for help in the collection for the saints in Jerusalem because Paul understands this relationship between treasure and heart, between blessings received and praise given, between giving and God. This offering for the saints in Jerusalem is an opportunity for the Christians in Corinth to discover new blessings and joy in the worship of God. Giving is an act of praise and worship.

Giving is an exercise of the heart. Giving is a measurement of our vision of life. Our giving shows the size of our hearts. There is a narrow view of life, a stinginess of spirit, a miserliness of perspective that sows sparingly, cautiously, tentatively. There is a bigness of the heart that sows widely, sows broadly, sows recklessly. It was a casino night for the American Heart Association and some friends took a minister as a guest. Everyone was given ten dollars in chips and more chips could be purchased, with the money going to the American Heart Association. That minister spent the night at the roulette wheel putting one chip on red one time, then maybe two chips on black the next time, and all night he never got more than two chips ahead and never more than three or four chips down. At the end of the night, the minister was depressed to discover that he was such a timid, cautious human being and sowed so sparingly. Look at your giving. Look at what you give away to others and to what you give those gifts for. The giving, the sowing, says so much about what you believe about the fertility and abundance of creation and about how life operates. If the pie is limited, and everyone is trying to get more than his or her share, then one must be very cautious and careful, but if the greatness of God is that God is a God of creation and a God of abundance, able to feed 5,000 from two loaves of bread, and if God has created the world in a way that the more that flows through you the more that flows into you, then we sow abundantly by giving away generously.

But "each one must do as he has made up his mind, not reluctantly or under compulsion for God loves a cheerful giver." Giving ought to be a decision that is a part of a planned approach to life. The offering ought not to be what one decides to give on the spur of the moment when the plate is passed. The gift ought not to be made out of some challenge so that some feel trapped and compelled to give to avoid embarrassment. Nor should giving be some impulse reaction to an appeal to the heart strings. Our sowing grows out of the honest assessment of just how richly blessed and graced we have been, a calculation of what resources we have and what expenses we will be having, and a giving that is as generous as we can make it.

Giving for the believer is a critical act of witness. Giving is a significant testimony of faith. Giving is at the heart of testimony to the faith that one believes and acknowledges that gifts have been given to him or her. All human giving is in response to blessings that have been given. Our giving to others is a statement of acknowledgment that we know blessings and gifts have been given to us, and to give those gifts in the name and to the glory of God is to bear witness that we recognized that the gifts we have received have been given to us from the gracious goodness of God. A cheerful giver is a giver who has an abundance of gifts, so that they are not anxious about what they will eat or what they will wear, and out of that abundance of blessings, which they acknowledge, they give in thanksgiving to God.

It is a tragic part of our consumer economy that we are never invited to see ourselves as those who have too much. Always there is the message, "You need more. You need to shop. There are more tools, there are newer cars, there are better computers, there are lower interest rates, there are different things needed, so you need to buy, to get more, to shop." There is no extra out of which we can become cheerful givers because we are always feeling that what we have is needed to get the next new thing.

Giving away a portion of those blessings is a testimony of faith that we believe that the God who gave us gifts in the past will continue to bless us with gifts in the future. Giving is a statement of faith in the goodness of God in the past and in the future.

Our giving is a bearing witness of our faith in the power and goodness of God. God has enriched us so that we are able to give. There will be others who see that as a display of the power of God. God is able to bless with such abundance that his people are able to give to others. They will hunger for such blessings and become part of the people of God. The more who become a part of the people of God in Corinth, the more stories of blessings and thanksgiving will be told. The giving will rebound and rebound to the enrichment of the whole people of God. The cheerful giver who declares that God has blessed them with gifts so abundant that they are able to give much to others is a shining light for the power of God to keep and sustain his people, and so more will seek those blessings. The more who come, the more God's power will be seen and more stories will be told. The giving is a showing forth in witness of God's power and love.

Strange as it may sound to us, the greatest good that comes from the act of giving is the producing of thanksgiving to God. Giving not only begins for us out of thanksgiving for what we have received, but there is the marvelous result that giving creates thanksgiving. When the saints in Jerusalem receive the gift, there will be great praise and thanksgiving for the marvelous love of God that has been at work in this matter. The ones who receive the gift will give thanks to God for the gift. They will give thanks for the ones who made the gifts. They will give thanks, both private and public prayers, for the gift itself. There will be prayers of thanksgiving for the love of God in Christ Jesus that was the connection between the saints in Corinth and the saints in Jerusalem. We give because it is one of the great ways to praise, honor, and bring hymns of thanksgiving to the God who blesses.

It is fascinating to some that Paul never mentions the situation in Jerusalem. Paul does not explain in this letter why they need the help. Paul does not tell how desperately hungry they are or how badly oppressed they are or how deeply in debt they may be. There is no effort here to create sympathy in our hearts for the poor victims. No tender pictures of children feeding in the streets are given here. Nothing in Paul's discussion about the act of giving is related to the condition of the recipients. Giving is a matter for our hearts. The decision for sharing grows out of my response to my situation. Giving is the response of our heart to our discovery of how blessed we are by the love and goodness of God. Our giving is the thoughtful decision of our faith in recognition that we have sufficiency for our lives and for our obligations, and out of that abundance we will give to others. We will give as our act of praise and thanksgiving. We will give as our testimony of our faith that God has blessed us in the past and God will continue to bless us in the future. We will give so that others may see the abundance of God and desire to open themselves to that goodness. We will give out of our thanksgiving so that there will be a choir full of praise and thanksgiving from those who receive and those who are blessed by the gifts. But our giving is not caused or in response to the needs of the victims. Our giving as children of God is out of the profound awareness of how much we have been blessed by God's goodness to us.

Lectionary Preaching After Pentecost

The following index will aid the user of this book in matching the correct Sunday with the appropriate text during Pentecost. All texts in this book are from the series for the Second Readings, Revised Common Lectionary. (Note that the ELCA division of Lutheranism is now following the Revised Common Lectionary.) The Lutheran designations indicate days comparable to Sundays on which Revised Common Lectionary Propers or Ordinary Time designations are used.

(Fixed dates do not pertain to Lutheran Lectionary)

Fixed Date Lectionaries *Revised Common (including ELCA)* *and Roman Catholic*	**Lutheran Lectionary** *Lutheran*
The Day Of Pentecost	The Day Of Pentecost
The Holy Trinity	The Holy Trinity
May 29-June 4 — Proper 4, Ordinary Time 9	Pentecost 2
June 5-11 — Proper 5, Ordinary Time 10	Pentecost 3
June 12-18 — Proper 6, Ordinary Time 11	Pentecost 4
June 19-25 — Proper 7, Ordinary Time 12	Pentecost 5
June 26-July 2 — Proper 8, Ordinary Time 13	Pentecost 6
July 3-9 — Proper 9, Ordinary Time 14	Pentecost 7
July 10-16 — Proper 10, Ordinary Time 15	Pentecost 8
July 17-23 — Proper 11, Ordinary Time 16	Pentecost 9
July 24-30 — Proper 12, Ordinary Time 17	Pentecost 10
July 31-Aug. 6 — Proper 13, Ordinary Time 18	Pentecost 11
Aug. 7-13 — Proper 14, Ordinary Time 19	Pentecost 12
Aug. 14-20 — Proper 15, Ordinary Time 20	Pentecost 13
Aug. 21-27 — Proper 16, Ordinary Time 21	Pentecost 14
Aug. 28-Sept. 3 — Proper 17, Ordinary Time 22	Pentecost 15
Sept. 4-10 — Proper 18, Ordinary Time 23	Pentecost 16
Sept. 11-17 — Proper 19, Ordinary Time 24	Pentecost 17
Sept. 18-24 — Proper 20, Ordinary Time 25	Pentecost 18

Sept. 25-Oct. 1 — Proper 21, Ordinary Time 26	Pentecost 19
Oct. 2-8 — Proper 22, Ordinary Time 27	Pentecost 20
Oct. 9-15 — Proper 23, Ordinary Time 28	Pentecost 21
Oct. 16-22 — Proper 24, Ordinary Time 29	Pentecost 22
Oct. 23-29 — Proper 25, Ordinary Time 30	Pentecost 23
Oct. 30-Nov. 5 — Proper 26, Ordinary Time 31	Pentecost 24
Nov. 6-12 — Proper 27, Ordinary Time 32	Pentecost 25
Nov. 13-19 — Proper 28, Ordinary Time 33	Pentecost 26
	Pentecost 27
Nov. 20-26 — Christ The King	Christ The King

Reformation Day (or last Sunday in October) is October 31 (Revised Common, Lutheran)

All Saints' Day (or first Sunday in November) is November 1 (Revised Common, Lutheran, Roman Catholic)

U.S. / Canadian Lectionary Comparison

The following index shows the correlation between the Sundays and special days of the church year as they are titled or labeled in the Revised Common Lectionary published by the Consultation On Common Texts and used in the United States (the reference used for this book) and the Sundays and special days of the church year as they are titled or labeled in the Revised Common Lectionary used in Canada.

Revised Common Lectionary	Canadian Revised Common Lectionary
Advent 1	Advent 1
Advent 2	Advent 2
Advent 3	Advent 3
Advent 4	Advent 4
Christmas Eve	Christmas Eve
Nativity Of The Lord / Christmas Day	The Nativity Of Our Lord
Christmas 1	Christmas 1
January 1 / Holy Name of Jesus	January 1 / The Name Of Jesus
Christmas 2	Christmas 2
Epiphany Of The Lord	The Epiphany Of Our Lord
Baptism Of The Lord / Epiphany 1	The Baptism Of Our Lord / Proper 1
Epiphany 2 / Ordinary Time 2	Epiphany 2 / Proper 2
Epiphany 3 / Ordinary Time 3	Epiphany 3 / Proper 3
Epiphany 4 / Ordinary Time 4	Epiphany 4 / Proper 4
Epiphany 5 / Ordinary Time 5	Epiphany 5 / Proper 5
Epiphany 6 / Ordinary Time 6	Epiphany 6 / Proper 6
Epiphany 7 / Ordinary Time 7	Epiphany 7 / Proper 7
Epiphany 8 / Ordinary Time 8	Epiphany 8 / Proper 8
Transfiguration Of The Lord / Last Sunday After Epiphany	The Transfiguration Of Our Lord / Last Sunday After Epiphany
Ash Wednesday	Ash Wednesday
Lent 1	Lent 1
Lent 2	Lent 2
Lent 3	Lent 3
Lent 4	Lent 4
Lent 5	Lent 5
Passion / Palm Sunday (Lent 6)	Passion / Palm Sunday
Holy / Maundy Thursday	Holy / Maundy Thursday
Good Friday	Good Friday
Resurrection Of The Lord / Easter	The Resurrection Of Our Lord

Easter 2	Easter 2
Easter 3	Easter 3
Easter 4	Easter 4
Easter 5	Easter 5
Easter 6	Easter 6
Ascension Of The Lord	The Ascension Of Our Lord
Easter 7	Easter 7
Day Of Pentecost	The Day Of Pentecost
Trinity Sunday	The Holy Trinity
Proper 4 / Pentecost 2 / O T 9*	Proper 9
Proper 5 / Pent 3 / O T 10	Proper 10
Proper 6 / Pent 4 / O T 11	Proper 11
Proper 7 / Pent 5 / O T 12	Proper 12
Proper 8 / Pent 6 / O T 13	Proper 13
Proper 9 / Pent 7 / O T 14	Proper 14
Proper 10 / Pent 8 / O T 15	Proper 15
Proper 11 / Pent 9 / O T 16	Proper 16
Proper 12 / Pent 10 / O T 17	Proper 17
Proper 13 / Pent 11 / O T 18	Proper 18
Proper 14 / Pent 12 / O T 19	Proper 19
Proper 15 / Pent 13 / O T 20	Proper 20
Proper 16 / Pent 14 / O T 21	Proper 21
Proper 17 / Pent 15 / O T 22	Proper 22
Proper 18 / Pent 16 / O T 23	Proper 23
Proper 19 / Pent 17 / O T 24	Proper 24
Proper 20 / Pent 18 / O T 25	Proper 25
Proper 21 / Pent 19 / O T 26	Proper 26
Proper 22 / Pent 20 / O T 27	Proper 27
Proper 23 / Pent 21 / O T 28	Proper 28
Proper 24 / Pent 22 / O T 29	Proper 29
Proper 25 / Pent 23 / O T 30	Proper 30
Proper 26 / Pent 24 / O T 31	Proper 31
Proper 27 / Pent 25 / O T 32	Proper 32
Proper 28 / Pent 26 / O T 33	Proper 33
Christ The King (Proper 29 / O T 34)	Proper 34 / Christ The King / Reign Of Christ
Reformation Day (October 31)	Reformation Day (October 31)
All Saints' Day (November 1 or 1st Sunday in November)	All Saints' Day (November 1)
Thanksgiving Day (4th Thursday of November)	Thanksgiving Day (2nd Monday of October)

*O T = Ordinary Time

About The Authors

James L. Killen has pastored a variety of congregations during a 45-year career in the ministry, ranging from a small open country parish in northeast Texas to Trinity United Methodist Church in Beaumont, Texas, a 2,000-member church with a television ministry serving all of southeast Texas and southwestern Louisiana. A graduate of the University of Houston and Perkins School of Theology at Southern Methodist University, Killen's work has appeared in several publications, including *Preaching*, *Pulpit Digest*, *Circuit Rider*, *The Upper Room*, and the *Abingdon Preaching Annual*. He is the author of *What Does The Lord Require?* (CSS).

Richard W. Ferris pastors two Disciples of Christ congregations in the Akron, Ohio, area, Barberton Christian Church and Firestone Park Christian Church, and has served other congregations in Ohio, Michigan, and North Dakota. He spent several years in a tentmaker ministry, working in such places as Junior Achievement, a mental health agency, and a rehabilitation hospital to support his church work. Ferris received his B.A. degree in journalism from Ohio State University and his M.Div. degree from Lutheran Theological Seminary (now known as Trinity Seminary).

William G. Carter, the senior pastor of First Presbyterian Church in Clarks Summit, Pennsylvania, has received national recognition for his preaching and writing. He is the author of four books published by CSS, and his sermons and articles have appeared in numerous outlets, including *Journal for Preachers*, *Presbyterian Survey*, *Preaching*, and *Lectionary Homiletics*. Carter's preaching has been featured on *The Protestant Hour*, an international radio ministry reaching over two million listeners each week.

A graduate of Princeton Theological Seminary (M.Div.) and the State University of New York at Binghamton (B.A.), Reverend Carter is also a highly regarded jazz pianist, composer, and arranger who has studied and performed with such noted artists as Dave Brubeck, Phil Woods, and Bob Brookmeyer. He is the pianist and leader of the Presbybop Quartet (www.presbybop.com), which has recorded four CDs of original material plus jazz versions of favorite hymns. Carter has traveled widely presenting contemporary worship services and frequently weaves his music into his ministry.

Jeff Wedge, a freelance writer of magazine articles and contract technical work with over 200 appearances in print, is the founder and corporate officer of a company for development and delivery of training. He is an active member of Hope Lutheran Church in Daytona Beach, Florida, where he serves as a Lay Assisting Minister and Lay Preacher. A former parish pastor, Wedge holds an M.Div. degree from Lutheran Theological Southern Seminary. He is the author of the CSS titles *A Bucket Full Of Miracles* and *Mrs. Johnson's Rummage Sale*.

Rick Brand is pastor of First Presbyterian Church in Henderson, North Carolina, and has served other congregations in North Carolina, Texas, and Pennsylvania for over 35 years. He has also served as General Assembly Commissioner in 2000 and with the Presbytery Commission on Ministry. Brand's sermons have appeared in several publications, including *Preaching Magazine*, *Homiletics*, *Pulpit Digest*, and *Emphasis*. He is a graduate of Davidson College and Princeton Theological Seminary.

www.ingramcontent.com/pod-product-compliance
Lightning Source LLC
Chambersburg PA
CBHW050133240426
4367SCB00043B/1652